in this place
together

in this place together

A PALESTINIAN'S JOURNEY TO COLLECTIVE LIBERATION

PENINA EILBERG-SCHWARTZ
WITH **SULAIMAN KHATIB**

BEACON PRESS, BOSTON

BEACON PRESS
Boston, Massachusetts
www.beacon.org

Beacon Press books
are published under the auspices of
the Unitarian Universalist Association of Congregations.

24 23 22 21   8 7 6 5 4 3 2 1

This book is printed on acid-free paper that meets the uncoated paper
ANSI/NISO specifications for permanence as revised in 1992.

Text design and composition by Kim Arney

Some names in the text have been changed to protect individual privacy.

The epigraph quote "The Land is a witness" previously appeared in Shelley Elkayam's
poem "The Crusader Man" in the anthology *Keys to the Garden: New Israeli Writing*,
translated and edited by Ammiel Alcalay (San Francisco: City Lights Publishers, 1996).
Reprinted here with permission.

The Rumi epigraph previously appeared in "The Guest House," *Rumi: Selected Poems*,
translated by Coleman Barks with John Moynce, A. J. Arberry, and Reynold Nicholson
(New York: Penguin Books, 2004). Reprinted here with permission.

The English translation of the Darwish epigraph previously appeared in Mahmoud
Darwish, *In the Presence of Absence*, translated by Sinan Antoon (Brooklyn: Archipelago
Books, 2011). Reprinted here with permission.

Library of Congress Cataloging-in-Publication Data
Names: Eilberg-Schwartz, Penina, author. | Khatib, Sulaiman, author.
Title: In this place together : a Palestinian's journey to collective
     liberation / Penina Eilberg-Schwartz with Sulaiman Khatib.
Description: Boston, Massachusetts : Beacon Press, 2021. | Includes
     bibliographical references.
Identifiers: LCCN 2020035460 (print) | LCCN 2020035461 (ebook) |
     ISBN 9780807046821 (hardcover) | ISBN 9780807046845 (ebook)
Subjects: LCSH: Khatib, Sulaiman | Palestinian Arabs—Biography. |
     Arab-Israeli conflict—1993- —Peace. | Palestinian Arabs—Politics
     and government—1993–
Classification: LCC DS126.6.K5546 E45 2021 (print) | LCC DS126.6.K5546 (ebook) |
     DDC 956.9405/5092 [B]—dc23
LC record available at https://lccn.loc.gov/2020035460
LC ebook record available at https://lccn.loc.gov/2020035461

*Imagination is a secret companion
who helps you correct typos in the
book of the universe.*

—MAHMOUD DARWISH

The Land is a witness.

—SHELLEY ELKAYAM

*Meet them at the door laughing,
and invite them in.*

—RUMI

CONTENTS

A NOTE ON
TRANSLITERATION

For the Arabic transliteration, we've tried to use spellings that would allow non-Arabic speakers to approximate proper pronunciation of Palestinian dialect (i.e., *fellah* over *fallah*). We often favored the most common transliteration of words or names over those in line with a more consistent approach (i.e., Jneid instead of Junayd). Occasionally we chose a transliteration in favor of a friend's preferred spelling of their name over the more common one (i.e., Aljafari instead of al-Jafari). And when an apostrophe appears at the end of a word, it indicates an "ah" sound—so that, for example, Bi'r al-Sab' sounds something like "Beer al Saba." Though this is the case for the word *tatbi'* (normalization), we used *tatbi'a* to help non-Arabic speakers recall the approximate pronunciation of this frequently used word.

For the Hebrew, we used *ch* for "chet," and an apostrophe when separating two vowels that should be pronounced distinctly. We used *kh* for "khaf," in part because this letter in Hebrew seems to map best onto the Arabic letter *kha'*. We tried to balance consistency with use of the most common transliterations. Occasionally, we favored the more common transliteration over the most consistent one (i.e., Mizrahi instead of Mizrachi). Other times, we chose an inconsistent transliteration to help non-Hebrew speakers approximate proper pronunciation (i.e., Khevron instead of Chevron).

A NOTE
FROM PENINA

Before a crowd of Israeli Jews at a peace demonstration—in the same square where an Israeli man, certain he was right, shot Yitzhak Rabin—Sulaiman Khatib stood on a stage. It was 2014, the war in Gaza not yet over. In Sderot, and sometimes in Tel Aviv, Israelis were ducking for cover. In Gaza, the death count was rising. That summer would see the deaths of approximately 70 Israelis, more than 2,200 Palestinians.

Looking down at a piece of paper, holding a microphone, Sulaiman wore a shirt that read "Combatants for Peace." On his chest, two silhouettes threw their weapons behind them, as if recklessly. From the stage, Sulaiman began to speak to the crowd in his Arabic-accented Hebrew. It was a rare moment of solemnity for him, his words slow and deliberate.

"My name is Sulaiman Khatib. I've come from Ramallah. . . . We, Israelis and Palestinians, call on both sides to act in courage and wisdom, to immediately stop the war in Gaza—and to start a serious dialogue." He spoke the Hebrew words that had taken on their own life and rhythm from frequent use. "*EIN pitaRON tsava'I l'sichsOOCH shelanu.*" It meant what it always had: *There is no military solution for our conflict.*

When he stepped offstage, his phone began to ring. It was his friend Ra'ed, calling from the Palestinian town of Yatta.

"I saw you on Al Jazeera live!"

"*Wallah,*[1] really?"

Sulaiman was surprised. Combatants for Peace received mostly international or progressive Israeli press. Palestinian TV didn't

often cover their actions. When it did, Sulaiman was sometimes
called a traitor to his people; an '*asfur*: the Arabic word for bird
that, for many Palestinians, meant a spy for the Israelis. Someone
who, among other things, normalized the occupation, practiced
tatbiʻa.

For a moment, Sulaiman felt a little afraid to go home to Ramallah. *It only takes one stupid person,* he thought. But by this time, he'd
grown accustomed to feeling fear and meeting it —or sensing it and
burying it. It wasn't always clear which acts of imagination and era-
sure were needed to build a new story from an old one.

Two years later, a bit of wind blows as Sulaiman drives me down
a West Bank road. The sky is darkening as we approach a famous
junction near a number of Jewish settlements. Young Israeli soldiers
stand at four corners, guns on their shoulders. As we drive by, Sulaiman's shoulders inch toward his ears.

Sulaiman Khatib—or Souli, as many know him—is a Palestinian peacemaker from a village northeast of al-Quds, the Palestinian
name for Jerusalem. He is cofounder and codirector of a binational
nonviolent movement called Combatants for Peace, created by Israeli and Palestinian ex-fighters and ex-prisoners. He is a person
who's been through much, who seems able to lightly hold burdens
that would bring others to the ground.

Soon after we pass the soldiers, Souli turns to me and smiles. My
jaw is clenched, not yet ready to let go. *Ajaki,* he says, laughing out
his favorite word. It's a play off of Arabic slang from the streets of
al-Quds, a word that moves between meanings, from "You get it?"
to a nod of agreement. But the way Souli repeats it—like a song, or
a punch line—it seems to mean nothing at all, or too much to name.
His hair bounces over his eyes. When I first met him, it was shaved
close to his head.

We are headed somewhere, but we're not sure where. It's something Souli likes to do sometimes: get in the car at night and drive,
without any destination, without any sense of what will come next.
In this way, Souli's driving seems like a kind of dreaming, a thing he
does often. It's linked to his way of existing firmly in reality while

somehow escaping it entirely, living somewhere else, somewhere others can't quite find him.

Where he is now, in reality, it's been almost fifty years since Israel took over East Jerusalem, the West Bank, and Gaza; over ten years since Israel withdrew settlers from Gaza, but kept control of its borders and so much else. Souli is not sure how many years it's been since he acquired his nickname. He's not sure how many years it's been since he was only Sulaiman.

For years now, Souli's fans have told him to write his story. "It's so cinematic," they say and touch his shoulder while he smokes.

"They think I'm a visionary," he explained to me once, grinning.

People do think this, I've seen it, and it's because of what happened after one big bang of a moment many years ago, when at the age of fourteen and five months, Sulaiman stabbed an Israeli and was sentenced to fifteen years in jail. The length of his life until then.

Some people talk about him as if he were a prophet because, when he was released from jail over ten years later, he went searching for a way to participate in joint nonviolent activism and reconciliation with Israelis. Among many other things, he worked alongside a handful of Israelis to create Combatants for Peace, resisting the occupation and modeling a shared, peaceful future. Because of this, some people read his life as a textbook for transformation. They want it written.

"Why not have someone write the book in Arabic?" I'd asked him at the beginning.

"Palestinians know this story," he said, waving his hand at a nonexistent fly. "Palestinians know that za'atar[2] is a religion, that land is a religion. They know what the olive trees, figs, and pomegranates mean to us."

And he's right. Some parts of his story—the violence and fear, the redemption and lack of it, the sacredness of land and of memory—are old news to Palestinians. A person does not need their daily reality narrated back to them. But Souli's relationship to reality, as many friends have pointed out, is a bit strange. There's something different in his way of seeing, and it doesn't seem so only to me—a white American Jew—but to many of the Palestinians and Israelis around him.

Strangeness has always seemed to me like a path toward truth or, if not truth, some better version of our world. So it was Souli's strangeness that made me finally say yes when he asked me to write this book, or to help him write it. At the beginning, it wasn't clear to either of us what he was really asking of me.

"We'll see!" he said the day I agreed to work on the project, sitting in a café in San Francisco, blinking at all the light coming in. "Life is a journey!" he said, as if in answer to a question I hadn't asked. Laughing, he picked up his fork. I rolled my eyes. He often said things that would annoy me coming from anyone else, but somehow, when he said them, they were true. I took a bite of his banana bread. I laughed, too.

I met Souli in 2006, in my mother's house. When I walked into her wide-windowed dining room, and saw the lean man slouching in a chair, legs crossed, I knew very little of him.

"We have the most *amazing* new friend," my mom, a rabbi who speaks in capital letters, told me. "He's a Palestinian peace activist."

At the time, my mother, the first woman ordained by the Jewish Conservative movement, was engaging in dialogue about Palestine-Israel. It was a tense time for us, filled with many painful conversations about Zionism in which I angrily tried to unravel something I knew was precious to her, something she hoped would stay precious to me. I argued that it was not possible for a state to be both Jewish and democratic; she argued that no state (and no democracy) is perfect, and that the Jewish people deserve a safe space in the world to grow and govern—just like all other people. Our conversations pushed her further along a path she was already traveling, seeking out alternative narratives. Souli's story was one of many beginnings for her. It was a story she could hear.

I don't remember much of that initial encounter. I remember Souli, with tight, dark skin and close-cropped hair, getting up from his chair to shake my hand. I remember we ate and joked, that I invited him to come see my friends play banjo and musical saw in a café.

I remember later that night, when I went downstairs to fetch a book or something else I'd forgotten, and Souli was there, standing in the doorway of my younger stepbrother's room. He smiled at me, said goodnight.

Behind him, I saw my stepbrother's bed and the full-size Israeli flag hanging over the headboard.

"They have you sleeping there?" I asked. "Under that flag?"

I was so angry. They couldn't have given him someplace else to sleep, or taken down the flag?

He laughed. "It doesn't matter, *habibti*,[3] calm down."

I didn't know it then, but this would be the first of our many political disagreements.

It wasn't until two years later that I heard him tell his story. He wrote to tell me he'd gotten another visa to the US and would be giving a talk in Berkeley. He wanted me to come. When I got to Cafe Leila, I hugged him and sat with a bunch of mostly white, gray-haired people in their fifties and sixties. Amid the sound of forks on plates and scraps of conversation, he began.

I don't remember what he said exactly. He changed focus erratically, traveling from place to place without warning. He spoke about stabbing two Israeli soldiers. He made jokes about jail—"Now I'm a couchsurfer, but then I was a jailsurfer. They took me from jail to jail, so I was traveling for free!" I sat there wondering at the nonchalance of his storytelling. He was light when he talked about his history; he didn't place weight on anything.

When he finished, people clapped and asked questions. Someone wondered how he kept going, even in the darkest times. "I had to have something inside myself," he said, "to know there was part of me living outside the jail."

I saw it in him, how he seemed able to tear down anything in his way. Not with violence, but with something metaphysical, alchemical. He acted as if certain things that appeared solid were just a mirage. I wanted to know more about it, this physics-defying capacity. I wanted to know what it meant for him to transport himself elsewhere, to walk through walls. And I wanted to know whether *anyone* could follow. Or whether, for some, the walls stayed solid.

————•——

After his talk in Berkeley, before he flew to the next place, Souli and I spent every day together—walking, sitting on trains, making sure we never felt hungry, arguing about Palestine and Israel. I wanted him to be angrier; he wanted me to see the traditional Israeli narrative, too, to understand not only the occupation but also the mistakes Palestinians had made along the way.

After he returned to Ramallah, we stayed friends online. Though he often asked me to visit him, I never did. I'd been working intensely on issues of peace and justice in Palestine-Israel, yet I hadn't visited the Middle East since the week-long vacation I took with my mom when I was ten years old. I'd never traveled to the West Bank or Gaza.

Time passed, and our communication grew thin. Our exchanges were limited to brief messages with little in them: a cartoon face or a heart, and nothing else. So I didn't take it very seriously when, years after our last meeting, Souli sent a Facebook message asking me to help him work on a book. I said no. I didn't think I was the right person for the job. I was neither Palestinian nor Israeli, and this meant there were many things I could not know, the knowledge that comes from living in a place. I was a leftist, perhaps not someone Israelis would feel moved to listen to. And I didn't understand what Souli meant when he said he wanted to incorporate "my story," too. I didn't like the idea of a white American Jew telling a Palestinian story. I could hear the critiques. *It's his story. Get out of the way. It's not for you to tell.*

He wrote multiple times, and I said no just as many, until he was there—sitting across from me in a café in San Francisco. Seven years had passed since we'd last seen each other.

Over a small plate of banana bread, Souli asked again. He wanted me to help tell his story, to weave in Israeli stories, and my own— not to forget the importance of American Jewry in this conflict. As I listened, as time passed in its strange way, I knew that he was asking for the impossible. I knew that the result would be a tangled book, knotted with starkly unresolved issues of representation. But I also knew that the book's questions of ownership and form might have something beautiful and distinctive to say about who Souli is, about the place he comes from, about what has happened there.

I looked out the window and turned back when I felt his hand on mine. He pressed it, offered a question: "How can these two narratives—Palestinian and Israeli—exist in one homeland?" He shrugged as if there were little left to say. "That's the big question we have to share."

This book, a vehicle for telling (one version of) Souli's story, takes that question and peers at it through the lens of a larger and messier question: What does it really mean to share space?

When I arrive in Jerusalem/al-Quds to work on the book, it quickly becomes clear that Souli and I want to discuss different things. He avoids talking about jail, and instead speaks repeatedly and in generalities about what I already know. He moves quickly to other people's stories, wrapping them into his own, picking them up along the way—like the lucky coins his father used to spot on the ground. Throughout our conversations, we struggle with each other over which past is most important to tell. In many cases, he prefers to ignore the past and tell only stories that point toward the future.

This may have something to do with his tendency to look outside the frame, and, in a sense, outside of language. He speaks fluent English, but translated directly to the page, something essential in his words seems lost. In this book, to simulate the fluency he communicates in person, I will quote him while "correcting" his grammar, smoothing his syntax, making his tenses match. I want him to sound how I imagine he sounds in Arabic—though it's only an imagining. I understand these changes as a kind of trespassing; he doesn't.

Where there are holes in his narrative—so many things Souli doesn't recall or doesn't want to say—I slip into them, imagining my way into the small gestures of the story. These are intrusions Souli reads and approves before they make it into the final text. Because he wants his story—especially the beginning, before jail—told *as story*.

He doesn't remember (and I can never know) exactly how hard he could kick a soccer ball, *precisely* when he first thought to use violence as resistance, the way he waved his hand at his mother when she asked him questions. Though he remembers his aunt telling him she could predict the weather, he can't recall exactly *how* she told him. To speak of these things now, *as story*, is to imagine them. And yet, they happened.

So when it comes to his experiences, I tell the story based on what he's told me, but imagine my way into certain minor details, the way he's learned to imagine himself into the stories of people who've lived very different lives than his. All past dialogue is re-imagined rather than explicitly remembered; the same is true for the exact sequence of events and duration in which they occurred. And due to the incredibly sensitive nature of this material, we have changed some names to protect the identities of those involved. Though what follows is faithful to the conversations I've had with Souli and with many others, it is not a work of history.

I am made nervous by all this slippage, but Souli remains unworried. Maybe it's already clear to him how much memory is an act of interpretation, how every telling requires intrusion. Even when he relates his story, in his own voice, he's only telling versions. That's how it is for all of us. Developing a story is the act of deciding what to emphasize, what to leave out. And Souli doesn't think this is a bad thing. On a collective level, he struggles both with and against this phenomenon to build a story—*a third narrative*—that includes Jewish and Palestinian histories, and all the places they overlap. His whole life has led to this reimagining. This, he thinks now, is how the world will get better.

When I talked about this act of imagination with a reporter, she looked at me with sharp eyes and told me that the Palestinian story is very real and has been ignored for a long time. I remember her saying, "It doesn't need you to imagine it."

Reliving this moment, I feel her words physically, a sharp pain in my stomach. I see her as she might see me: another Jew occupying Palestinian space. I see myself this way too, sometimes. Which is why I hope to make this occupation more *visible*, to remind myself endlessly that my presence here, even if I were to hide it, changes the story Souli tells. Making myself invisible won't erase the power I have, so I would rather see it towering above me. It serves as a reminder that this book is a place where the two of us are sharing space. A reminder of the responsibility that Souli has given me: to shape how he is seen and even, as I would find sometimes, to shape how he sees himself.

Power travels across so many lines, and I've decided there is no neutral place from which to write. A book is a place full of danger— of a man's story overtaking a woman's, of a European Jewish story overwriting that of a Palestinian.

When I tell Souli what the reporter said about imagination, he laughs. He tells me to relax, that Palestinians are not just victims, that they have at least one enormous power: to make Israel legitimate in the eyes of the world, or not.

Among others, this is one of the powers Souli has over me.

A NOTE
FROM SULAIMAN

Power is very strange. Growing up in Palestine, I believed that the Israelis were evil, that the only way to have a meaningful life with freedom and dignity was through armed struggle. But over the years, I have discovered other, greater forces. The power of love and forgiveness. The power of story and noble silence. The power of humanity, which is bigger and more powerful than any kind of violence. It is the only way for me to live.

Getting to this point has been long and complicated, and I hope to make it a little easier for others. I want to reach the ones who share my reality, and also the ones who don't, but who are connected, emotionally or politically, with the land and the place and the conflict. Who see Israel and Palestine only through the eyes of the media. It's maybe, I feel, my duty.

By telling my story, I want to humanize the headlines as much as possible. To show the complexity and the beauty and the ugliness and the pain and the hope. To share what I went through, what our communities—both Palestinian and Jewish—continue to go through. I hope to use my little bit of knowledge to give a different look, from different sides.

My goal is not to prove a logical point, or to offer evidence of who was the first one here, of who is the bad guy. I don't want to write one more book in the line of books serving PR purposes. To shame and blame the other. I don't want to be part of this game. What I want is to change the game, and the rules of this thing we call conflict. I want to rewrite how we fix this story in our minds, and how we learn it.

To hold multiple narratives is not easy. It is not easy to carry contradictions in your soul. It's much easier to see one side of the story, to blame the other, to live in victimhood. To feel that all the world is against you, that everyone wants to kill you.

But this is not reality. The history of Palestine and Israel has been told in many ways, and if we want a better future, we must gather the pieces and form them into a new, shared story. There's an old anger we must recognize, but there are new opportunities and possibilities we must recognize, too. 'Ali ibn Abi Talib, a sacred figure in Islam, spoke about treating others as we want to be treated. In Hebrew, there is this same concept: *ve'ahavta leray'akha kamokha*, to love or wish for your neighbor as you wish for yourself. In Christianity, this is the life of Jesus. In other, very old Mideast traditions, this is the reconciliation process of *sulha*. People were practicing it here thousands of years ago, and we still practice it today.

Love is not easy, but I really believe in the connection that's deeply there. I've seen people open their hearts and eyes, and move from fear to trust. I believe truly, as Mandela said, "No one is born hating. . . . People must learn to hate, and if they can learn to hate, they can be taught to love, for love comes more naturally to the human heart than its opposite." It's painful, of course, but we have to look for that love and goodness and activate it in others. We need to see things from new, less tired eyes. Because we are tired, and traumatized. We need to heal, and I want to help in this healing journey. I do this for myself, and for people wherever they are.

I know that there are no quick results, no quick solutions. We don't have the answers yet. I'm at peace, a bit, with that. Perhaps it's my own privilege, or perhaps it's my weakness. I don't know. I am still learning.

This Passover, I went to the Sinai with a group of Jewish, Palestinian, and Egyptian friends. We discussed the Jewish story of slavery and freedom, and the Palestinian story of indignity and the fight for freedom. We discussed salt and water as a symbol, during Passover, of Jewish survival, and we discussed how Palestinian prisoners use the same salt and water to survive hunger strikes. As we talked, the moon came up slowly, slowly, and lit the desert and mountains. We fell silent, and we all prayed in our different ways. I felt, really, the history of this land. Thousands of years.

We started to dance, a spiritual dance, and one of the Israelis came up to me. She'd never met a Palestinian before, and we hadn't really spoken. But by the sea, under the full moon, she said to me one sentence. *I can't believe we are enemies.* That's it.

Maybe it's too spiritual for some people, but I feel the land has its say. I have a firm belief in this. And the way things are—the wall and everything—they will not last. Every stone has a different story, and they all exist together. We can learn from this, from the olive trees and the za'atar and jasmine. From the stone and the valley, the birds and the moon and the sun. There is a deeper connection.

I have a vision of this different reality. And with this book, I am putting it out there, expressing my real true soul into words. Not just for people to read, but to maybe understand, maybe open their hearts. It's a challenge, but I hope people will focus on the message and not on me personally. I am not a devil or a hero. I'm just passing a message through me. I feel it is a mission, you can say. A sacred mission. To make people listen to the ones they call the other, and to not be afraid of their shared dreams and their longing, for the same water, the same stones.

As a friend of mine said, to do this work, we have to keep one leg in reality and one leg in the dream. Perhaps, in this way, in this place together, we can begin to change the bigger picture—the big reality of this land.

PROLOGUE

It is too obvious but still important to say: in a contested story, no one agrees on the beginning.

Souli will tell you that his particular story began in Hizma, a village less than ten kilometers northeast of Jerusalem's old city. It began when his father worked for the Jerusalem municipality cleaning streets and other public things that needed to be cleaned. It began before he learned to play the wooden flute.

But, of course, this story also began before Sulaiman was born, before his father was born. It started before then, but no one agrees when—whether in one of the myriad religious conquests of Jerusalem, or much later.

Hillel Cohen, a professor at Hebrew University's Department of Islamic and Middle Eastern Studies, identifies "year zero" as 1929—when violence broke out between Palestinians and Jews in British Mandate Palestine. Many others point to 1948, when the newly declared state of Israel fought against Egypt, Lebanon, Jordan, Syria, and Iraq. When over seven hundred thousand Palestinians were expelled or fled, when Israel kept them from returning home. Still others believe the trouble began with the war in 1967, when Israel won another victory against Egypt, Jordan, and Syria, seizing the Sinai Peninsula, the Golan Heights, Gaza, the West Bank, and East Jerusalem.

Others go further back. According to Souli, in the broadest sense, the conflict really began the moment a specific idea was born: that Jews should "return home" to the land of "Palestine, Israel, Canaan, the Holy Land, or whatever you want to call it." A dream, he says, that existed for thousands of years.[1]

Still, it's not clear whether Souli thinks the dream itself was the beginning of the conflict, or whether the beginning was something the dream gave birth to along the way—between the first exile of the people we now call Jews from this land approximately two thousand years ago, and the story we see unfolding today.

Which takes us to this particular beginning, in 1982, long after all the suggested beginnings, when Sulaiman was ten years old and Hizma was a place with white houses and green and brown grass. When you walked through its streets, you could smell jasmine and other sweet smells I don't know how to name.

in this place
together

PART ONE

CHAPTER 1

Ta'mira

Shimon had red hair, and because his teeth were the biggest teeth they had ever seen, Sulaiman and the other boys from Hizma liked to call him "Shimon *Abu Snan*"—Shimon, father of teeth.[1] This was a very good name —(a name is good when it's true)—because these teeth were so big, they could have given birth to all the other teeth in the world. Shimon lived in Neve Ya'aqub,[2] the Jewish village just next to Hizma, and Sulaiman would meet him there often in the flat grove between their two villages. The grove was the home of some dark green trees and a few delicate deer who startled easily at the way the boys shouted—in Hebrew and Arabic—while they played soccer.

Sulaiman stood guard between two stones that made a goal out of a space where before there'd been nothing. Shimon stared at him, reaching his leg back for a breath that felt like forever, and kicked. The ball came toward Sulaiman like an unstoppable force, but when he looked down, it was in his hands. He hadn't expected to catch it. Shimon was two years older, and, like his teeth, he was huge, a little wild, and very strong.

Shifting the ball to his hip, Sulaiman clapped Shimon on the back and shyly teased him in Arabic. He knew some words of Hebrew from his father, and though he sometimes tried them out on the boys from Neve Ya'aqub, he often spoke to them in Arabic, trusting they would understand the language of his body even if they didn't understand the words themselves.

The grass was bright with sun by the time they said goodbye. Shimon left, walking with arms swinging toward Neve Ya'aqub and its houses made from stones that looked something like, but not exactly, white. Sulaiman watched him and clapped his hands together, laughing. He couldn't believe he'd beat Shimon and couldn't wait to tell his friends Hanif, Fadi, and Mohannad.

The voice of a goat startled him. He'd almost forgotten the family's herd and donkey were with him. He cooed at the animals lovingly, mockingly, and walked over to the donkey he'd tied up to a trunk at the edge of the cool grove of trees. He pulled out a bottle of water from its harness and drank so quickly some of the water missed his mouth and wet the front of his shirt. His foot caught in a root. It was better not to take the goats here; they preferred the open hills, not this low ground. But he'd had a feeling Shimon would be here today and hadn't wanted to miss a chance to play. *I'll make it up to them*, he thought, looking up into the hills that were covered in the kind of grass the goats liked best to chew.

Together they picked their way through the sparse yellow grass and dusty rocks, following a little road someone had made with their feet a long time before. He tried to avoid the sharp nettles that scratched his ankles and fell back, watching the animals at the front as they began to bend their heads down to the earth.

When he was young, the family had just two goats, and then the two became five and now the five had become seven. The goats gave the family all the milk and cheese they wanted and didn't need much in return. And when Sulaiman took them out with his friends and their herds, the goats kept to themselves. The first in each group wore a little bell around its neck, and all the goats seemed to know which family was their family, and which bell was their bell. That's why it was wrong for a shepherd to think of himself as a leader of goats.

Sulaiman tried as much as possible to let the animals go where they liked; he thought they deserved it since they spent all day in his family's backyard, in the pen underneath his bedroom window.

Sometimes, when they were behind that wire netting, he looked into their eyes and thought he saw an accusation, or a challenge. It seemed to mean something very clear: they wanted to walk out free into the world. Today the herd picked its spot in a wide circle of dry grass next to a cave. When he peered into it, he found only a wave of cool air, the smell of wetness. There were many little caves like this out in the hills, usually named after a family, or something from history, or a bird. There were two twin caves called the *yehudiat* (Jewish women). And there were big ones near the village cemetery, and the ancient Roman graveyard that lay below it, called *tawabin al-rumiya*, the Roman ovens. No one knew when the names started. When a person was born their name was born, and it was the same with caves.

Many families in Hizma had caves of their own. Sulaiman's family had one along the road to Jericho where they used to bring the goats to keep them warm during cold winters. When his grandfather Ayed was alive and still young, he had also lived in that cave during winter. Sulaiman's parents had even used the cave as a hiding place in 1967—back when Hizma was still controlled by Jordan, and uncles, cousins, and siblings could visit one another whenever they liked.

But 1967 changed everything. In the years before, Palestinian militias—based in Jordan, Lebanon, and Syria—began launching more raids into Israel, fighting to return home. In 1966, Israel had killed close to twenty people in a raid on the West Bank village of al-Samu'; then came 1967. The year that Israel destroyed several Syrian fighter planes. The year that Egyptian president Gamal Abdel Nasser removed United Nations peacekeeping forces from the Sinai, brought soldiers to the Israeli border, and blocked Israel's access to the Red Sea. The year that Nasser organized an Egyptian alliance with Jordan, stating that together, they would destroy Israel. The year that Israel attacked Egypt and proved Nasser wrong.

When the fighting broke out, Sulaiman's mother had just given birth to her first son, Karim. As the family ran, Said guarded Sarah, who carried the new baby under her arms in a little bundle. They hid in their cave and prayed for a pan-Arab victory, hoping to win back the land taken from them in 1948, in the war that followed the creation of the state of Israel, the war that everyone Sulaiman knew called *al-Nakba*, the Catastrophe. But after six days, when Sarah emerged, Karim in her arms, she found the opposite had occurred: more death, more Palestinian refugees. The pan-Arab alliance hadn't only failed to win back land. Egypt lost the Gaza Strip and Sinai Peninsula; Syria lost the Golan Heights; and Jordan lost the West Bank—a territory it had annexed after the Nakba, a swath of land that included East al-Quds and a little village called Hizma. When the sounds of war stopped and Sulaiman's parents left their cave, they found they now lived in territory taken by Israel. They had entered the cave in one country and left it in another.

Breathing in the cool air of the cave, Sulaiman decided to sit. He tied the donkey to an olive tree and pulled the wooden flute from his back pocket. He played for the goats and they came a bit closer, but one of them, a *shami*,[3] stayed behind. Sulaiman spoke to him and he came, looking annoyed, as if distracted from some monumental task. Sulaiman laughed, stuck out his dry tongue, and realized how thirsty he was.

At his feet, he made a small fire to heat some mint he'd found beside his house. He searched for rainwater in the small holes of rock surfaces, but summer made everything dry. Instead, he took the jug of water he'd placed in the donkey's saddle, and even though the water wasn't made fresh from rain, the tea was just what he needed. He drank it slowly, lingering longer than he needed to, and when the air started to look a little dark, he gathered the goats and began the walk home.

When his house came into view, he stopped for a second, lifted his face to the sky and smiled into the light breeze that smelled like jasmine, maybe like something else he didn't recognize. It had been hot, but now the evening brought a perfect kind of cool. His father's sister Fatima had been right that morning when, drinking coffee in the kitchen with his mother, she'd said it would be a beautiful day.

She is always right about the weather, he thought as he approached the line of white houses at the edge of town. One day about a year before, he'd practically sprinted out the door when she'd grabbed his wrists with her surprisingly strong hands.

"*Istanna shwayya*, wait. Today will be very hot. Make sure to take extra water, to rest more."

"*Khalas*,"[4] he said, smiling, "let me go. It's cool now. What makes you think it will be so hot?"

She waved the back of her hand dismissively and started to walk away before she turned back, locked eyes with him, and said, "A boy like you may not believe it, but my skin knows."

He didn't believe it. She had been overly dramatic for as long as he could remember. But soon he realized that every prediction she made was right: when it would rain, when it would grow too hot to go out at all, on what particular day the olives would be ripe enough to pick. She would look to the west for clouds, smell the air, and determine if the weather was going to be hard or easy. He knew it had something to do with her fingers, something to do with the moon.

Maybe, he thought, *she knows because she's been alive for so long.* Maybe she'd watched the rain and the heat all that time—memorized their patterns, learned to trust their timetable. Because even when the rain came late and the *fellahin*[5] started to worry, Fatima sat in her chair with a little smile. Weather wasn't like people at all. It didn't make mistakes.

The following morning, Sulaiman walked the dirt road toward school. When he entered the classroom, his cousin Sadiq was already there, bright eyes flicking to both sides before he waved Sulaiman over. Today they had a geography lesson with Wahid Qudsi, the fattest and meanest of all the teachers. Sadiq pulled out a piece of chewing gum, and Sulaiman understood right away. They chewed until the gum lost its flavor and then, before Qudsi came in, they went up to the desk at the front of the class, sticking their pieces of gum on the ends of their teacher's chalk.

Sadiq and Sulaiman had only just sat down when the door opened and Qudsi crashed in. The other kids tried not to giggle as he picked up the chalk, but when he began writing and couldn't, their laughter burst out, unstoppable. Qudsi's ears grew red and swollen, and without even turning around, he shouted, "Sadiq! Get out!" This only made everyone laugh harder. Sulaiman smiled. At least this time Qudsi had only sent Sadiq out of the room. Last time, he'd made Sadiq stand on his feet for the whole period, wearing a white basket over his head. The kids kept laughing for a long while, even after Qudsi threatened everyone with more homework, and the laughing had to go on in secret.

Sulaiman thought these games were much better than paying attention. He felt trapped inside the classroom, counting the minutes until he could get outside, play soccer with his friends, or just walk in the hills alone, with the goats. His mind wandered to Ta'mira, to one piece of his family's ancestral land—a plot of several dunams,[6] filled with figs and grapes where he and his parents sat every Saturday. He dreamed of the clean soft stone he would put under his head, just as his grandfather Ayed had done before him. Lying there, he could find the quiet that escaped him at school and at home. He could lose himself in something, some dream, though he didn't know its shape yet, its weight and color.

When Saturday arrived with the sounds of birds, Sulaiman jumped up from the floor, off the mattress his mother had woven from sheep's wool. He ran downstairs into the kitchen, where his father bent over a pan of *shakshuka*, stirring and poking at the mixture of tomato, egg, and spice with the seriousness of a scientist.

Sulaiman smelled the bread before he saw his mother. Sarah came up the stairs holding the round soft bread she'd taken fresh from the *tabun*[7] oven outside, right near the goats.

"*Sabah al-khayr*, Sulaiman," she said, "are you hungry?"

His stomach grumbled, and his father smiled a small smile. "Sit down, then," he said.

His younger brothers Aziz and Fadel came out of their room, rubbing their eyes. Sulaiman winked at them, tore off a piece of bread, and stuck it right into the *shakshuka*'s yellow yoke. Closing his eyes, he took as long as he could to swallow. He was still just a few bites in when Said rose from the carpet where he sat.

"Hurry up, Sulaiman," his father said.

Sulaiman nodded and began to eat faster. "Where's Karim?" he asked.

Sarah picked up his half-eaten dish. "Your brother's not coming today, *habibi*. He's at Fatima's house doing schoolwork."

Sulaiman sighed. Since his grandfather Ayed had died a few years before, Sulaiman's older brother Karim had been responsible for looking after their aunt Fatima. She wasn't married and used to live with her father, but now that he was gone, she lived alone. There was fire in her blue kohl-lined eyes, and when she laughed the whole world shook. She'd done well, building a business from sewing golden thread into head coverings she sold to wealthy women from Bayt Hanina, a neighborhood of al-Quds. With the money she earned, she didn't just take care of herself, she took care of Sulaiman's whole family.

She gave them things, taught them history and stories. When a new child was born, she helped choose its name. Like other mothers, she seemed very old and asked them too many questions. She shouted when it was important, and whispered when it was still important but she didn't want the neighbors to hear.

Since Karim began living with Fatima, Sulaiman hadn't seen much of his brother. The school in Hizma only went to the ninth grade, and now that Karim was in high school, he took the bus to the Rashidiya school in al-Quds. He spent a lot of his time there, was distant from the rest of the family somehow. Maybe it had to do with love. A month before, he'd asked Sulaiman to give a note to a girl in the village named Nayla. Sulaiman knew how angry his brother would be if he read it, so he used all his powers not to peek inside the little piece of paper. When Sulaiman asked Karim what had happened, he wouldn't say a thing.

Sarah was just closing the picnic basket she would bring to Ta'mira when Sulaiman took off running, flashing through the doorway. "I'll race you!" he shouted back to his little brother Aziz, and headed toward the hill that led down to the family land.

He laughed when Aziz finally caught up with him, small chest heaving, and together they walked until they arrived in the clearing. Sulaiman picked a few pieces of stray grass from the packed ground and flopped down. Sweaty and tired, he pulled over a stone, brushed the dust out of the cracks, and pet it like a small animal. He made it his pillow until his parents arrived, walking slowly with little Fadel.

Sulaiman watched as Sarah walked around each tree, as if saying hello, wiping the dust off the leaves with a light touch, bending down to clear the dry leaves and dirt that had gathered around the trunk since the previous week. It seemed like those trees had been there forever, and maybe this is why his mother touched them the way she'd touch her own mother, who was very old, but still alive. The way you touch someone or something that has given you everything possible to give. Sulaiman had never seen anyone else touch a tree the way she did, as if it were human, as if it knew it were being touched.

As she paused at each tree, she sang traditional working songs. The formula was always the same, but she changed the words to fit the time of year: the olive harvest, the wheat harvest. Sometimes she would add a name: one of the family's lost relatives who had gone off to South America and disappeared. Or the name of Sulaiman's uncle who, living in Jordan in 1967, at the time of the *al-Naksa*,[8] now wasn't allowed to come home. Sometimes when she sang these names she cried. This—the cleaning and the singing both—was the work that had to be done to keep the land feeling loved, to keep it looking beautiful, to make sure it didn't forget that it belonged to someone who cared for it.

But it's not that it belonged to them exactly. When Sulaiman's grandfather Ayed was alive, the two of them would often walk together to Ta'mira. Ayed explained that the land didn't belong to people at all; it was the other way around. He taught Sulaiman that the oldest trees were called *rumani* because the Romans brought them here a long time ago, and that the other trees were called *baladi*[9] because they were from here, like their family. With the sky high above them, Ayed would lie down to take a nap. Instead of a pillow, he would always use the same soft stone.

Sulaiman's grandfather and the land had understood each other because they were both very old and somehow related. When Ayed died, the family cleaned his body just as they cleaned the land—very,

very carefully. Then they wrapped him in the whitest sheet Sulaiman had ever seen before carrying him through the main street of Hizma, to the graveyard near the mosque, where they dug a hole to put him in.

Everyone was at Ayed's funeral. The Israeli government even allowed Sulaiman's uncle a permit to enter briefly, to stand by the grave of his father, to visit the place he was born—the first time since 1967.

It was still a little strange visiting Ta'mira with Ayed gone. Sulaiman rested an ear against his stone until Sarah looked toward him and made a clicking sound. "Sulaiman," she said, "come help!" It was the height of summer, so while everyone else cleaned around the fig and grape trees, Sulaiman was responsible for grabbing the jug and pouring water over their roots. He remembered his mother's words when she first taught him to water the trees. *Iskihum*, she'd said. *Let them drink.*

When Sulaiman finished his work, his mother was still dusting the olive branches and pulling off their dead parts. Her work looked finished to him, but she kept going before joining the others in the shade. They rested, and the birds whose names his mother knew kept singing their usual songs.

Like always, they ate the food his mother had packed: lentils and watermelon, Coca-Cola and apples, vegetables and bread, cucumber and *lebne*.[10] After they were full, Said placed three stones in a circle and carefully stacked a pile of olive wood between them. He started a fire and pulled out a satchel of black tea with a bit of mint. Saturday tea was better than any other tea, because as Said took small sips, some extra life appeared in him.

During the week, Sulaiman's father seemed distant. His mother Sarah was the social one—talking, telling stories about how, when she was young and very beautiful, Said had started walking her home from school, and how his family didn't like it because her skin was darker than his. Even Aunt Fatima hadn't approved. *But I was the most beautiful one*, she would say, and laugh.

Sulaiman always felt close to his mom and her stories, but it was different with his father. Every day, except Friday and Saturday,

Said woke while it was still dark and went to work for the Israelis, cleaning the streets of al-Quds, in the part some people called West Jerusalem. By the time Sulaiman and his siblings rose to eat the *lebne*, za'atar, olive oil, milk, and eggs his mother set out for them, Said was already gone. And when he came home at night, they only saw him for a quick dinner before he went straight to bed.

Sometimes it was different, too, when Sulaiman went with his father to al-Quds for a haircut. When the hair grew long around his ears and his mother frowned, he'd get on the bus in Hizma at noon, after school. Fifteen minutes later, he'd climb off the bus at the *karaj*[11] near the Jerusalem Hotel, under the sign that read "Hizma-Quds Line." His father would walk quickly across the dirt lot toward him, looking tired but somehow comfortable, like he was in his own house. And then he'd kneel to the packed dirt and pick up something shiny. Wherever he went, Said was always finding coins on the ground.

From the Jerusalem Hotel, they'd walk west, past vendors who nodded and smiled at Said, up the hill toward a street called *Ha-Nevi'im* in Hebrew and *al-Anbi'aa* in Arabic—two words that both meant "the prophets." Sulaiman would listen to the sound his father's adult shoes made on the pavement, would go home later and beg his mother to put something on his own shoes so they'd make that *tiktac* sound. After a several-minute walk, Sulaiman listening to his father's shoes, they'd reach the barber with the head of white hair that stood out in all directions. While the Israeli Jew cut Sulaiman's hair, his father came alive, speaking a Hebrew too complicated for Sulaiman to understand. It was like watching a line drawing fill with ink and color.

Something similar happened to his father over tea at Ta'mira. Said smiled, and something got soft and somehow light in his face. He drank his tea slowly, and for the last hour, no one did anything but find all the best ways to sit and lie on the ground.

When the light started to darken, Said began singing one of his Saturday songs. Sarah started gathering the dried edges of bread wrapped in napkins and throwing the bundles back into her basket. The music made the cleaning into a kind of a dance. Sulaiman watched, wanting to know how to make the sun go higher so they could stay there, and keep staying there.

He looked out at the land—toward the ancient quarry, just a bit farther than the ancient graveyard where his relatives dug for rusty treasures to sell in al-Quds—and followed his family home.

CHAPTER 2

Ra's al-Tawil

Later that year, Sulaiman caught an image on television, or the image caught him: piles and piles of bodies. Israel had invaded Lebanon, hoping to weaken Palestinian guerrilla groups gathered there. Overnight, Israeli soldiers had cast light into the sky: from planes and from the ground. Inside the camps, Christian Phalangist militias had moved through the streets conducting a massacre, killing hundreds of the Palestinian and Lebanese civilians who lived there. The Israeli soldiers provided light; they waited outside until it was done.

On his aunt Shamsiya's television screen he saw them, the pictures of bodies, filmed in unreal shades of black and white, lying in terrible positions all over the ground. He wouldn't forget them.

He would forget the details of what happened a couple years later, when his older brother Karim appeared in his aunt Fatima's house, or maybe his parents' house, bleeding. The doctor arrived, followed by soldiers. It was almost certainly the middle of the night. This is usually how the army made sure all family members and neighbors were in bed. The village *mukhtar*[1] knocked on the door; Sulaiman couldn't remember later if the soldiers who entered were cruel or polite. He couldn't remember whether he saw them drive away, heard the tire wheels on the dirt as the crying started, or whether he just heard Fatima talk, between tears and fists, about what the soldiers looked like—what they'd said and done.

Whatever happened the night of the arrest, Sarah began to cry and wouldn't stop. The whole family was awake even though it was late, the sky outside completely black. Maybe there were stars, but Sulaiman couldn't see any.

The morning after, Sulaiman woke to the neighbors pacing about the house as if they'd always been there, as if there was nothing strange at all about this moment. They made breakfast, fluffed pillows, moved things from one place to another and back again. One woman named Hajar did the laundry, and another named Khadija walked by, calling, "Sarah is the queen, the princess of Ibrahim. And Hajar is the servant!" She was referring to the story of the first Sarah and Hajar, from the Qur'an: Sarah, who was barren and offered her handmaiden Hajar to her husband, Ibrahim, to bear his children. Hajar, who gave birth to Ismail and found herself alone with her son in the middle of a desert, without enough water.

Sarah laughed between tears, but not Said. He didn't laugh or cry; he just walked around with a faraway look, his face still, and hard, and dry.

When the guests started to arrive, Sulaiman took his post at the front door beside his father, and after greeting each person, went to serve coffee. He carried it around on its silver tray and poured the thick brown liquid into many little silver and white cups. Then he perched somewhere nearby until more people came and he had to stand again. There weren't enough places to sit.

The guests continued to come, staying for hours to drink coffee and tea and smoke and talk about Karim, or sometimes, to talk about anything else, pretending nothing was wrong. They came to express their sadness about a son locked away, to give gifts, simply to do what is always done when something difficult happens. They came out of devotion to the principle of *sumud* (steadfastness), and sometimes for other reasons that Sulaiman could feel but not quite understand.

Weeks passed and Sulaiman's hands grew tired from holding, and pouring, and serving all the people on all the couches. No one had news of Karim, but Sulaiman kept expecting to see him walk down the road from Fatima's house. He sneaked glances at his mother, because it seemed wrong to look. She always sat in the same place on the far side of the room, hands folded lightly in her lap. Her crying was quieter now; sometimes it seemed like it had stopped completely, until he'd see one tear squeeze itself out, as if trying not to bother anyone.

That's how it was when Karim's friend Sami arrived. As the young man walked through the door, Sulaiman could sense Said stiffen beside him. Sami was older than Karim, in his early twenties, and he hung out in the nearby community center. Everyone in the village knew he was political, that he talked often about fighting for their country. Sami leaned forward to kiss Said's cheek, but Said waited a long moment before offering it back to be kissed. When the young man reached out to place a hand on Said's shoulder, Sulaiman's father pulled away, microscopically, almost invisibly.

"It's okay," Sami said, "we have to struggle. Your son is a hero."

Sulaiman turned to watch the young man walk into the living room where Sarah sat, and when he looked back, his father was gone.

That night, Sulaiman lay still on his mattress. He could smell the goats on the warm, heavy air and hear his father's voice traveling up from downstairs, through his open window. Through the sounds of the night, he could only make out certain words: *Jewish, municipality, money, criminal, bad luck, job.* He could hear his mother respond with something more like a flute than a voice; he heard only the melody of it.

"You should have known," his father's voice grew louder. "You shouldn't have let him spend time with those people."

Said didn't want his children to fight the Israelis. He wanted them to have money, to study. He saw no use in struggling to change the system. He wanted only to work and live, to build new floors in his house, to make a good life under the circumstances he'd been given. And now that he was the father of a political prisoner, he was afraid he'd lose his job working for the Israelis in al-Quds.

Through the window, Sulaiman imagined he could hear the sound of his mother's tears leaving her eyes, reaching toward her chin. He knew that she didn't want her children to fight either, but he could tell she wasn't angry. She just wanted her oldest son back.

Sulaiman liked the older boys who came and sat and spoke respectfully to Sarah, the ones who made his father disappear. They were tall and smart and strong, and he felt their lives were important somehow. He wasn't sure how, even if she'd wanted to, Sarah could have stopped Karim from spending time with them. They were men, and not even a mother could stop a man from doing what he wanted. Now, with Karim somewhere else, Sulaiman was the oldest son of the house. *Which means,* he reminded himself, *that I'm a man now.*

Karim appeared in court multiple times. Once, when a court guard saw the shoes Sarah clutched to her chest, he backed away yelling. He thought she'd brought them to throw—shoes as weapons. Someone had to calm him down, to tell him she was just a mother worried about her son's feet. It would be many months and many court dates later that someone finally read Karim's sentence: fifteen years.

The new reality that settled in was, in many ways, just like the old one. In the house, the love songs of 'Abd al-Halim Hafiz came in through the radio and Sulaiman played soccer in the little grove. But once in a while, he and Sarah went somewhere else. They took the same bus that Karim once took to school, and after about five minutes, they got off in Bayt Hanina. They waited for a second bus to Ramallah, and when it arrived, Sulaiman turned the other way so his mother's face could turn gray and then back to its normal color without anyone to witness it.

Ramallah was only fourteen kilometers away, but it was still a foreign place. The bus ride to the new city made Sulaiman nauseous, so his mother brought a lemon for him to smell. She carried it in a brown paper bag and handed it to him when the bumpy road began to turn his stomach. The lemon helped, but when the Israeli prison appeared, a faint sick feeling returned.

The building looked so big, like he'd never be able to find his brother inside it. As he stood and waited to pass through security, he opened and closed his hands, as if he'd only just realized they were his and wasn't quite sure what to do with them. He watched a female guard pat his mother down, saw the look that hung about Sarah's face and settled into her shoulders until they reached the room where Karim sat, on the other side of a mesh divider. Sarah could

touch her son through the wire, but just his fingers. Sometimes, Sulaiman noticed, this touching made her cry. Not Karim, though. He
looked big, like the other prisoners, who said words like *al-ihtilal*,
the occupation, words like *Arafat, PLO, enemy, struggle, hero*. Sulaiman held onto the words, organized them in his mind, compiling
a dictionary he knew he shouldn't speak out loud.

Over many months, he learned that most of the prisoners' families were refugees from the war of 1948, the Nakba, unlike Sulaiman's cousins, who were refugees from the Naksa, the 1967 war.
Until these visits, he hadn't met many refugees at all. He knew only
the small community that lived in a few houses at Hizma's edge. After 1948, they'd come from a place called Ishwa', west of al-Quds.
When Fatima talked about their struggle, it seemed like she wasn't
talking about them at all. "Israel took the seaside," she often said,
"and gave us the mountains." He understood, when she said this,
how much she missed the sea.

Though Sulaiman accompanied Fatima or Sarah to the jail almost every two weeks, Said's visits were infrequent, brief. When he
came, he sat in silence. Once, in front of all the prisoners, Sulaiman
saw a tear come from Said's eye. He'd turned away from his father,
embarrassed.

Sulaiman understood what his father didn't: that his brother was
part of a changing world, one that refused to stay the same. He
knew that *sumud*, steadfastness, had something to do with it. That
changing the way things were and rooting down deeper were linked
somehow. Slowly, he felt the edges of his world creep wide.

Now the oldest boy at home, Sulaiman began to sleep in his
grandfather's house, in the big room off the balcony across from
Fatima. Though she seemed to rule over whatever space she was
in, Fatima never lived alone. His parents thought someone needed
to be there to help her, and Sulaiman was glad to be chosen. He
loved the old stone house: its dark basement that stayed cool and
smelled like earth, its garden of pomegranate, fig, and lemon trees;
its stone stairs leading up to a balcony that looked out over the valley and hills. He loved the little holes in the flat stones of the front
yard, where Fatima always made sure there were bits of bread for

the cats and pigeons and chickens. He loved Fatima and her talent for picking pomegranates and presenting them to him at just the right moment. If Sulaiman was ever about to get hungry or sad, a pomegranate would miraculously appear. But it wasn't a miracle, it was only Fatima.

Living with his aunt meant that Sulaiman had to do whatever she asked, running to the little market down the road to get something for her kitchen, but mostly he had freedom. He could go wherever he wanted, moving easily between his family home and Fatima's, as if the road between them were just a hallway. He felt stuck only when he saw the soldiers at the entrance of the village, stopping cars and looking at people's papers, telling them whether or not they could visit their family, whether or not they could return home from work.

It was one day, after seeing the soldiers, that Sulaiman and his cousin Asif first visited the community center between Sulaiman's two houses. When they first walked in, Sulaiman looked around nervously. He nodded at Sami, the young man who'd told Said that Karim was a hero, and glanced at a few other older boys—disappearing into couches, smoking hookah, and drinking coffee. He followed Asif to the ping-pong table, where they played until his stomach hurt from laughing at his cousin's jokes and it was time for dinner.

They began to visit the community center often. After school they bought sandwiches and Coca-Colas; they went to the center to play ping-pong, pool, and foosball, to listen while the older boys talked. Sulaiman heard them speak the new words he'd learned sitting next to refugee families at the jail: *PLO*, *Arafat*, and a new word, the name of the center—*Shabiba*.

Sulaiman felt the lines of division traveling through the village, between his father and the boys playing ping-pong around him. While his father and many others accepted the status quo, a small number of people, like the boys at the Shabiba center, were seen as "PLO people." The PLO (Palestine Liberation Organization) was created to organize different Palestinian political groups fighting for freedom and a return home. The boys at the Shabiba center supported the PLO's mission to establish a Palestinian state and reject

Israeli rule. Sulaiman understood their message but couldn't trace its details. He didn't know that Shabiba was a youth movement born in the early 1980s, around the time the PLO had been pushed out of Beirut, into even more distant exile. He didn't know that the movement and its center were affiliated with Fatah: the party of Yasser Arafat, the dominant party of the PLO. He didn't know because people rarely spoke the word *Fatah*. Israel had deemed the party illegal. It was dangerous to even whisper its name.

On his way back to Fatima's one day, Sulaiman chose a detour through the hills. Taking his time, he heard a strange noise from the hill called Ra's al-Tawil, not far from the center of Hizma. It sounded like drills, like heavy stones falling. By the next month, a building or two had appeared, as if by magic. He didn't think much of it. He didn't wonder what it meant. He didn't connect it to Neve Ya'akov, his friend Shimon's home to the northwest of Hizma, or to the 1967 war, or to the other Jewish settlements growing in a ring around the eastern section of al-Quds.

It wasn't until later that year, during a performance at the brand-new Palestinian theater in East al-Quds, that he heard Palestinian national music for the first time. The songs were so loud in the big hall that their vibrations settled under his skin, found space between his tissues and ligaments and bones. The songs reminded him a little of the ones Fatima sang during the wheat harvest: about lost things, a longing for home.

Though he kept playing soccer in the grove with Hanif, Fadi, and Mohannad, he began to feel differently around them. These old friends didn't know how to listen for the most important thing: the way the world sounds when it's changing. He could tell they didn't have a secret dictionary, didn't understand the things the prisoners did. They were looking in the wrong direction, like his father, and he didn't want to be like them. He wanted to be someone who understood.

That spring, about a year after Karim's arrest, on the first day of Ramadan, Sulaiman was standing on the rose-and-white checkered floor in front of his family's house, trying to decide if there was time to play soccer before the *iftar* meal.[2] When he turned around, his eyes met a green uniform, an impossibly wide waist, the black ridges of a gun. When he looked up, he recognized the face of Captain Tzahi, the head of Israeli army intelligence in the central West Bank. Captain Tzahi knew everyone in Hizma, and everyone in Hizma knew him. He asked to speak with Said and, after Sulaiman led him inside, he asked if the family had heard the news. A year after his arrest, Karim was being released in a prisoner exchange. They hadn't heard, and when Captain Tzahi told them, it was a sudden thing, as if someone had flipped the whole world from the bottom up. The house became busy, food had to be made quickly, everything altered so rapidly that Sulaiman could almost hear it—like the sound of a foot stepping on glass, or a gun shot in the air at a wedding.

They waited for a few hours before a Red Cross vehicle rolled up to the front door and Sulaiman saw his brother's feet, then his knees, then the rest of him—the whole thing so fast and strange, it didn't seem even a little real.

They'd waited one year and a handful of hours for Karim. The families of his friends would have to wait much longer. Their sons were sentenced for ten and thirteen years, and they would serve that whole time. But not Karim. A distant relative in the PLO leadership had put Karim's name on a list, so he was released early, not dumped on the street like prisoners usually were, but delivered right to their door where the whole family waited.

When Karim appeared, everyone grabbed him. Everyone wanted to touch some part of him—a piece of his shirt, his elbow, his shoulder, like he was something they could rub for good luck—before forcing him onto their shoulders and into the air. They walked him down the street, a long line of people. Even the ones who were just clapping their hands, it was like they were carrying him too.

For days after Karim's release, there were songs and sweets and endless cups of coffee and tea that Sulaiman might have spilt, just once, as the long line of neighbors came in and out of the house, and Sulaiman nodded to each, wearing a face that made him look like a man, like the brother of his brother.

When an older boy named Adil walked in the door and nodded, Sulaiman tried to hide his excitement. Adil's family house stood just next to Fatima's, and in its second-story window there was often a girl surrounded by yellow light. Every evening, Sulaiman looked up at that window where he could see Adil's younger sister Samira; she seemed to be always moving, doing some kind of dance with pencils.

He'd heard the gossip: Adil's family was politically active. A few of his brothers were in jail and his father was involved in the PLO somehow. There weren't many families like that in the village, so when Adil came to visit after Karim's release, Sulaiman watched the older boy carefully. He was nineteen years old, and to Sulaiman he looked like a grown man.

Adil talked like the guys at the Shabiba center. He said that Palestine was being held down like a bird in a cage and needed to be freed. He sang revolutionary songs from memory. And though Karim wouldn't answer any of Sulaiman's questions about jail or revolution, Adil was happy to talk. He gave Sulaiman the feeling that he was different, important. That if he wasn't a leader yet, he'd soon become one.

CHAPTER 3

A Hidden Place

In the family house, where the doors were always left open so-the wind could move sweetly through the rooms, Sulaiman began closing his. On the second floor, he listened to cassette tapes for hours. *Musiqa thawriya*, he learned to call it, "revolutionary music." It was illegal, and this deepened the lyrics all about *hanin*, a word with many others inside it: *longing* but also *hope, yearning, blossoming*. When he listened, he closed his eyes, imagined running off in uniform to fight for his family's freedom. He pictured Samira and all the girls of the village gathered in one window—somehow they all fit—waving to him as he left.

Sulaiman played along with his wooden flute. He practiced with his breath, learned how to move it back and forth to make the shaking sound he liked. He played until his lips and fingers were sore.

When he emerged one day, his mom was there, applauding. "Another artist in the family!" she said, and clapped her hands together.

"You have our family's blood in you, for sure," she said. "Going back a long time, we've played flute and sung behind closed doors. We have warm blood, artist's blood, and a lot of us also like the taste of sweet things."

He waved the back of his hand at her, didn't say anything in return. He let her think he was just becoming an artist, not considering big historical questions that would change everything, that would save them from the strange toy houses multiplying on Ra's al-Tawil.

The next day, Sulaiman found the huge key to his father's storage room downstairs and went secretly, looking over his shoulder the way a boy does when he's trying to keep a secret but just learning how. When he opened the door, he saw his grandfather's stone pillow from Ta'mira sitting among old coins, an ancient-looking radio, and a mess of papers and cups. Pulling one of his cassette tapes out of his pocket, handling it like glass, he slipped it into his Walkman, and pressed play. Trying to imagine the sound of the singer Abu Arab's voice filling his body, he waited for his favorite line, the one about greeting the land of his ancestors, the one that ended *The melodious bird is still singing for our return.*

Sulaiman played the tape again and again until it became scratched and worn, until the black ribbons inside came out, dancing to the music the way some people dance for rain: to make it true.

After dinner at his parents' house, he slipped bits of bread into his pockets when no one was looking. He ran to the kitchen and kissed his mother on the cheek, just once instead of the usual three times; she was too busy with her soapy hands to offer him the other side of her face. On the checkered patio, he kissed his father a full three times—left cheek, right cheek, left cheek—and sprinted the few yards, under the stars, to Fatima's house. The black metal gate was open but he scrambled up the beige stone wall anyway, to practice. It was good to know how to climb things; kids in Hizma learned to do it very young. His cousin Asif could scramble up the tall cliff wall near the spring of 'Ayn Fawwar[1] like a little goat.

Sulaiman sat on the top of the wall for a moment. To his right were some leafy bushes he knew were green, even though he couldn't see them in the night; past them were a cluster of blossoms that glowed white, even in the dark. And past those, a bit to the left, he saw the lights of al-Quds, where his father worked, where the barber lived with his wild white hair.

When he felt the beginning of a shiver, he jumped down from the wall, ran through the grove of trees, and straight up the stone stairs. Fatima sat on the patio, looking at the sky.

"You're so late!" she swatted at him.

She sounded angry, but he knew she wasn't. They sat and drank tea while Fatima spoke in the way that she did—he couldn't tell whether she was talking to him or to herself—about the strange people moving into the new buildings on Ra's al-Tawil. It was her new favorite topic. These people were Jews, like the people in Neve Ya'aqub, but they were different; they spoke Russian, didn't even know Hebrew. She spoke about how Jews had lived in Neve Ya'aqub before the Nakba.[2] They'd traded with the people of Hizma—chickens and almonds, figs and milk. But these new people were from somewhere else. It felt like someone had transplanted them from outer space.

Sulaiman listened to his aunt talking, almost singing, about the land that was disappearing, going, piece by piece. To describe the new buildings on Ra's al-Tawil, Fatima used a word Sulaiman hadn't heard before: *mustawtana*, settlement.

"What do they think they're doing?" she yelled at the sky. He'd heard her repeat this question many times already, while his mother sipped tea on the couch, fingering her prayer beads, twisting her white sleeve around her long fingers. "The *mustawtana* started building on land belonging to Hizma families. They didn't try to buy it. They didn't even ask whose it was. They must know we'd never sell."[3] As Fatima continued, raising her hands to the sky, Sulaiman didn't say anything, but he let an anger rise inside him, a hot heat, a righteous, good feeling.

Then, as if joining a song that had already begun, Fatima changed course, lifting her voice to sing the old family *ghazal* about a cow her mother had loved very much, who'd died too soon. She sang until she got tired, and she and Sulaiman returned to the room off the balcony, where the smells of the garden floated into the emptiness where Sulaiman's grandfather once slept.

On his mattress, Sulaiman strained to see what he knew was there: the dresser next to Fatima's mattress, the picture someone had painted a long time ago, a small pot of flowers. He looked up at the ceiling, tried to imagine it was transparent, that he could see all the way to the stars. As he felt his eyelids close, he willed them to stay open. This was the hardest time of day. After school, and the goats, and pretending to be a boy in front of his mother and father. He was so tired.

When enough time had passed, and he could hear Fatima's breathing, slow and heavy, he slipped out from under the blanket and stuck his pillow underneath. It looked like a body curled up in a ball. He tiptoed down the stairs, opened the black gate as quietly as possible, willing it not to squeak, and headed out into the street.

He'd recruited his cousins to form a group, and the three of them had started to go, secretly, without their families knowing, to Najla's cave. It was a huge, old cave, surrounded by figs when the season was right. No one knew if the cave belonged to anyone—if Najla was alive or not. This made it a hidden place. The boys brought candles or a flashlight, called each other by secret names. One of Sulaiman's names, his favorite, was Jabal, "Mountain."

That night, he waited for Asif and Sadiq in front of their school, just before the mosque and the well. It was strange how different their school looked in the dark, how it was the same building but also somehow wasn't. When he heard his cousins' footsteps, he began to pull out the cans of white, red, and green, one at a time.

"Okay," he said, handing the paint to his friends, making sure his voice was at its deepest. "Ready? Go."

They began to shake and shake the cans, pulled off the caps, and sprayed mists of paint on the walls. When they stepped back, Sulaiman had drawn a Palestinian flag and a wobbly picture of Handala, a famous cartoon of a Palestinian boy, like them. Handala's creator, Naji al-Ali, had lived in a refugee camp in Lebanon, a camp like Sabra and Shatila. Handala saw all the things that happened and didn't look away.

Asif and Sadiq each wrote "Free Palestine" so that their part of the wall read "Free Palestine Free Palestine."

Sulaiman looked at the drawings, which were important because they were illegal, at least twice over. Painting on the walls was prohibited, and so was the Palestinian flag, which is why Sulaiman spent his time in math class sketching secret Palestinian flags in his notebook. He hated math and he hated how his teachers never spoke the word *Palestine*, which was another sacred, prohibited thing. They never mentioned that they weren't free, never said anything that made Sulaiman feel he was learning about himself. Adil had told him that Palestinian teachers in the West Bank and Gaza worked under the Israeli Army's Civil Administration, and that if they said the wrong thing, they'd lose their jobs.

When he grew tired of looking at their wall, Sulaiman whispered in Sadiq's ear, "I'll race you!" and took off running. Even though Sulaiman had a head start, Asif and his long legs reached the cave first. But Sulaiman had already prepared his surprise. Breathing heavily, grinning at his two friends, he lifted a sheet off a small object in one of the cave's dark, wet corners: a small wooden radio with gold knobs. He'd stolen it from his father's secret room of old things.

Sadiq clapped his hands and rubbed them together as if trying to start a fire. Asif ran out to collect figs, and when he returned, the boys huddled together, filled their mouths with the wild fruit, and wiggled the radio dial until they heard words coming through the static. The PLO was calling to them with ghost voices—barely audible, but still somehow very loud. Here, the volumes of the world's regular channels were reversed: the secret revolutionaries were loud and everything else slightly turned down and less true. The voices told Sulaiman what he already knew. Like prophets speaking from far away, they said the only way to be alive was to fight.

The boys, imagining themselves as a tiny militia, concocted plans. Sulaiman wrote them down in a notebook hidden, along with copies of the secret magazines *al-Bayadir al-Siyasi*[4] and *al-'Awda*,[5] in small holes in the cave's floors and walls. He recorded what they said, what they did, what they planned to do. Tonight, they had memorized the words to a song and made resistance art on the wall of their school. He didn't write down what was also true: the whole thing was fun, a little like a game.

Sulaiman knew his father only wanted him to be a good student—to stay away from politics and throwing stones. But the expansion of Pisgat Ze'ev—the name of the settlement growing on Ra's al-Tawil—kept shrinking the space he could move through. Soon, the construction would cut the road between his home and al-Quds. Soon, it seemed, there would be more soldiers than normal people.

Though there had been an Israeli army training camp near Hizma for as long as Sulaiman could remember, the soldiers seemed to come through town more often now. He could no longer ignore the guns firing nearby, the sounds of barely grown men learning how best to shoot. It seemed that every night he looked out the window, there was the shape of a jeep, the sound of wheels on dirt, headlights shining too bright in the inky dark. He could hear the quick thunder of tear gas, Fatima's soft steps as she ran through the house in her slippers, closing all the windows. Sometimes, if Fatima spotted an army jeep outside, she would close the windows just in case, and they would wait together to see what happened after the soldiers entered a neighbor's house.

Sulaiman hated this waiting. It didn't make sense to see the soldiers and do nothing. To just hold prayer beads or lift hands to the sky or go to work in Jerusalem, like his father, and bring home the dry cracker the Jews ate once a year, or the too-sweet cakes they ate all the time. Throwing stones was something that made sense.

Standing at the entrance to Hizma, Sulaiman watched as a soldier took an ID card from a hand stretched out of a car. The soldier shook his head, pointed. The car followed the soldier's finger and turned around. As if calling him, Sulaiman heard the sounds of the songs he'd begun listening to, urging his people to be brave, to resist, to never give up. He reached down to the ground and pulled up a small handful of rocks, tiny smooth stones and little rough ones that scratched his palms. He swung an arm back, like he'd done the night before, throwing tiny Palestinian flags onto electrical lines—so the bits of fabric hung like undeniable reminders that his people were here, that they would never leave. It was the same now, as he took a deep breath and spun his arm forward, so hard he thought it had come out of his socket. He opened his palm with the stones inside. He let go. There was a sudden, hook-like feeling in his stomach, and then he turned and ran, dirt spitting out from his heels.

That first time he threw stones he was afraid, but not the next time. That's the way it always was with frightening things. He gathered Sadiq and Asif, and together they sat and waited for the army jeeps to come into Hizma, or they headed to the post where the soldiers stood at the village's entrance, checking IDs. Sometimes they waited for a long time, like the people in American movies who sat on bridges, fishing. They joked and talked about girls. How Adil's sister Samira seemed to dance in her window as she did her homework. How Lina, a favorite of many boys in their class, had looked at Sulaiman and winked, how other boys said she'd winked at them too. Everything was built around a thing that would happen, but the bulk of the action was the waiting itself. Sulaiman was growing more and more tired of this waiting; he felt he almost couldn't do it anymore, couldn't sit in school playing games with his teachers who didn't understand a thing.

That's when summer came.

In the summer of 1986, Sulaiman stopped taking out the goats. With the school year finished, he looked for a job, hoping to make a bit of money. He took the first thing he found, in the growing settlement of Pisgat Ze'ev. Alongside a Palestinian citizen of Israel from Haifa, he painted the iron railings of staircases in the new houses. It seemed like the town's construction had only just started, but there was already a main road with bakeries, cafés, stores, and all those people speaking Russian to each other as they carried their groceries home. They seemed pleasant enough, and somehow, the Pisgat Ze'ev he worked in became a different thing than the one he imagined attacking while sitting in the cave with Asif and Sadiq, or walking with Adil at night. As if one had nothing to do with the other.

On days he didn't work, he and Asif would walk all the way to the blue pools of 'Ayn Farrah[6] under an old monastery, where all the children in Hizma learned to swim. On the way, they'd stop in the valley, shouting up at a hole in the cliff where they knew a monk lived alone, practicing secret languages only the angels knew. They called out, asking the monk to drop the secret ladder and let them up into his house of God, but no one ever appeared.

Sulaiman began visiting al-Quds without a chaperone, leaning against the walls of Salah al-Din Street to look at the girls walking by. With his pocket money, he bought a small red knife like the one all the boys bought when they became men. It cost ten shekels. Sulaiman kept the knife at his hip and took it out only sometimes—to cut an apple, or let a bit of it show, just a little, when a girl walked by, slipping on the smooth rocks of the old city. He marveled at how pretty girls looked when they fell. And then, as if it weren't strange at all, his mind turned down another path: into the cave, where no girls were allowed and no girls slipped, where he had finally collected a good supply of plastic bottles, strings, and gasoline.

He didn't know exactly what he was planning for, but he knew he was getting ready for *something*. With Asif and Sadiq, he practiced making Molotov cocktails, putting gas in a bottle, lighting the string that balanced half in and half out, and throwing it at nothing in the empty space beside the cave. He hesitated, always, and then went off running.

They began to talk of doing something special that September, for the anniversary of Sabra and Shatila—that terrible massacre in Lebanon those few years before. Something that would add to the Palestinian band Firqat al-'Ashiqin's tribute, their song "Ishhad Ya 'Alam," which Sulaiman often sang pieces of to himself, calling to Beirut as to a dear friend and saying: *We didn't raise the banner of surrender.*

Singing and walking near the stone quarry one day, Sulaiman saw an old construction worker blowing up parts of mountains to make room for new houses. He watched as the man, bent-backed, took the black powder he used for explosions and hid it in a big hole where a piece of mountain used to be.

Sulaiman brought Asif back with him that night, and they collected the powder. They didn't tell Sadiq, who had lately developed a nervous twitch in his eye. As the boys crept back to their cave, Asif mentioned that his friend Farid's house had just been demolished because it was built without an impossible-to-get permit. As the cousins whispered, they laid out their supplies. They placed the powder inside a piece of broken water pipe, a bullet in front. Asif lit the bottom of the device with a match, and as he threw it, it exploded. Both boys pretended they hadn't jumped clear off the ground, nearly flying from fear. A small whimper split the quiet. The blast had been weak, but the heat of it had burned Asif's hand.

Sulaiman decided that neither Sadiq with his nervous eye nor Asif with his singed hand would be ready for anything when September came. He thought about what Asif had said about Farid. He barely knew the blond-haired boy, but he knew enough to guess he'd want revenge for the loss of his home.

That night, Sulaiman crawled into bed in his family house, where he still sometimes slept. Sleep didn't come though, and as he lay there, he imagined he could smell the gunpowder and damp dirt of the cave on his shirt. *Tomorrow morning*, he told himself as his eyes finally closed, *I'll wash well before I go into the kitchen.* He didn't want his mother to sense that smell, and know.

The next morning, Sarah watched him over the tea kettle. "Sulaiman," she said, pausing. "Where did you go last night?" She twisted her long white sleeve around her hand, covering the tips of her fingers.

"We were looking for birds."

"Birds? Where?"

"*Yamma*,[7] relax! In the hills, in the trees, in the sky."

"At night?"

Sulaiman took a gulp of tea and flashed a smile. "Yes! What do you think? That the birds disappear in the dark?"

She paused and looked at him. When he didn't say more, she sighed. She pushed her worry away. He was only fourteen years old.

CHAPTER 4

'Ayn Farrah

The morning of August 21, Farid's mother was in Mecca for the Hajj. It was later that she told Sarah she'd seen a *ru'ya*, a vision of her son passing by, that she'd seen blood. But Sarah didn't see any visions from God. She just rose early to knock on the window of Sulaiman's room. "*Yamma*," he'd said the night before, "wake me early. I want to go hunting while there's still fog."

She had to knock several times before she heard his voice and knew he was awake. She went to warm some milk, to prepare the *khubz* (bread) to bake in the stone *tabun* outside. She placed the milk on a table and when Sulaiman came in, he wanted to sit and drink next to her, but she shook her head. She had too much to do. She asked him to bring something from Fatima's, then left to tend to the goats and bread.

But when Sulaiman finished his breakfast, he didn't go to Fatima's. He met up with Farid and together they walked the path along the cliff face, high above the valley. Sulaiman had his red pocket-knife, the one he'd bought in al-Quds, and Farid had a more traditional knife, something stronger. It was August, and very hot, but each boy wore the traditional Palestinian *kufiya*[1] around his neck. It was August, and they were two boys headed out to steal guns from the soldiers who were often at 'Ayn Farrah, guns they could use for the anniversary of Sabra and Shatila, just one month away.

When they reached the water of 'Ayn Farrah, the sun was directly above them, a ball of light too bright to see. Then they heard the voices. A big group of Israeli tourists were walking into the clearing around the spring's first pool. They carried bags, wore sunglasses, joked, laughed. At the back of the group, two men wore the green uniforms of IDF soldiers. Those two men—about nineteen or twenty years old—looked just like the soldiers who checked IDs at the entrance of Hizma. Each of them had a big bag—big enough, Sulaiman thought, to hold a gun.

The group waded into the first pool in the valley, and kept moving until their voices faded into an echo and eventually Sulaiman and Farid couldn't see them at all. The two men in uniform stayed behind for a moment, then walked with their bags up the dirt path toward the monastery. Farid and Sulaiman followed. The boys entered the holy courtyard and found the two Israelis, their backs to the door.

Sulaiman could still hear the distant calls of the large group, likely gathered around one of the springs below, where he'd once learned to swim. He reached down to his pant waist, ran his fingers over the red pocketknife, made sure it was still there. When one of the Israelis turned around, Sulaiman smiled. The Israeli smiled back.

Sulaiman began to recite the few words of Hebrew he knew from his father, from big-toothed Shimon, and the Israelis laughed. Sulaiman sat beside one, Farid beside the other. The Israelis offered them tea, and they all drank together. At some point, Sulaiman began to sing.

In the invisible pauses between words and gestures, Sulaiman wasn't sure he should continue. But it was like he was an actor in some play, as if an engine were running in his chest, somewhere beneath his ribs, propelling him forward. After an all-too-brief interval, the Israelis were standing up, hoisting their bags onto their shoulders and turning to leave the monastery. Sulaiman could feel Farid's blue eyes before he saw them, asking the question. Sulaiman looked at the other boy, this boy he barely knew, and blinked once, hard.

They attacked. Sulaiman was a second late, so the Israeli next to him was ready, standing up in his green uniform, yelling. Sulaiman and Farid had knives but the men they fought were stronger and bigger. If the Israelis overpowered them, Sulaiman was sure they'd reach into their bags, grab their guns. With all their voices raised loud, Sulaiman felt certain the group below would hear and come with the whole army behind them.

The Israeli that Sulaiman struggled with held him off; he was strong and Sulaiman couldn't see a way out in any direction. They fought for an hour. Half an hour. Ten minutes, maybe. Hands, a little knife, and stones. The moments passed as in a dream. He could die, he was sure of it, in a second.

Something shifted and Sulaiman stopped trying to win; instead he began to work only on freeing himself from the tangle of arms and blows. Somehow, he pulled himself away, and suddenly he was with Farid and they were running, without bags or guns, remembering to be afraid. They ran and ran and it seemed they would never stop running.

Sulaiman didn't look back. He didn't know if the Israelis were on the ground or were chasing after him, if there was any blood. He didn't know, wouldn't until later, that these two young men were on a backpacking trip after the end of their army service. That they'd worn their army uniforms only to make it easier to hitchhike. That there were likely no guns in their bags.[2] He only ran, not realizing they'd left their *kufiyat* behind, that the Israelis were using the checkered cloths to dress their wounds.

Somehow, they made it back to Hizma. They found themselves leaning over the well near the mosque, drinking from cupped hands, but the moment didn't last long. Suddenly, there was noise on all sides: sirens, the slicing sound of helicopters, dogs barking, unintelligible words through a loudspeaker.

They started running again until they reached Ta'mira, crouching down between the olive trees. But the voices of the soldiers followed them, crackling through the air in Hebrew-accented Arabic: *Sallem nafsak*, give yourself up. Something in Sulaiman's stomach fell before he realized, *They don't know where we are. They are just saying it. If they saw us, they would come.*

For a moment, he thought it might be nice to lie down, to find a stone pillow like his grandfather's. But before the thought was finished, he and Farid were lifting each other from the ground, running again. They ran a long time before they stopped, and by then,

the cramping pain had come and gone from Sulaiman's belly. As if
something was in there, trying to get out.

Outside the town of Jaba', they let themselves slow down but
didn't stop until they reached Mukhmas, the village where Farid's
mother was born. Sulaiman kept waiting to hear shots fired, to feel
the choppy wind that meant another helicopter. But there was
nothing. For a moment, Sulaiman thought he might throw up. The
two boys stood in front of Farid's family house for a while, until Farid
led the way in.

The news spread as in a wind. Two Israeli men had been stabbed,
one in the back, the other in the left shoulder and right rib. They
had survived, and described their attackers: one boy with big black
hair and one blond boy with a shining gold tooth.

As soldiers searched Hizma, Sarah held tightly to the ends of her
sleeves, counting her prayer beads, making every promise to God
she could think of if only He kept Sulaiman safe. For a little while,
she held onto the hope that it wasn't what it seemed.

A curfew was called, and the soldiers gathered all the men and
boys between the ages of thirteen and thirty in the courtyard of the
school. The Israelis instructed them to open their mouths, and they
went through the group, one by one. The children's jaws opened
and the soldiers peered into the dark spaces of all the little mouths,
searching for a gold tooth, for some kind of secret, but they didn't
find one. All the boys and young men in the village were counted
but two.

Sulaiman stayed with Farid's extended family in Mukhmas, waiting. Farid's family watched the news on their TV, heard reports of
a stabbing in 'Ayn Farrah, a giant search. But if they were suspicious, they didn't say anything to Sulaiman. He stayed there, as if
completely on his own. He sat in different places in the house and
walked around the small quiet village that he'd only visited once or
twice before.

It wasn't real until he and Farid saw their own faces, drawn
in black pencil, staring out from the television screen, heard the
broadcaster announce that one of the suspects had a golden tooth.

Sulaiman looked away from the charcoal sketch of his hair, his eyebrows, his chin, and looked over at Farid. As if for the first time, he saw a light inside the older boy's mouth, blinding him. After one night or three, Farid left to have the dentist pull the gold from his mouth. After one night or three, Sulaiman's grandfather—Sarah's father—arrived to drive him home.

When Sulaiman first returned to Hizma, everything was quiet. It was a sharp kind of silence, crouched in on itself. As he got out of the car and walked toward his family house, a neighbor saw him and started. "You're still here!" she said. Everyone thought he'd already been arrested. At least that's how it seemed to him: everyone in the world knew what he'd done.

When Sulaiman walked into the living room, he saw Sarah sitting there, as if she'd been waiting for him in that one spot all the time he'd been gone, waiting as if for a million years. She cried, or she didn't, and then she grabbed him and held him, ran her fingers through his hair, slapped his face lightly, symbolically. She shook so much it felt like her shaking would enter his body.

"Where have you been?" she asked again and again in different ways.

"Bird-hunting," he smiled weakly.

She stared unbearably into his face until he was able to pull his arm free, finding a place to stand across the room. He wanted desperately to get away from her eyes trying to catch his, from his siblings running around asking him where he'd been, from his father's face like a stone. He was tired of pretending.

As soon as he could get away, he did. Walking up the stairs to his room, more heaviness came with each step. He didn't usually notice the time it took to get from one floor to another, but tonight it seemed the stairs spanned the distance between Jaba' and Mukhmas, the road he'd traveled what already felt like a long time ago. He was so tired. Still, when he lay his head on the pillow and closed his eyes, he couldn't sleep. The night air stayed warm. He waited for the army to come.

It was around one in the morning when the sound of shouts and heavy boots arrived. Sulaiman was neither awake nor asleep. The soldiers burst in around him, pulling him through the house, past his mother and father. He felt his father's eyes, wondered briefly if this might cause trouble for his job in al-Quds, and turned away from Said toward Sarah. He smiled at her, lifted his fingers into the shape of a *v*, for victory.

He hid behind the smile for a moment, tried not to wonder where he was going, or whether he'd made a mistake. Outside, he saw a brief glimpse of Captain Tzahi standing beside one of the jeeps, felt a hood drop over his head and down to his shoulders. His wrists were too thin for the handcuffs; he could feel the cold metal rings slipping down to his knuckles. The hands on his back and arms pushed him into the car.

Every breath he took was filled with the smell of urine and sweat, as if the hood had never been washed. But Sulaiman was more concerned by the darkness. He couldn't see anything, not light or shapes or the other people sitting beside him. He felt an emptiness in his stomach, the car going then stopping, another body pushed into the back, the car starting again. Everything was black.

PART TWO

CHAPTER 5

Shibl

It should have been a thirty-minute drive to Ramallah, but it felt like two hours, maybe three. There was just a little air in the hood, in the back of a van with small holes in place of windows. It was hard to breathe through the smell of vomit. Soldiers stopped here and there to throw more handcuffed people into the back. No one knew where they were going; no one knew where they were.

When the van finally stopped, Sulaiman was lifted up under his arms. He stood, still hooded, in the dark. Or he sat crouched in a small cell of cold cement, until eventually, a soldier took him and put him in a room for *chakira*—the Hebrew word for "investigation" that to Palestinians means torture. Sitting and waiting, he looked down and saw ten thin fingers twisted together. For a moment it seemed they belonged to someone else.

In the days that followed, they did different things, too many to remember. They put him in a misshapen chair at a terrible angle to the floor, his body bent into unbearable shapes, his hands behind his back.[1] They made him stand for long periods of time. They grabbed his hair and slammed his head against the wall.

At the beginning, he denied everything. They beat and threatened him, but he kept denying that he'd ever taken a small red knife to a spring. Then, at some point, another officer came in. He looked down at Sulaiman and said, "Oh, you're young. You're from a good family. Your father works in the municipality and he's a good man.

We want you to go back to school. It starts in a few days. Just tell us what happened."

Sulaiman knew it was a game, but he went with it, played it like it was real. Because what if it were true, what if this officer could save him from the other who beat and threatened him?

While Sulaiman was deciding what to do, what to say, they put him in a cell alone. He couldn't see anyone, but he could hear the shouts of other prisoners, could hear the guard calling the next in line for investigation. In that cell where he waited, there was a small window, very high up, letting through just a narrow shape of light. He looked up at it, knew he was behind the sun. But he didn't know what time it was, or how many days had passed. There was just a little bit of food that looked dirty, one egg or some other small thing. Without clothes to change into, the smell of his body filled the space, and he started to feel he wasn't a normal person anymore. He was something else.

In this cell, he stole a few minutes of sleep before the soldiers took him back to the investigation room, or to one of the other rooms, where, depending on how much pressure the officers wanted to apply, Sulaiman was made to sit in the crouched, bent chair with the hood over his head—his hands cuffed behind his back—or made to stand for what seemed forever until his knees gave, and the guard would yell or beat him until Sulaiman forced them straight again.

Fighting to stay on his feet, he tried to picture a future in which he'd buried all these memories in muteness, where they couldn't quite reach him. As his knees shook, he closed his eyes to escape what was around him, to imagine himself away from the smell, from the pain. He shut his eyes tight until colors appeared, and then he used those colors to paint Hizma, to imagine walking into the hills with the goats and calling to them with his flute. He tried to hold on to this picture for as many moments as possible before he heard the footsteps of the guard and the voice barking out his name, calling him back to the investigation room.

It didn't take long for Sulaiman to confess. He said whatever the interrogators wanted, and more, everything inside him, all the words he could think of. Anything to end the torture. In the dark of al-Muqata'a, the old jail built during the British Mandate, he signed the document of confession, barely looking at the words, later unsure if he'd signed a paper written in Arabic or in Hebrew, a language he could not read, but he was done, he didn't care. He hadn't spoken to a lawyer or to his family for seventeen or eighteen days.

When he put down the pen, the guards ushered him into a shower where he stood under the water, washing off smells that had accumulated over two weeks. Then, clutching the white thermal pants the Red Cross brought detainees after their first fourteen days, he was transferred from the interrogation center in Ramallah to a jail in al-Khalil, the city Israelis called Khevron.

Sulaiman looked over the guard's shoulder as they climbed to the fourth floor of the Hebron jail, a section just for minors called the *ashbal*. In the new cell, Sulaiman's eyes darted first to the tiny barred window near the ceiling. He could almost imagine the perfume of the Wadi al-Tuffah, the Valley of Apples. He saw something green move, pretended he could feel the wind, and then the door closed behind him. He looked down from the window and around his new cell: nine boys on bunk beds stared at him amid a strong scent of urine and soap. A toilet stood in the corner. An older boy wearing a uniform pushed himself up and limped over. Sulaiman didn't meet his eyes right away; he looked at the pocket of the older boy's uniform, the same as everyone else's, with the three letters printed there.

Shin, Bet, Sin, short for *Sherut Beit Sohar.* Prison Service.

The older boy peered down at the figure in front of him, his skinny arms. "*Mabruk*² and welcome," he said to the top of Sulaiman's head. "What's your name?"

"Sulaiman al-Khatib."

"I'm Bassam al-Aramin. But everyone calls me Abu Arab."

Bassam read Sulaiman's silence as a question; he smiled and answered it. "I know all Abu Arab's songs. I'm always singing them."

He waited for Sulaiman to respond, but still he was quiet. "How old are you, Sulaiman?"

"Fourteen and a half years old."

"Why are you here?"

"I attacked two Israelis."

Bassam waited for Sulaiman to say more—to brag, like the others did. But he didn't say anything. Sulaiman looked into the older boy's eyes, as if mute, as if unsure what words were for. "Don't be afraid," Bassam said finally. "We take care of each other here. We're your family now."

Squinting down at Sulaiman, Bassam couldn't believe this boy had hurt anyone. He could barely picture him cutting the blossom from a flower.

Sulaiman wouldn't learn Bassam's story until later. His limp came from polio. When he was very young he saw an Israeli helicopter come down from the sky; he heard his aunt scream as a soldier struck his cousin's face. He and his friends formed a group, found weapons they didn't know how to use, tested a grenade so heavy they could barely carry it. His friends left him behind when they attacked Israeli soldiers, because he couldn't run fast enough, but he got seven years in jail anyway and cried when he heard his sentence because he'd wanted it to be longer, like those of his friends. Though Sulaiman didn't know Bassam's story then, he saw something in the older boy's eyes that he liked.

That first night, he slept for hours upon hours. When he woke at seven the next morning, it was from the sound of a door opening. It was the best night of sleep he'd had since before the incident at 'Ayn Farrah.

He imitated the others, standing in a circle as two guards counted them and then left, closing the door behind them. The door stayed closed as the boys did sit-ups, read, and told jokes until, after a while, it opened again. They were led outside, and Sulaiman looked around. The yard—*chatzer* in Hebrew, *fura* in Arabic—was small. There were some drawings on the surrounding walls, as if someone had tried to make it look like a school. *It looks nothing like a school*, Sulaiman thought, and then stopped. He couldn't believe it. Huddled in a corner—in the real, fresh air—were Asif, Sadiq, and, standing a bit apart, Farid. Sulaiman embraced Asif and Sadiq, let go before he wanted to. He shook Farid's hand.

"How are you, Farid?"

"I'm fine, Sulaiman. How are you?"

"Fine." The two didn't have much to say to each other, or if they did, they didn't know which words to use.

Farid wandered away as Asif began telling jokes. Sulaiman let his friend's voice fade into the background, thinking how strange it was to be outside again. During the long days of interrogation, everything around him had been dark, narrow, and closely walled in. But here, though they were surrounded by tall walls and wire, though the wind smelled of gasoline from the busy city of al-Khalil, there was at least a little space.

The older boys walked, laughed, yelled, sat in corners of sun, and scribbled on pieces of paper. As Asif and Sadiq talked about the interrogation without talking about it, Sulaiman saw a few of the older boys approaching.

"Hi," one of them said. "We are the welcome committee. We're here to help you get adjusted as quickly as possible. My name is Ahmad Aljafari."

If you didn't look at Ahmad closely, he seemed very serious. But Sulaiman saw something like laughter hiding in his eyes, and he recognized his name. Sulaiman knew the story of Ahmad's uncle Ali, who'd participated in the political prisoners' hunger strike in 1980, and had died after the Israeli administration force-fed him.

"The first business is where you will sleep," another boy on the welcome committee said. "To help us decide, please tell us—are you *rifaq*, comrades? Or *ikhwa*, brothers?"

Sulaiman, Asif, and Sadiq looked at each other, confused.

"Neither," Sulaiman finally said. "We're *awlad khalat*, maternal cousins."

Ahmad exchanged looks with the others before the corner of his mouth twitched. The twitch spread from one boy to the next until they were all doubled over, laughing. One of them threw back his head and shouted between his hands, "*Awlad khalat! Awlad khalat!*"

After everyone finally caught their breath, Ahmad looked at the boys from Hizma. "No," he said, smiling in the subtle way that, for him, was huge. "'Comrades' means you are with the Popular Front, and 'brothers' means you are with Fatah."

For a long time, this had been the policy in jail. You couldn't be independent; you had to decide which party you belonged to, with which organization you would spend your life. But Sulaiman and his cousins didn't know which party they were with; they had only ever been themselves. To the confused stares of the younger boys, the welcoming committee explained their options. There was Fatah, the secular nationalist party led by Yasser Arafat; the Popular Front, led by George Habash, which believed Marxist ideology and the Palestinian revolution were inseparable; and the Democratic Front, which had split from the Popular Front for reasons Sulaiman couldn't quite grasp.

After the boys listened and discussed, Sulaiman lifted his chin. He told the welcome committee, as if he'd known all along, "We are *ikhwa*, brothers." He knew almost nothing of Fatah; he chose it because it was attached to Arafat's name, and Arafat was a hero, like he wanted to be.

After they'd chosen, Ahmad launched into his orientation speech, though it took longer than usual because he kept having to stop when another member of the welcome committee would suddenly clutch his side and yell, "*Awlad khalat!* Cousins!"—causing the rest of them to start laughing again.

Between these outbursts, Ahmad explained what the newcomers should expect from life in jail; that while Palestinian political prisoners from different parties lived and studied separately, they all worked together in the *nizam dakhili*, internal organization—a complex system of self-leadership that functioned across all the Israeli jails. Each political party had a financial committee that distributed canteen funds, a security committee that monitored prisoners collaborating with the Israeli administration, and an education committee to determine a curriculum of study. Each party also had a revolutionary council, which acted as legislature, and a central committee that acted as executive government.

Standing above all those committees was a managing council with representatives from each political party. Sometimes they called it *Lajnat al-Hiwar*, the Dialogue Committee, and sometimes *al-Lajna al-Nidaliya*, the Struggle Committee. This group was responsible for talking to the prison's Israeli administration on behalf of all the jail's Palestinian political prisoners.

This system of government, Ahmad continued, was entirely democratic. Elections took place regularly and in secret. Names were written on tiny pieces of paper that were passed around until the votes were counted and the leaders chosen. In the *ashbal* section of Hebron, the prisoners thought of themselves as men, even though not one of the hundred or so boys was older than nineteen.

With a certain awe, Sulaiman, Asif, and Sadiq tried to blend into their new life. But the following day, as they jogged around the yard, a prisoner they hadn't met stood in their way, a stern look on his face. He glanced over his shoulder, broke out in a grin, and yelled, "Look! It's the kids from the esteemed *awlad khalat* party!"

From then on, everyone, in almost every jail, knew the *awlad khalat* story. The joke passed everywhere.

In those first days, Sulaiman learned the clockwork of his new life: an hour in the yard in the morning, two study sessions after breakfast, then lunch, another hour in the yard, two more study sessions, dinner, and then the door closing and staying closed until morning. There wasn't enough to eat, and though his stomach grumbled, he grew accustomed to the sound. For lunch, all the prisoners in the room put their individual portions of food into a large tray, layering bread and rice and soup until they could almost pretend it was *mansaf*.[3] They called it *fatta*, a mix of everything together, and the appearance of so much allowed them to trick their stomachs into feeling more full. When it grew cold, as it often did in the old building, Sulaiman's cellmates taught him to wear multiple pairs of the long white thermal pants the Red Cross had delivered. He learned, with the others, to ration the limited water they had available.

The prisoners who'd been in jail longest were his teachers in all this, though they were still young. In their study sessions, which they called the Revolutionary University, they spoke of transforming the jail from a place of torture and humiliation into a place where they could grow stronger. They summoned the wisdom they'd learned while spending a few nights in other prisons with adult prisoners, and sometimes communicated with these prisoners using secret messages wrapped in plastic casings, held under their tongues when being transferred from jail to jail. They swallowed if necessary.

The older prisoners taught them to devote much of their days to studying, and they did. In books hand-bound by prisoners themselves, they learned the history of the prisoners' movement, of everything. This unshakeable commitment to learning made sense to Sulaiman right away. For the prisoners, learning itself was a form of resistance, a way to make sure Israel couldn't successfully steal the most precious thing. Through reading, they took back their time.

It was still dark one morning when Fatima and Sarah boarded the Red Cross bus in Hizma. The humanitarian organization sometimes sent buses to pick up the prisoners' families; many lived far from where their relatives were kept. From their seats, they watched the light rise in the sky outside the window, the little figures appearing beside the road. Nothing moved quickly enough. This was the first day they were allowed to visit Sulaiman.

The trip to Hebron was supposed to take two hours, but it took longer. There were so many mothers and fathers and brothers to pick up along the way, the bus starting and stopping again and again. The men and women spoke or stayed silent. They sat and wondered if their children would look the same, or if the days had left a mark.

As Sarah and Fatima waited for the doors of the jail to open, they passed through security and hoped the guards would not touch them. Sarah tried to keep breathing. She'd done all this before.

When she saw Sulaiman, it was through the squares of the metal mesh divider. She put her fingers up against the metal so that, through the small holes, the pads of her fingertips could touch his. Sulaiman looked past her, for his father. Said wasn't there. Only two family members were allowed to visit, Sarah explained, and he hadn't wanted to. She didn't need to tell Sulaiman how angry his father was. He already knew.

Some unidentified mixture of pride and grief collected in Sulaiman's chest. *They see now that I'm a man,* he thought. But the words disappeared when they began telling him what had happened in Hizma, just after the army had taken him.

Not long after Sulaiman's bed was left empty, an Israeli army truck had pulled up in front of Sarah and Said's courtyard. Sarah looked out at the vehicle—filled with cement and sand, blocking the gate—and assumed the worst. The army was there to destroy her house: a way to punish all of them, all of her children, for what her third eldest had done. She'd seen houses destroyed for less.

The soldiers piled out in front of Said, and he learned why they'd come. They began placing concrete slabs inside Sulaiman's room, and as they barred the door and windows with wood and iron, making the room unusable, Said stood behind them.

"I have many children," he said. "Where will they sleep?"

Sarah heard one of the soldiers reply, an answer without an answer in it: "Let them sleep in this other room. You can sleep on the balcony."

In a way, Sulaiman's family was lucky. According to Regulation 119, a rule passed by the British in 1945 and then adopted by Israel, a military commander could claim ownership of any property from which they *suspected* that a firearm had been fired, or whose residents had abetted any act of violence or intimidation. Once the ownership had been transferred, the army could destroy the house without compensation.

The policy was supposedly used only for deterrence, not punishment. According to Israeli court rulings, the army was supposed to demolish only in cases that were regarded as severe terrorist attacks, and where the demolition was regarded as "proportional" to the value of future deterrence.[4] If someone killed (or attempted to kill) an Israeli, it was normal for the entire house to be demolished. Whatever the intention, in homes like Sulaiman's, with eight children and two parents, this was a punishment for the whole family, even for the children too young to understand what exactly they were being punished for.

For Sulaiman, it felt impossible to listen to his mother speak of this, but he somehow did. The guards stood behind them for thirty minutes as Sarah touched Sulaiman's fingers through the mesh, as she cried and told him that no matter how much they cleaned, the whole house smelled like dust and metal. When he looked at his mother's face in that moment, he saw a look he imagined she wore

whenever she walked by the closed room, the look of someone delivered a physical blow.

He tried not to think of it, to focus instead on Fatima talking
and talking about other things: how they'd given the guard a small
bag of coffee they'd been allowed to bring. She told Sulaiman they'd
written his name on it, and gave the guards some money he could
use at the jail's canteen. Sulaiman held himself straight and nodded.
He already knew what would happen next. Later, the Israeli woman
who ran the canteen would work with the prisoners' financial committee to distribute the money the families brought. No matter what
his family gave, every prisoner would receive the same amount and
had the same choice: cigarettes or the Israeli chocolate Egozi.

Still, Fatima wanted him to know how much they'd given. She
wanted him to know they'd found a lawyer he'd meet soon, and
then, as if the visit had never started, Sarah wiped her tears with her
sleeve and the whole thing was over.

After Sarah and Fatima left, the *awlad khalat* party went back to
its routine and tried to forget their mothers and rooms at home.
There was walking and running and laughing in the yard; Asif trying out new jokes, practicing imitations of the bulky guard Paper's
surprisingly squeaky voice; Sulaiman and Sadiq trying to guess what
exactly their siblings were eating back at home.

Inside the cell, they attended mandatory study sessions their
leaders had planned. They learned about Arafat and the history of
the PLO. They began to learn Hebrew. "You need to learn the
language of *al-ihtilal*, the occupation," his teachers told him, "in order to defeat it." Sulaiman passed the time this way, waiting for the
moment the door would open and the guards would take him to
Ramallah for his day in court.

After a couple of months in Hebron, the day came. Sulaiman was
stuffed in the van, driven back to Ramallah, to the same jail of his
chakira, interrogation. This time, he stayed in a different section, a
room with forty other prisoners, all adults. He was the youngest one
there, so the others called him *shibl*, son of the lion. It made him feel
strong, bold enough to speak with men who were three times his
age, from all parts of Palestine, from everywhere.

Before the trial began, Abed Asali—the lawyer Fatima had found—came to visit. Asali was from East Jerusalem, a small busy man with a muted, tired sort of concern on his face. He sat with Sulaiman and told him what he knew—that because Sulaiman had signed a confession, there was no choice but to plead guilty. Sulaiman felt a pain in his stomach but smiled through it.

"That's not a problem," Sulaiman said, imagining what a hero might say. "Their court is not legitimate anyway. That's what I will tell them."

After Asali left, Sulaiman sat in the Ramallah jail with the others, waiting for his trial.[5]

As the days blended together, the central radio kept the time. It went on twice a day, once at midday and once in the evening, when it played Umm Kulthum, the famous Egyptian singer. The prisoners would lie down and put towels over their eyes, try to be alone, remembering. The songs were about memories, about love. Some people cried, but for Sulaiman it was different. He was young and didn't have any loves to remember, not the kind Umm Kulthum sang of.

The night before he went to court, he looked at all the *munadilin* (freedom fighters) around him, and felt proud to be with them. They made him feel strong as he dreamed different versions of what he could say to the judge the next day. He tried not to think too much about his mother, about whether she was all right. But in the cold, old room built during an earlier, British occupation, it wasn't easy to melt these things away; it wasn't easy to sleep. The room was so crowded the men had to lie very close together. Sulaiman could feel someone's breath on his neck.

For Sulaiman's court date, Asali made the commute from East Jerusalem. He was tired. This case was one among many hundreds he fought, defending Palestinians accused of everything from murder to stone-throwing to membership in an illegal political organization. Sometimes, in the case of administrative detention, the Israeli army jailed Asali's Palestinian clients without any charge at all. He was used to all of it, along with the biggest problem in these cases: they simply couldn't be won, hardly ever.

It was the same for the few other human rights lawyers he knew—impossible to navigate the two different court systems for Palestinians and Jews. If a Jewish settler in the West Bank committed a crime, they were tried in a civil court. But Asali's Palestinian clients were tried in Israel's military courts, which almost always handed over guilty verdicts. So he aimed low; he fought for lower sentences, asking the court for mercy because his clients were poor or young. He only spoke about the context of occupation when defending an adult client who'd killed someone, when there was no hope of mercy from the court.

"Always, when there is occupation," he'd say at these times, "there are people who resist. And people, they were not born murderers. They were born human beings and they want to live. They want their liberty and they want self-determination."

He didn't make this argument to help his clients; he made it because it was true, and he made it when there was nothing else to say or do. This argument never resulted in a lower sentence. The judges would always respond in the same way. "We are not the Knesset here," he heard them say many times. "We are here to judge; we are not political."

The difference in this case was Sulaiman's age. He was so young. In that moment, before the wave of the first *intifada* (uprising), a fourteen-year-old defendant was still unusual.

So there Asali was again, in the late fall of 1986, fighting another unwinnable case. He watched Sulaiman enter the courtroom, the gangly boy walking with his head high, wearing his brown prison uniform, trying to convince himself he wasn't afraid. Farid entered too; they were on trial together.

When Sulaiman got to his seat, he looked around the wide, old courtroom, to the high desk at the front of the room, the three judges who sat there. The guards kept his hands cuffed and he sat on a bench off to the side as the court moved quickly through various cases before his. He tried to smile at Sarah and Fatima, who stared at him from the front row.

When the guards led Sulaiman to his place at the defendant's desk, he was able to whisper a request to his aunt, something he would never have asked his mother. He'd heard how sometimes, at the end of a trial, the women would ululate, sing out sounds of triumph to show they weren't afraid. He knew Fatima would like this act of celebration, the same sound she made at weddings, and that his mom would hate it, find it too defiant, too political. But he wanted everyone to know he was proud for fighting, that he wasn't afraid.

When the time came, when Sulaiman was invited to speak, he thought about what he'd heard somewhere. That he was young, and if he said sorry, they might give him a shorter sentence. Though he'd also heard that, if he got a longer sentence, he was more likely to be released in a prisoner exchange, like his brother.

When the time came, in court, he didn't say sorry. He raised his voice and rejected the authority of the judges. He said, "No, fuck you. You are the occupation, and we don't recognize you." Or he sat in stony silence. It didn't matter; the sentence would likely have been the same. Fifteen years for him, eighteen for Farid. When he heard the years called out, he felt proud, would have felt prouder if the sentence were longer.

He stood and raised his fingers into a *v*, for victory. And then, again, the palms on his back, the hands pushing him out of the court and away from his mother with tears in her eyes, away from Fatima, tipping her nose to the ceiling and pouring out the clear tone of her song like a royal bird.

CHAPTER 6

Clockwork & Prayer

After court, after Sulaiman was transferred back to the Hebron jail, he spent days and nights asking himself what had happened, how he had managed to get here, to lose his freedom. Other times, if he tried hard enough, he could listen to the other boys in his section and feel like listening was a kind of traveling. He could almost force himself to forget the smallness of the world he was living in, and how for the first time in his life, he had no hills to wander through.

Reading seemed another way of traveling, so during the four daily study sessions, Sulaiman devoted himself to the Revolutionary University. At first, the older boys controlled the books, making sure the students believed Fatah's mission before they began to read freely. Sulaiman loved this early reading about Fatah, the movement he thought would one day bring his people freedom. It was a movement that belonged in the great tradition of revolutions, like those in Cuba and Algeria—movements that eventually succeeded, even if they took some time. Movements that always returned what needed to be returned in the end.

He became a disciple of Sakher Habash's book *Principles of Revolutionary Conduct*. Sitting on the cold floor, legs crossed, wearing two pairs of thermals and rubbing his hands over his thighs for warmth, he took notes in a notebook he'd bought from the canteen, with money distributed by the financial committee.

A revolutionary should tell the truth and be kind.
A revolutionary has to be willing to die for what is right.
He should never hurt a woman or a child.
He may attack a soldier, but if the soldier surrenders,
    he cannot shoot.
A revolutionary must practice honor and mercy.
A revolutionary should be an example for his people.

He embraced the clarity and vision in these values, the sense he had of how many ways there were to be *Fatahwi*. Fatah was home to those with left-leaning politics like Salah Khalaf, whom they called Abu Iyad, and people like Khalil al-Wazir, also known as Abu Jihad, who was more traditionally nationalistic and centrist. Each leader had their own followers in jail, but somehow, they could all live together. Their interior disagreements weren't important yet. The most important thing was freeing Palestine first. The social revolution, Sulaiman learned, would come later.

In this way, he learned to think of Fatah as *his* movement, to see all the boys and men who belonged to it as his brothers. As the boys around him cycled in and out—most serving six months to a year for minor offenses like stone-throwing—Sulaiman continued to study. He still had Asif and Sadiq to laugh with in the yard, but their sentences were only for a year and a half. Unless a prisoner exchange occurred, he would stay in this place for fifteen years: studying, doing push-ups in the yard, standing twice a day to be counted.

Sometimes, when night came, Sulaiman would lie in the dark and pretend he was staring up into one of the olive trees on Ta'mira, his head resting on his grandfather's stone pillow. Sometimes, when his dreaming was interrupted—when the bony guard Elvis decided to rattle his keys all night so they couldn't sleep—Sulaiman would remember to feel angry for all of his Fatahwi brothers who couldn't return to the places of their grandfathers' stone pillows and houses and trees and first memories of love. He trained himself to see their losses as his losses too. They all had been closed off from what was most precious, closed off behind cement and iron, together.

They were all here together, lying in their bunk beds or, when there was overcrowding, lying on the ground with their bodies touching. On those nights, a hand would sometimes brush against his, bringing some heat. He didn't speak of this, though he wondered why people were sometimes suspicious if he walked in the yard with his friend Ruhi, holding hands. In the years of jail to come, he'd hear the stories of people falling in love, but this kind of falling was forbidden here.

As boys were released, prisoners were shuffled around. The Palestinian leadership had a rule that everyone should spend time equally with everyone else, so as not to fall in with favorites or cliques. But when Sulaiman was transferred into Room 8, with Asif and Sadiq, he had trouble containing his excitement. He was happy to be with his friends, and Room 8 had a glow about it. It was famous for the time a boy used a knife hidden in his shoes to bust open the high, tiny window. He'd tied sheets together in the night and rapelled down the wall of the prison all the way to the ground. Miraculously, he hadn't been caught.

In Room 8, Omar and Suhail—two older boys from al-ʿArrub refugee camp—began to show Sulaiman special attention. They pulled him aside to tell him jokes or to give him an extra piece of Egozi chocolate. Both boys, Sulaiman knew, were on the Fatah prisoners' security committee in the *ashbal*. They were responsible for identifying and investigating boys who might be sharing secret information with the Israeli administration.

One day, Omar pulled him aside. "Do you want to learn the system of codes the prisoners have developed? If I teach it to you, you'll have to guard it carefully."

Sulaiman nodded, and listened to what Omar said, focusing on the piece of chocolate he was eating, turning his mind away from the sour smell that came from the toilet at the room's edge.

He was glad Omar and Suhail trusted him with this secret language that just the three of them, among all the boys in the *ashbal*,

would hold and keep safe. To learn, Sulaiman began with simple things: the words for house, mother, blue. Then he moved
to the more complex: the name of the *shawish* (representative) in
each room, and eventually longer sentences that circled around the
names of boys he thought might be '*asafir* (birds)—collaborators
with the Israelis.

One day, Omar and Suhail asked Sulaiman to watch Yunus, a
boy from al-Jalazun camp. Everyone thought he was acting strangely,
and he had access to secret information the Israelis magically seemed
to know. Sulaiman started to observe Yunus, took notes in careful
code, and hid the notebook under his mattress. At night, the bind-
ing poked into his stomach, just above the hips. He wondered what
the guards would do if they found the notebook beneath him during
a regular *taftish* (search). He liked to imagine Paper, the Israeli head
of prison security, poring over the notebook's pages, not able to
understand a thing.

The notebook gave him a special feeling of secrecy, similar to
what took him when opening the pages of a Qur'an he'd borrowed
from Nasri, an older boy from Jericho. The feeling reminded him
of carpet between his toes, of quiet things that couldn't be spoken.

Though he'd hardly ever prayed before, he began to pray five
times a day, diving in completely. He didn't tell anyone that his favorite part was not the words themselves but the act of bowing to
the ground. The art of it felt like playing the flute, the wonder of
other daily gestures from home. To get closer to this feeling, he affected a deep seriousness, refused to read anything but the Qur'an,
and pored over the same words again and again, like they were in
a code he hadn't yet learned, like it was a waste of time to do anything else.

Asif and Sadiq watched as Sulaiman began casting imperious
glances at the unholy books they were reading, even calling their
secular books *haram*, forbidden. It seemed he was playing the role
of someone else, someone his cousins didn't recognize. So Asif and
Sadiq decided to play a joke to bring their Sulaiman back. They
slipped a piece of paper to the prisoner librarian. When their order
arrived, they stayed behind when everyone went out to the yard
for their hour of fresh air and light. They slipped the books under

Sulaiman's pillow and hid their laughter behind solemn faces. That night, when Sulaiman prepared for bed, he found one book about Che Guevara and another about Lenin beneath his head. He threw them at Asif and Sadiq, yelling, trembling as if their words could have slipped into his ear while he slept.

But just as quickly as Sulaiman's religiosity came, he let it fall off. Around his fifteenth birthday, on March 9, 1987, he began to feel very bored of prayer—especially when plans for the hunger strike took on a clear shape.

CHAPTER 7

Mayy wa Milh

The knowledge came quickly: nothing in jail was free. The only reason Sulaiman had anything—a bed, a blanket, access to books and pens, time in the yard, organized representation—was because someone had fought for it, and won.

After Israel's victory in the 1967 war, the population of Palestinian political prisoners in Israeli jails increased dramatically. But there was little time to plan for this shift. Israel saw the political prisoners as *mechablim* (terrorists). The idea was to get them out of the way first, and think of what to do with them later.

At first, there were no pencils, pens, or paper in the jails unless they were smuggled in like drugs. The prisoners slept on thin mats on the floor. They had to speak to the prison guards saying, *Ya sidi*, Sir, yes sir. If they wanted water, they'd have to say, "Sir, I want water, sir." If they forgot a "sir," the guards could beat them. The hunger strikes of the 1970s had won improvements, but not enough.

When Fatah leader Qaddura Fares arrived in jail, the prisoners were still sleeping on the floor. Together with the other men, he asked the prison administration for bunk beds. The administration refused, citing "security reasons." A prisoner, the Israelis pointed out, could easily bang another's head against the bed. Qaddura thought this was ridiculous. If someone wanted to hit someone else, they didn't need a bed to do it.

In 1980, still without bunk beds, the prisoners in Nafha prison launched a hunger strike. It lasted around thirty days, and the prison administration began force-feeding prisoners through a tube into the stomach. Sometimes, the tube hit a prisoner's lungs, and by the end of the strike, Ahmad Aljafari's uncle and a prisoner named Rasem Halawah were dead. It was an especially difficult strike, but not long after, just a few years before Sulaiman's arrival in Hebron, the political prisoners finally won their bunk beds.

Because of past hunger strikes, Sulaiman now had a blanket, a bunk bed to sleep on when there wasn't overcrowding, access to paper, pencils, and books. Because of the strikes, the prison administration even recognized certain aspects of the prisoners' system of self-organizing. But there were many things left to struggle for. The prisoners wanted more humane security searches for their mothers and aunts and sisters. They wanted longer family visits, more time in the yard, better access to news of the outside world through radio and television, and more food and medical care.

Before they began to strike, the boys in Hebron waited for a message. The prisoner leadership was presenting a list of demands to the prison administration, and if these were not met, they would launch an open hunger strike. An open strike meant you could choose when you began but not when you ended. It meant you could die.

In preparation for the inevitable, prisoners carried secret messages in capsules under their tongues. When one of them was transferred to another prison, or when a lawyer came to visit, they passed these messages to their brothers in other prisons, and to student leaders at Birzeit University. In conjunction with the strike, Birzeit students planned protests, telling the prisoners' stories to the world and making sure the world heard. The students risked so much by doing this: if the Israelis found them with a capsule that came from inside a prison, they would face arrest.

On a family visit day, an older boy named Rafiq handed Sulaiman a capsule and nodded, as if that small movement said enough. Sulaiman stared through the plastic at the flimsy piece of paper rolled up inside, its pen marks carrying a message for someone he would likely never meet.

"But I'm not being transferred," Sulaiman said finally. "What should I do with it?"

"Give it to your mother during the visit," Rafiq smiled, and made a motion as if slipping a pen or cigarette behind his ear.

When Sulaiman sat down in front of Sarah, she began talking. He didn't hear her. He was looking sideways, up at the guard, checking to make sure he wasn't looking. When he passed the capsule through the wire mesh, he saw the fear burn up into his mother's eyes, but he nodded to her quickly, watched as she raised her hand to slip the capsule under her white headscarf. Her eyes widened. Sulaiman looked up and saw the guard looking at her, annoyed or bored. He heard his mother's breath quicken and his did too, until he saw that the guard's face wasn't changing. The man understood what he saw, but wouldn't do anything with it. Like they were in some game, with rules Sulaiman couldn't name.

After Sarah left, the guard silently returned Sulaiman to his cell, where the study sessions had turned entirely to preparations for the strike.

"Don't be afraid," Rafiq said. "The worst thing is surprise. But you'll know exactly what to expect."

Sulaiman listened carefully as the older boy spoke. "You will feel hungry at first, but not for long. The mouth will begin to smell, to taste strange and bitter. You will take the water and salt to help with this, but also to give your body what it needs to keep going. The point is not to die, but to win. And whatever you do," Rafiq said, looking around seriously, "don't talk about food. You will want to, but you'll be sorry if you do."

And then, they heard the news. The prisoner leadership had made its final requests; the administration had returned a hard no. The Struggle Committee had determined the minimum achievements they needed to win before eating again. The strike would begin the following day.

That night, Sulaiman tried to imagine hunger—what it might look like if it were a physical thing. He wasn't afraid, or didn't think he was. He trusted what he'd learned in the study sessions: the water and salt would keep his body fluids high, keep his heart pumping blood. They'd learned this from their brothers, the Irish, who'd struggled in the same way, and won. The most famous Irish hunger strike, he'd learned in a study session, lasted a whole seven months. Before that strike, the Irish freedom fighters petitioned for the right to wear their own clothes and not the uniforms criminals had to wear. One of the Irish heroes decided that if he couldn't wear his own clothes, he wouldn't wear any! He put on a blanket, and like a crazy person, wore only that until the others joined him and the prison was full with naked men wrapped in blankets. Sulaiman thought about these proud men, and when he imagined them walking around in makeshift shawls, their bare legs sticking out, he laughed and laughed until he fell asleep.

By the next morning, a new round of capsules had found their way into the world. And when the sun rose in the refugee camps and in the cities, the words *mayy wa milh* (water and salt) had appeared on the walls, as if by magic.

When the guards delivered breakfast the first morning, Rafiq shook his head, and the Israelis retreated with their trays. Sulaiman followed the others: lying on his bed, trying to fidget as little as possible to keep his body from wasting energy. He moved only his mouth, singing along to songs his friends used to distract themselves from the constriction in their stomachs.

By the second day, the prisoners forgot for a moment that they were supposed to act like men and not boys. They began talking about food, the way their mothers made bread or *maqluba*,[1] or how the best *mansaf* in the world could only be found in the city of al-Khalil—not far at all from where they sat. These thoughts were so pleasurable they hurt.

The pain spread in tendrils through his arms and legs, and that night, Sulaiman found it very hard to sleep. As he waited, he took himself on trips, dreaming. He walked across the chessboard of his family's patio and into the kitchen where Sarah had laid out bread and olive oil and za'atar, where she poured sweet tea, and where fresh air came in through the window and tousled his hair.

He left his family's house, counting his steps, placing one foot in front of the other, then giving up the count to run toward Fatima's, finding himself under the pomegranate trees, full with the smell of their tart, red juice. He climbed to the balcony, and lying under a dark sky, he counted the stars. Breathing in the crisp night air, he finally felt calm enough, far away enough to sleep.

This is how he learned, without naming it, that a person needed something big inside himself to survive in a small place. Some of the other boys didn't know this, he could tell, because they cried out in their sleep.

In the days that followed, he'd often forget where he was, climb too quickly from his bunk, fall dizzy against the wall. One particular day, he noticed something strange; it took some time to understand what Rafiq had told him. The guards were eating barbecue chicken down the hall, trying to get the prisoners to break. There was no pleasure in the way this smell hurt. It felt heavy, almost unbearably hard. Before this, before jail, he'd never been hungry. He looked for something to hold, he went back and forth between *sumud* (steadfastness) and regret. All of it came at once, and seemed, sometimes, to make a mess inside him.

Though it seemed to take forever, the smell of barbecue faded, and by the seventh day, other things had taken hunger's place. Sulaiman's limbs seemed to belong to some body other than his own; the space between his bones ached. He asked his friend Hisham to tell a funny story, something to distract him from a sour smell that had taken up residency under his skin.

And then one day, the Israeli doctor came. He furrowed his brow and told each of them they were hurting themselves, that they should stop for their health. They looked back at him. One of their demands in the strike was adequate health care and medicine. But this was the same doctor who showed up during interrogations; the one who seemed less interested in treatment and more interested in extracting information. This was the same doctor who came for normal visits with only aspirin.

The prisoners just looked at the doctor and said nothing until he took his small medicine bag and left. As soon as he was gone, they began laughing, a weak and labored sound that clanked through their bodies. They made a skit to distract themselves, with Hisham playing the doctor and Sulaiman the patient.

"Hello, Sulaiman! What's wrong?"

Sulaiman clutched his side with one hand, his forehead with the other. "Doctor! Help me! I'm dying!"

"Poor thing, but not to worry," Hisham said, pulling something invisible from his pocket. "Have some aspirin!"

It had been nearly two weeks, and one morning Sulaiman noticed how thin his arms and thighs had become. He'd entered a fog in which everything was a little softer and darker than usual. It didn't lift until the thirteenth day,[2] when Rafiq walked into the center of the room and said some words that Sulaiman couldn't make out.

Rafiq repeated them again. "It's over."

When the words landed, a strong tug pulled something in Sulaiman's gut straight up to his forehead. He wanted to dance, but could barely stand. He looked at the others. He'd never seen people look so tired, or smile so wide.

Soon, the door opened again and prisoners from the kitchen appeared with small cups of milk. In all his dreaming about the strike's end, Sulaiman had imagined gulping down the milk, shoveling food into his mouth with both hands. But when his cup arrived, all he could do was take tiny, slow sips. The milk felt heavy and strange and slow as it slid down his throat.

After the milk, the kitchen sent mashed potato, soup, a little piece of bread—these soft, soft things. When the newer prisoners grabbed at the plates, those with experience told them to slow down. Patience, they said, was something they all needed to guard and practice.

Going to the bathroom hurt, and the following morning, Sulaiman saw clumps of hair on Sadiq's pillow. Even though his friend was pale and thin, he looked proud. The prisoners hadn't won all their demands, but the administration had agreed to some, including an additional fifteen minutes for family visits and a little radio to share among the cells. They'd had a secret radio already, hidden in the wall. But now they could place it in the open, each small victory a treasure to hold and keep.

The radio looked different now that it was legal, now that they'd fought for it and won. When it made it to Room 8, Sulaiman and the others gathered around it like worshippers at a shrine. Someone twisted the knob, looking for *Sawt al-Thawra* (the Revolutionary Voice)—a program that came in stately and static-filled every night. All the boys pressed together, shoulder to shoulder, hoping to hear what their exiled leaders had to say.

The space was too tight and the signal too weak, so they assigned one person to sit with his ear right up against the tiny speaker. That boy wrote down what he heard and passed his report to the other rooms: battles had been won, all Palestinian fighters of the revolution must stay strong, one day soon the struggle would be over. If Sulaiman closed his eyes and focused on the static, it almost felt like he was still in Hizma, in Najla's cave. As if he could still feel the damp, still listen to Sadiq and Asif talking about girls, until it was time to race home before his mother woke in the early dark to bake bread in the *tabun*.

But he wasn't in Najla's cave, and Sadiq and Asif wouldn't be in jail much longer; their sentences were almost finished. Farid had an eighteen-year sentence and would stay, but it wasn't the same. Asif was their only real link, besides what had happened in 'Ayn Farrah. And because of that, they looked at each other as briefly as possible, each smiling in his own small, strained way.

When it was time for Asif and Sadiq to leave, they lingered saying goodbye to Sulaiman, knowing a long time would pass before they saw him again. As former prisoners, they wouldn't be allowed to visit. It was one of the hardest things. In this strange place, all Sulaiman had were the people. With his friends, he could speak of home, of their little village, of their families. There was a common language between them. Now, without his friends from home— among prisoners from so many unfamiliar places—he'd have to keep this language alive without anyone to help him.

On October 1, 1987, an alarm went off in all the cells, and Sulaiman looked up from his book. Huge men in masks were pouring through the doors. This meant *qam'*, trouble.[3]

The men crashed into the cells, overturning the rooms. They pushed and pulled the prisoners into the hallway, down four flights of stairs, outside to the yard. They were policemen, or guards, or soldiers—it was hard to tell; Sulaiman couldn't see their faces. In the yard, in the cold air, they stood in two rows with sticks and gas masks. They made everyone from the *ashbal* take off their clothes and walk naked in a line between them. They yelled, beat the boys as they passed. They made them stand, reach to the sky, and sit down over and over, looking for capsules hidden inside them. Sulaiman tried not to look at his friends, to see their humiliation as the blows fell. But it was impossible not to see.

As the officers' sticks fell on shoulders and ribs and shins, Bassam looked over at Suhail. They had learned the revolutionary teaching that *if you smile in front of the enemy, he will cry*. So Bassam turned to Suhail, began telling jokes about the color of his underwear. They began to laugh and their laughter seemed to make the blows rain down harder.

Bassam stopped joking, raised his voice with the sense that he needed to do this, this small thing to prove he was human. He kept yelling and yelling until he was pulled aside. All the blows began to focus on him, on the ground, sticks falling on his back, until—suddenly—a body fell on his, a sort of shield. It was the Israeli prison guard Herzl.

Months and months before, Herzl had approached Bassam in his cell, looked at the leg that caused his limp, and shook his head. "You shouldn't be a terrorist. You're not well. Why are you here?"

Bassam looked back at him, and waited a moment before saying, "We are freedom fighters. You are the terrorist."

"How can you say that?" Herzl asked, but it wasn't really a question. "We give you land to live on and still you want to settle more, occupy more. You kill us. You should be in school now, not here in jail. But you choose killing over learning."

"Okay, okay," Bassam smiled. "Maybe we are the settlers and occupiers like you say. Maybe until now I've been brainwashed. If you convince me, I will stop fighting."

They began to talk whenever Herzl was on shift and his superiors weren't around. After nearly a year, they became something like friends. "I respect that you're fighting for your honor," Herzl told him one day. "I would be happy to live in a state next to yours." After that, when Herzl left the prison at the end of his work shift, he would sometimes come to shake Bassam's hand. And once, just recently, Herzl had reached into a hidden pocket of his jacket and passed Bassam an Abu Arab tape. Bassam stared down at the cassette, then up at Herzl, wonderingly. Herzl knew that everyone called him Abu Arab. They both knew bringing Palestinian national music to a prisoner could get him in unimaginable trouble.

But it was a sign of something, and Bassam felt the sign again now, as the guard's body sprawled on top of his own. He heard Herzl yelling, "Don't touch him! He has a problem in his leg and a problem in his heart. You'll kill him!"

The guards lifted Herzl from Bassam, then Bassam from the ground. They put him in a small room and locked the door. Bassam expected to stay there for a long time, but five minutes later, the door opened, and guards brought him back to his cell. Herzl came in after and looked at him. He opened his mouth and closed it again.

"I'm sorry," he said, his voice trailing.

Bassam looked at him closely. "It's not your fault."

That evening, Bassam asked another guard about the men that had poured into their cells while the prisoners were waiting for lunch.

"They were soldiers from the army," the guard said. "On a training mission."

They held each other's eyes. Neither man knew it, but the first intifada was about to begin.

CHAPTER 8

Abnaa' al-Intifada

The intifada was named for what it was: an uprising, a "shaking off." Five years had passed since the PLO's exile to Tunis, since Arafat said goodbye to his people in Beirut and left on a big boat. In the years since, from 1982 to 1987, some Palestinians in the West Bank and Gaza had been reconsidering notions of resistance. Their leadership was far away, and it seemed the neighboring Arab countries had long since abandoned them. If they were going to break free, many felt they'd have to do it alone. They would need a special kind of strategy, one that might work for an army-less people fighting an army that seemed impossibly strong. Activists discussed and practiced boycotts, strikes, demonstrations, and nonviolent reclamation of West Bank land taken by settlers. And a network of women's committees, established over many years to build mutual aid and resistance, grew into a force that would shape what came next.

As with most things, people disagreed on how the intifada began. Some liked to point to the sparks in Gaza, but before the sparks, there was a bigger, growing heat. By spring of 1987, around sixty thousand Jewish settlers lived in the West Bank. And over two thousand Jewish settlers held a disproportionate amount of territory in Gaza, leaving more than 565,000 Palestinians feeling crowded into the remaining bit of land by the sea.

One thing always touched another, and that April, a pregnant Israeli settler was killed in a firebombing attack near Qalqilya. The

Israeli army increased its arrests using administrative detention, jailing Palestinians without charge, and used live fire on student protesters, shooting and killing a business student. December of 1987 brought the moment many would later call the intifada's beginning, when an Israeli was stabbed to death in a Gaza City market. Not long after, an Israeli truck crashed into two vehicles stopped at an army roadblock, killing four Palestinian workers. Israeli media called it an accident. Palestinian media named it an act of revenge.

In the demonstrations that followed, some Palestinians threw stones and some burned tires and hurled Molotov cocktails. Many more took to the streets empty-handed, or armed only with a Palestinian flag, a piece of paper or cloth made illegal by Israeli military law, prohibited like many forms of organized protest in the West Bank and Gaza. Israeli soldiers arrived on the scene with tear gas, with bullets of rubber-coated steel. These soldiers were trained to respond as if any kind of Palestinian resistance was an act of war. In those days, when many Palestinians worked inside Israel, many Israelis felt violence could erupt anytime, anywhere. No Israeli soldiers died in the clashes that December, but by the end of the month, the Israeli army had killed over twenty Palestinians.

Throughout Palestine, leaflets circulated calling for noncooperation and protest: boycott of Israeli goods, tax refusal, strikes, the raising of flags and ringing of bells. Israel imposed curfews, closed schools, made mass arrests. But street art kept appearing on the walls in certain places, certain cities—signed by *abnaa' al-intifada* (children of the intifada).

Before the first intifada, Israeli prisons held few Palestinian youth like Sulaiman. Most political prisoners were men from refugee camps: Tulkarem, Dheisheh, 'Arrub. The people who'd resisted then were from specific families—families that other parents told their kids not to follow. But after the intifada started, it changed. Resistance became a thing that belonged to everyone.

The Israeli army implemented a policy of broad sweeps: it arrested those throwing stones, and also anyone who *knew* the ones throwing stones, just in case. In Hebron, tiny twelve-year-old boys appeared in the *ashbal*, smoking in the yard as if they were men. For the first time since his arrest, Sulaiman felt old.

The prison grew crowded with people from around the country. For a while, new boys slept on mats on the floor, sharing stories of the villages, cities, and refugee camps they came from. One of the young prisoners told Sulaiman about his life growing up in the Dheisheh refugee camp. In passing, he mentioned that his family had originally come from Egypt. It made Sulaiman pause. The idea he'd grown up with was this: the Israelis were not from here and the Palestinians were. But this boy's family was originally Egyptian. He identified as a Palestinian, but in a way, he wasn't, not like Sulaiman was. It was a small thing, and Sulaiman didn't give it much space. It was pushed away by endless reports from outside.

Each new story pulled him in. Thousands were showing up in the streets and Palestinian women were leading the way. When Israel closed the schools, women arranged alternative classrooms—in living rooms, under trees. Palestinian women organized boycotts of Israeli products, too, and helped teach neighbors to cultivate the land, to grow vegetable gardens wherever they could.

He heard stories about Bayt Sahur, a village near Bethlehem where the villagers had called for a nonviolent intifada and were refusing to pay Israel's taxes. In response, the army had cut the town's phone lines and imposed curfews. Soldiers entered homes, taking furniture and other things more valuable than the taxes owed. The villagers discarded their IDs, issued by Israel's Civil Administration, in great numbers—even when threatened with arrest. In the streets of Bayt Sahur, where the villagers had invited Israelis interested in peace to come and visit, soldiers shot tear gas and rubber bullets.

But Sulaiman's favorite story was the one about the cows. Some people in Bayt Sahur were practicing self-reliance, and bought eighteen cows from an Israeli kibbutz to supply their community with dairy. For the Israeli army, these cows crossed some invisible line. One day soldiers appeared at the new farm, counted the cows, took pictures of them, and demanded that the farm close within twenty-four hours. That night, the villagers hid the animals, prompting the army to conduct a massive cow hunt the next morning, searching for the cows as if they were the revolutionary leaders Abu Ammar (Arafat) and Abu Jihad (Khalil al-Wazir) themselves.[1] Sulaiman loved thinking about the Israeli soldiers chasing cows, loved hearing of his people's resistance, and loved Abu Jihad's statements of support that made their way into the prison via capsules. But there were other stories too. Sulaiman heard about the army going into schools, gathering children in the courtyard, making them wash the abnaa' al-intifada slogans off the walls. He heard about an Israeli soldier firing at a Palestinian flag hanging from an electrical line, accidentally killing a person nearby. And one day, he learned that Shadi, the boy who'd escaped through the window of Room 8 using a ladder of sheets, had been shot and killed. Sulaiman didn't think much about whether or not it had been an accident. He just looked up at the small window from which Shadi had once fled.

November 1988 brought another surprising story, a shock. The Palestinian National Council, the legislative body of the PLO, had met in Algeria to sign a declaration of independence. Written by the beloved Palestinian poet Mahmoud Darwish, the statement noted that the 1947 partition plan, though unjust, provided the "international legitimacy" for Palestinian self-determination. In these words, the statement also implicitly recognized the Jewish state, and a future two-state solution. It was a momentous thing for Arafat to sign this statement, written by the poet of his people.

But by the end of 1988, the dream of any Palestinian state—whether from the river to the sea, or only in the West Bank, Gaza, and East Jerusalem—seemed as distant as ever. A little over a year into the intifada, many people were dead. It was hard to know the exact numbers, but it seemed Palestinian militants had killed four Israeli soldiers and eight Israeli civilians. And the Israeli army had killed over three hundred Palestinians. Sulaiman would keep hearing reports as far more Palestinians lost their lives, and even more were wounded and imprisoned. When Sarah came to visit, she recited long lists of names: new boys from Hizma taken to jail. Sulaiman couldn't keep track. There were too many.

Winter came again and brought the cold. It helped a little that there were so many new bodies packed into the *ashbal*, generating heat in Sulaiman's frigid cement cell. But there were problems with this too: overcrowding meant instability. People came and went more quickly than usual, and this made it harder to trust newcomers. Omar told Sulaiman to keep an eye out, that the Israelis had probably planted new collaborators among them, to listen to their conversations. They had to be very careful.

Omar, Suhail, and Sulaiman decided it was time to consult the notes they'd taken about their fellow prisoner Yunus: his erratic behavior, the way he overheard conversations the Israelis learned about later, what other prisoners said about him behind his back. They'd heard he was organizing a spy group, that he wanted to disrupt the prisoners' systems of leadership, their secret modes of communication. It made sense. There was enough to go on now; it was time to investigate, to get information from Yunus himself.

The night they decided they were ready, they waited until the last roll call, and exchanged glances as the guards closed the door for the night. They took Yunus to the area by the toilet, where the guards couldn't see him through the door's small window. They took off his clothes, so he stood only in his underwear. They played the same game Israeli intelligence played with them—good cop, bad cop. One of them poured cold water on Yunus; another asked him to confess, told him they'd go easy on him if he did. The boy's legs shook as freezing water dripped from his skin. He said nothing. They beat him, making sure to avoid his face, so the guards would see no marks.

The next morning, when the guards came for roll call, Yunus went straight to them, whispered something Sulaiman couldn't hear, and followed them out the door.

Omar nodded at Sulaiman. "Put on all your clothes," he said.

At first Sulaiman didn't understand—and then he did. They had two pairs of brown prison trousers and two pairs of long underwear from the Red Cross. Sulaiman stepped quickly into all of them. It was a little hard to walk, but his legs were padded.

Barely any time passed before they heard the alarm, before guards burst into the room wearing gas masks, holding out their black sticks. "Sulaiman, Omar, Suhail, out." As the guards pushed

Sulaiman through the hallway and down the stairs, using sticks against his legs, he was glad he'd listened to Omar. The extra layers protected him a bit from the blows. They still hurt, but he tried not to let anyone see it. When they got to the warden's office, the guard Paper was there, along with Abu Sabre, the Druze head of security: a huge, tall man, responsible for coordinating the *'asafir*, the collaborators, birds.

Abu Sabre looked at them.

"Who did this?"

Sulaiman's knees throbbed while he tried to think quickly. Suhail and Omar were supposed to be released soon, in just a few months. He didn't want them to serve more time. For him, though, another six months added to his fifteen-year sentence didn't make much difference.

Sulaiman looked up at Abu Sabre and Paper. "I did it."

The three boys were ordered to stand with their hands against the wall. The guards beat them, though it seemed they were only going through the motions, that they didn't care so much, that they were doing a chore. Afterward they sent Suhail and Omar back to the cell and took Sulaiman to *hafrada* (solitary confinement).[2]

Outside it was snowing, and in the small cement room without a bathroom, Sulaiman shivered. He tried not to think about Yunus, about his thin legs shaking under the freezing water. He tried not to think about whether or not he'd be out of solitary in time for the next family visit. He hadn't felt so alone since his interrogation in Ramallah.

A few days later, when Fatima and Sarah arrived for the next visit, they were told to turn around and go home. Sulaiman stayed in *hafrada* for thirteen days with little food and no one to talk to, though sometimes he could hear someone whisper through the walls, secret words meant for him or someone else.

The final time his mother and aunt came to visit in Hebron, Fatima gestured for Sulaiman to bring his face close to the mesh divider. She touched the hair above his lip.

"When did you become a man?" she laughed.

He pulled back, embarrassed. He had just turned seventeen.

A week or so later, a guard came into his cell at night; all the boys around him were preparing for bed. The guard told Sulaiman, as if it were nothing, to prepare his things for transfer the next morning. Sulaiman looked over his few personal belongings. He held the letters his family had sent, slowly folding them into a small box. Sitting in a circle on the floor, he stayed up late with his friends, telling jokes. He tried to share memories of Sadiq and Asif, who'd gone free a while ago, and Rafiq and Nasri, who'd been transferred without him, but none of the new boys remembered them. They all had shorter sentences—six months to a year—unlike Sulaiman. He'd lived in Hebron for nearly two and a half years; this jail had become a kind of home.

In the *posta*[3] the next morning, the van's metal seat cut into his thighs. From the back of the closed-in box, he could feel the world going by and, through a small hole, a microscopic breeze touched his cheek. He heard the noise of a city, sensed the light, and imagined people walking, the colors of figures passing on the street. He didn't know where he was going, but he hoped it was Jneid, a prison just outside the northern city of Nablus.

Before the Naksa, the Jordanians had built the structure as the foundation of a hospital. Only recently, in the mid-'80s, the Israelis had turned it into a jail to house the growing number of Palestinian political prisoners. Because Jneid was a newer building than some of the other prisons, the conditions were better. Sulaiman heard that the water came more easily there than in Hebron, that there was more food, more space in the yard. And some of Jneid's prisoners were important leaders in Fatah, men who'd led large-scale movements like the 1987 hunger strike.

If Sulaiman were transferred to Jneid, these important leaders would be his teachers. Instead of living among the transient boys of the *ashbal*, his cellmates would be men. They wouldn't talk about seeing their mothers in six months. They would have long sentences, like him.

He smiled and adjusted the capsule under his tongue. It was his turn to carry a message to the prison leadership in the next jail, wherever that might be. The plastic slipped easily in his mouth, reminding him to be ready, anytime, to swallow.

CHAPTER 9

Books & Gas

Sulaiman was taken to a jail in the city of Jenin. But since there was not a section for minors there, and since he was just barely seventeen, he was too young to stay. Instead, he was carted to a jail in the center of Nablus, where, in an old stone room crammed with thirty or forty men, he waited. Just outside the walls of his cell were the noises of the busy market. He waited like this—listening to the sounds of life outside—in a haze of uncountable days, until he was close enough to eighteen and the Israeli administration transferred him to Jneid.

Entering that prison, he felt like a person arriving in a new country, a foreign place with its own behaviors, sounds, traditions. When he got to his cell, Room 4, the men sat in a circle to share their names, where they were from, which jails they had lived in before. Looking around the circle on the floor, Sulaiman was glad to see a familiar face: Waleed, a young man several years older than him with a goofy smile and a wrestler's build. They'd met briefly in the Ramallah jail when Sulaiman was waiting for his court date. Waleed came from al-Jalazun refugee camp—not so far from Hizma—and he'd known Karim in jail, years ago now.

Waleed introduced Sulaiman to the others. There was Hatem, whom Sulaiman had met briefly in Hebron. Everyone used to think he was a collaborator with the Israelis, so when he got out, he'd stabbed an Israeli to prove them wrong. Now he was serving a long sentence and no one doubted him. To his right sat Maher, one year older than Sulaiman, who'd belonged to a group that had killed Palestinian collaborators; and next to him was Qaddura, who came from the village of Silwad, northeast of Ramallah. Qaddura carried a cigarette in his fingers, never bringing it to his lips, not even lighting it. He'd decided at some point that he wouldn't smoke again until he was free, and he hadn't. But he couldn't quit the delicate feeling of paper between his fingers.

When Qaddura got to his feet, he stood straight as a pole and carried himself like a king from some time when there were still many kings. He introduced himself as a member of Fatah, the jail's biggest party, and had the look of someone turning something over and peering at it from many angles. Sulaiman wanted to turn his eyes away, back down to the ground, but he found a way to hold his gaze straight.

"You'll be free before you know it," Waleed told him as the men left the circle, headed back to their beds. "Until then, and after, we'll take care of you. We are your family, your brothers. If you want anything, just say it, and we will bring it to you."

Sulaiman found that he didn't need much, that it was true what he'd heard: Jneid wasn't as cold as the prison in Hebron; it had more water and food than he was used to. There was even a television in his room, won through the hunger strikes. But the biggest change was living among adults instead of children. These men seemed like experts in the political systems the prisoners had built for themselves. They had ideas about how these systems might be improved, even transformed.

Around the time of Sulaiman's arrival, there was an election in Jneid. On a piece of paper, each man wrote the name of the prisoner he thought most fit to lead, and then all the papers were turned into capsules, hidden, transferred, found again, and counted. Once all the names were tallied, Qaddura became representative of Jneid prison, serving as the main go-between for prisoners of all political parties and the Israeli prison administration. He became a little like the mayor of a village.

Waleed, along with a group of friends who'd been transferred from Nafha prison, was chosen to serve with Qaddura on the

thirty-one seats of the revolutionary council. Waleed was also chosen to serve on the smaller central committee, which made sure the
revolutionary council's decisions were enacted.

The election marked a turning point: the younger generation
was taking over; leaders from past generations had lost their leadership positions. The older men drew their philosophy from the
culture of the 1960s and '70s, a generally more conservative time.
The younger men, who had been arrested while studying at university, were often more socially and politically liberal. Waleed, who
belonged to the younger group, felt that the older leaders were uneducated and prone to unnecessary strictness, that their mode of
operation often backfired.

For a long time, the old leadership had prohibited prisoners from
speaking to a prison guard unless there was no other choice. Only
each cell's *shawish*, representative, could speak to the Israeli guards.
If a leader on the security committee saw another prisoner speaking
to a guard, he might write the man's name down and hand it to the
security committee for further investigation. This, Waleed thought,
had taught prisoners to feel afraid of the guards. Waleed, and others
like him, had begun to say something different to their friends: *you
should be the one who is unafraid; you are the strong one, the guard
is the weak one. Talk to him freely. Let *him* be afraid of *you*.

The people with old ideas argued back: they said the new way
was less revolutionary, less true, less aligned with the struggle. They
insisted that the prisoners should listen only to songs with revolutionary content. Waleed responded that people needed a bit of
looseness to find strength. People needed small breaks, and not just
for their own sake: rest was a strategy for survival, maybe even a way
to win. These debates were rigorous, but no one revolted. Everyone
just sat on the floor of their cell, occasionally raising their voices.

Within these conversations, Qaddura listened to both sides.
Though more conservative and cautious than Waleed, he was committed to bringing more open-mindedness to the old ways. He held
onto stories about prisoners struggling to find balance between revolutionary discipline and modernity. Like the one about Tamer,
who had the job of reading the Israeli newspaper when it arrived,
blacking out the parts that were inappropriate, that might distract

the prisoners from their revolutionary studies. Like the people who'd had the job of newspaper examination before him, Tamer pored over the pages, especially the summer issue with pictures of women in bikinis. He looked for distracting legs and arms and skin to cover in black pen.

While performing his duty one day, Tamer paused over a photograph of a sculpture, the figure of a female nude carved in stone. He thought about blacking it out, but he couldn't do it; it was too silly. He bent down over the newspaper and when he was done, he left the picture of the monument untouched except for a simple caption underneath.

Qaddura always laughed when he remembered what it said.

Under the photograph, Tamer had written in big, clear letters: "THIS IS A STATUE."

To distract themselves from certain things—the lack of air, smells of the toilet in the room, summer heat, an inescapable longing for home—they focused on study sessions. After gathering together on the floor one morning, Qaddura asked, "Would anyone like to recite the values Habash sets forth in *Principles of Revolutionary Conduct?*"

Sulaiman jumped in, summarizing the text he'd read and reread in Hebron.

"The principles are like this," Sulaiman said. "Don't steal, help the community, knock on the door if you want to ask for water or food. Be in the community like a fish in the sea. Respect it, and don't look at their girls."

He'd learned these fundamental ideas well, but now in Jneid, with older and more knowledgeable prisoners, he could go deeper. He learned how Palestinians could be Muslim and Christian and secular and Jewish. He learned that religion had nothing to do with Palestinian identity. The problem was not with Jews and the Jewish religion but with the Western colonizers—the British especially, but also with America's support—who created Israel to ruin the Middle East, to control it. Palestinians needed to resist these foreigners claiming a right to the land. The goal was to free Palestine and to liberate everyone—including the Jews—from Zionism.

The point, Sulaiman learned, was that Fatah wasn't exclusionary; it could include anyone who loved freedom. And so they read all sorts of books about how to win this freedom. About the validity of armed struggle when your land is occupied. And about the brilliance of nonviolence too—of Gandhi and Dr. King. Any strategy that pointed toward liberation was welcome.

Aziz, a prominent Fatah leader, noticed that Sulaiman was reading everything he could, flipping the pages hungrily. He began creating reading lists for Sulaiman, covering one topic before moving to the next: five books of philosophy, then five books of psychology, followed by five books of history. Others had reading lists too, but since Sulaiman was young for Jneid, was again the *shibl* (son of the lion), some of the older leaders paid him special attention.

After poring over the handwritten catalogue in his cell, Sulaiman would order the books he wanted from the prison's library. He noted his selection on a piece of paper, which someone delivered to a section of the jail Sulaiman had never seen—an invisible place where a political prisoner named Jaber served as librarian for Jneid's Fatah-affiliated prisoners. Sometimes, when other prisoners requested a book first, Sulaiman waited a long time for it to appear. But eventually, as if by magic, Jaber arrived with his cart and Sulaiman's book.

In this way, Sulaiman read as much as he could—whenever he was not listening to a teacher speak during a session, whenever he was not outside moving his arms in circles, running, taking advantage of the brief time outside. He read all the books Aziz assigned to him and then asked for more. It felt so important, like he could suck the words from the page, swallow them, make the outside world a part of his body.

For the first time since Hebron, since he threw that book at Asif and Sadiq, he returned to Che Guevara's writing. For hours, he imagined Che in the woods somewhere, planning a revolution, peering out from behind a tree like the ones in Sulaiman's soccer grove at home. He even tried to look like him, growing out his hair until Waleed laughed at him, saying, "*Khalas*, Sulaiman. We're not in the mountains here. Cut your hair!"

He cut his hair and moved onto Frantz Fanon's writing about the French occupation of Algeria. He read and reread his favorite line in a poem by Abu al-Qasim al-Shabbi, a poet of Tunisia's struggle against French colonialism. The line was a song in itself, warning that anyone who failed to climb mountains would "forever live among the hollows." Poetry led to books of local proverbs, to Rousseau and Descartes, to all sorts of novels. Sulaiman loved *One Hundred Years of Solitude*, and another book, one about a bridge that led into the sea.

He could now read comfortably in Hebrew and he did, as a way to learn about the enemy, as a tool for struggle. He scrawled notes and quotations in a little notebook, like the one he'd once hidden in Najla's cave. Bits of novels and poetry, philosophy, and history. All the fragments he liked best seemed to bleed into one another. Poetry into philosophy. Novels into history. Khalil Gibran into the Egyptian feminist Saadawi, García Márquez into Fanon, Rumi into Sartre.

Everything was woven together for him: history and imagination and dreams, just one inseparable thing.

When Jaber's sentence was almost up, it was time to find a new librarian. The prisoner leadership always picked very carefully, and not only because the prison administration had to approve the choice. Because the librarian was able to leave his cell and work alone where no one could monitor him, no one could assess whether the Israelis had turned him into an '*asfur*, a bird. So the librarian had to be a trusted devotee of Fatah, but also someone who wouldn't cause trouble, who wouldn't do anything to anger the Israeli administration and spur collective punishment of the whole prisoner population. If the librarian did anything out of bounds, the Israelis might close the library, a sacred place for many of the prisoners, or worse.

When Sulaiman learned he'd been chosen as the new librarian, he couldn't believe his luck. He couldn't believe it even as he stood in the library that first morning, staring at the modest collection of books in wonder. Before then, he'd only traveled down the hallway in one direction, toward the prison yard. And now here he was: at the distant opposite end of the same hallway, in a section of the jail he'd never seen, in an impossibly beautiful world. It was a completely different way to leave his cell—not just for the two painfully brief daily periods in the prison yard, to visit the warden for punishment, or to put his fingers up against his mother's through the wire. The library didn't have a toilet tucked in the corner. Instead of his cell's wet smell of chemicals and urine, it had the lovely, dry scent of paper and dust.

Jaber—just days away from release—watched as Sulaiman walked around, running his fingers over the spines of the books. It was obvious which volumes had come from the Red Cross—faded and ragged—and which had been donated by families when the prison allowed it. He thought about how, if he'd been older, and come to jail in the 1960s or '70s, there wouldn't have been any books at all. The presence of the library was a sign that the prisoners were winning, slowly using the strategies of hunger strikes, boycotts, and negotiation to demand more and more of their rights from the Israelis. They did it in small steps and with patience, like revolutionaries often had to.

Since this was mostly a library for Fatah's political prisoners, only a small percentage of the books dealt with religion. Most were books of history, politics, and literature. Jaber showed Sulaiman the two catalogues: one the librarian kept and the other that was passed among the prisoners to make their selections.

Sulaiman watched as Jaber took a book from a new donation box, attached a label to its spine, and wrote the genre and author on it in tiny letters. He did it gently, like he didn't want to cause the book any pain. He showed Sulaiman how to shelve the books in the correct order; how to update the catalogue with the name of the book, the writer, and the subject; how to remove the listing of a book being replaced.

When time ran out and Sulaiman was ushered back to his cell, he felt like he'd left some holy place, like he should have removed his shoes.

Back in the cell, Sulaiman found his friends lying on their beds. Some men wore a pair of headphones, rigged to the precious television through a complex system of thin cables. This way, some could watch television while others slept, undisturbed. One Israeli guard had been so impressed with their makeshift system, he'd asked how to build something similar for his children.

Sulaiman flopped onto his mattress and pulled a pair of headphones onto his ears. There were only two or three channels, and the harsh light hurt his eyes, but he loved it anyway. Watching television in Room 4 was better than watching television in the other cells. Other room representatives changed the channel when a beautiful woman came on the screen, or when someone leaned in for a kiss, but Waleed pretended not to notice. He just turned away and grinned as Sulaiman stared with his mouth hanging open.

When Hakim, another leader on the revolutionary council, confronted Waleed about his laxity with the television, Waleed just shrugged.

"They are young," he said. "They are human beings, not walls. It's the worst thing to make these images strange to them. The more you make it mysterious, the more they want to watch."

Hakim threw up his hands. "You're going to make this prison into some kind of a nightclub!"

"You want them to just stare at the ugly faces of the guards all the time?" Waleed laughed. "Let them see something beautiful!"

There were different kinds of beauty in this place, but most had to be fought for, and won. So as a way to claim a corner for themselves, the prisoners started to mark the anniversary of the Palestinian Declaration of Independence. For Sulaiman, the statement—even with its implicit endorsement of the two-state solution—was a historic act of resistance. Arafat had declared the existence of a Palestinian state, whether or not Israel was ready to recognize it as reality.

That year, as the November anniversary approached, the Israeli prison administration gave approval for every component of the celebration but one. As part of the ceremony, the prisoners wanted to sing a Palestinian national anthem that had lived its life with various names: "*Fida'i*" (Revolutionary) and "*Biladi*" (My Country). The prison administration forbade it. They could do everything else—all the speeches, all the gestures—but the prisoners couldn't sing that

song. If they did, the administration told them, they could expect
tear gas.

This only made Sulaiman's friends laugh, tell jokes.

"Do you know why the Israelis need all those guns and
checkpoints?"

"Why?"

"Because they're so terribly frightened of singing!"

The prisoners decided that if singing was the only thing the administration prohibited, singing was the only important thing to do.
On the day of the celebration, Waleed stood at the small window
in the door of Room 4, looking out into the hallway as guards collected in gas masks. When he gave the signal to the others, they
began to sing.

My country, my country, my country, land of my ancestors . . .

Everyone knew the words by heart, how the song was an ode
to their land and to the *fida'iyin,* the revolutionaries who fought for
home. How the song went on to speak of conquering the impossible and climbing mountains, of winds and guns and battles, of a
return to Palestine, a place that was forever.

Everyone knew where the song was headed, but no one was
able to arrive there. Maybe Sulaiman was singing the first *my* or
country or *land* when the window in the cell door opened and the
guards started throwing in the gas. Suddenly there was powder everywhere and all the prisoners were on the floor—trying to escape
the gas, or already knocked down by it. Some were crying or yelling, some were quiet, their eyes closed tight as if they could squint
the burning feeling away. The guards rushed in wearing masks and
began lifting the limbs of the elderly and asthmatic, preparing to take
them to the clinic.

After the powder had cleared a bit from the air, and singing
might again be possible, Waleed stood. He looked around the room
at all the hunched figures. Maybe he asked them a question before
he started over from the beginning: "Will you let tear gas stop you
from celebrating our struggle for freedom?"

Or maybe he just made a great, directorial motion with his hands
and everyone began to sing again.

My country, my country, my country, land of my ancestors . . .

Immediately, gas came through again. Some men, as if just now waking, lifted themselves from the floor. Some threw soap or water at the guards. For a long time, it went on like this. Singing and gas, back and forth, as if the relation between the two things were written into a script somewhere. When it was over, Waleed looked around. It was late, and most of his fellow prisoners were in the clinic. He watched as the most recent powder settled into everyone's clothes and sleeping mats and blankets, and then something drew his eye. A blanket moving.

Looking closer, he saw a narrow figure kneeling on the ground, draped in a blanket from head to foot. It was Sulaiman. He sat on the floor like a child in a ghost costume, the cloth over his head, waiting for the air to clear.

As soon as the men could breathe again, some began cracking jokes, coughing through their laughter. The ones who could laugh this way survived. For others, it was different, as with two particular men eligible for early release. Each expected to go free, but for some reason—maybe singing "*Biladi*," maybe some other invisible whim—something changed. The day after they learned they were staying in this cement place, each was found hanging from a blanket, tied to the ceiling.

Sulaiman tried to find sense in it: they'd let themselves dream too much, and in the wrong way. He developed his own system that allowed him to dream and not dream, to be there and somewhere else at the same time. He used books in this way, studying English with Maher—who'd become one of his closest friends. English brought him closer to the British novels he'd read in translation, books in which sad lovesick men wandered through hills all day. Circling the yard in the evening, making the space bigger than it was, Sulaiman and Maher talked endlessly of studying in Europe or America, wandering through green hills in real life. About smaller trips they would take, once they were free. Driving to 'Ayn Farrah for a barbecue, or to the beach in Jaffa to look at girls or the sea, or both.

And when Sulaiman found himself thinking too much about something that hurt, he would pick up a book of Sufi poetry and imagine himself elsewhere, drunk on wine and in love with God. In this way, he used dreaming to suffer less, to live.

He balanced the dreaming outside the walls with an attempt to live exactly where he was and nowhere else, to zero in on the details of his life: the number of pages he'd read that day, how high his volleyball serve had arced, how precious the outside air had felt for the short period after lunch.

It was only at night, when he closed his eyes, that his mind wandered to his old bedroom in Hizma on the second floor. He imagined that it wasn't closed up behind iron, that he was lying under his old window, smelling the jasmine and the goats, listening to the voices of his mother and sister in the kitchen. He allowed himself this small luxury, but only for a minute. The wish for home, he knew, was a very dangerous sort of dreaming.

CHAPTER 10

A New
World Coming

In the fall of 1989, the first intifada was still seeping into Jneid.
Boys who were not quite eighteen kept arriving in greater numbers,
and soon there were too many *shibl* for any of them to be special.
Sulaiman, though not much older than these newcomers, was suddenly one of the veterans.

He pushed through his shyness and tried to assume the welcoming role others had taken with him. He explained things, pointed
out Waleed in the yard, short and fast, playing basketball with a
very tall new political prisoner from Nablus. What looked like a
regular game was part of Waleed's work of building relationships
and easing tensions between prisoners from the south and north.
There were significant cultural differences between them—regard-
ing food, styles of communication, systems of loyalty—and Waleed
often found himself playing mediator. Sulaiman helped him in this
work, joking about the giant and the dwarf playing basketball, trying
to make the newcomers feel at home.

As they breathed in the outside air, he told them secrets of this
place. How they could critique anything or anyone here, and this
was part of their revolution. He told them a story he'd heard about
the second caliph, 'Umar ibn al-Khattab, about how one Friday
night, when he was giving a speech in the mosque, somebody spoke
out and criticized him. When the guards went to remove the critic,

the caliph stopped them. He said: "Why do you make people slaves, when they're born free?"

The newer prisoners would nod, and Sulaiman would smile and continue with his little lecture. He spoke to them of 'Ali ibn Abi Talib, cousin of the Prophet Muhammad, who said that you should feel shame if you criticize someone else's behavior without looking at your own. He tried to recall the words of the thinker al-Shafi'i, though he couldn't remember the exact phrase. It was something like, "My opinion is right . . . but it could be wrong. And your opinion is wrong . . . but it could be right." Sulaiman spoke about how, with that lovely sleight of hand, al-Shafi'i kept this little space.

Sulaiman tried to call on these principles during the prisoners' weekly critique sessions. Every Saturday, all the men in his cell gathered together—to critique themselves and the other prisoners who shared the cement room. Someone might apologize for speaking out in anger; someone else might mention he'd forgotten to clean a cup three days before. The Saturday critique session was important. It was a mirror—a space where the men knew that, if they didn't behave well, it would be reflected back to them.

Though Sulaiman encouraged the newcomers to see the value in these meetings, there was often a silliness to them. Everyone had to say something, and sometimes Sulaiman couldn't think of anything to share. When it was his turn, he'd apologize for not washing a cup that he knew he'd actually washed. Still, he liked the practice, the philosophy underneath it, the inspiration of 'Umar ibn al-Khattab, of 'Ali, of al-Shafi'i. He liked how these traditions were somehow in conversation with secular Western philosophers he'd read, men who encouraged critique from the belief that nothing was sacred.

He embraced these teachings too. But just like al-Shafi'i, he kept a little space, because the sacred was real; it just wasn't what religious people said. It was the window on the wall, the pause between interrogations, the breath between a question and an answer. It was the voice of Fairuz crackling faintly and beautifully from the precious radio, or the smoke twisting up from a cigarette.

For years and years, Sulaiman had never touched a cigarette. And because he didn't smoke, he rarely drank coffee; to him, one didn't make sense without the other. Whenever he ordered from the canteen, he chose chocolate instead of cigarettes. Until Yasser asked for his help, he drank tea.

Yasser was older than Sulaiman, was always studying late into the night, smoking all the way through the dark. There seemed to be a direct relationship between the smoke he inhaled and his ability to absorb what was on the page, to speak to his cellmates so fluently about the material he learned. But to fuel his reading, Yasser needed more cigarettes than his ration allowed. And according to the ethics of the Palestinian leadership in jail, no one was supposed to get more than their fair share; everything from the canteen was to be distributed equally.

So when Yasser asked Sulaiman to start choosing cigarettes from the canteen instead of chocolate, they kept their deal secret. In order to make his sudden choice of cigarettes believable, Sulaiman would smoke a few every day in front of the *shawish*. Then he would slip the rest to Yasser—maybe from hand to hand, maybe directly into his older friend's pocket.

At first, Sulaiman gave Yasser seven cigarettes and smoked three for show. Then he handed over five and smoked five. And then, one day, he found he was unwilling to give even one cigarette away. He kept and smoked them all.[1] In his new life as smoker and coffee drinker—the one made him want the other—Sulaiman watched a decade close and another open up on his television screen.

He'd never lose it, the wonder of watching young Germans in jeans and jackets tearing down the Berlin Wall. And as 1990 unfurled, a similar joy arrived as he watched Nelson Mandela, hero of prisoners and fighters of injustice, released from jail. His wife, Winnie, walked beside him under a big sky, raising her fist, before Mandela raised his and the crowd roared. In the fall of 1991, Sulaiman saw Dr. Haider Abdel-Shafi lead a group of Palestinians to the Madrid Conference. Multilateral negotiations between Israel, Palestinian delegates, and neighboring Arab countries were about to begin.

On their shared television, Sulaiman and his friends watched the opening ceremony. When Israeli prime minister Yitzhak Shamir spoke of Israel reaching out "a hand in peace to its Arab neighbors," they laughed. It was ridiculous to think of this man painting himself a peacemaker. His government had refused to attend the Madrid Conference if the PLO sent its own independent delegation. Shamir, Sulaiman knew, saw the PLO as a terrorist organization. But Shamir's biography was a coveted book in the prison library; it had circled through the jail and many prisoners had read it. They knew he'd belonged to the Lehi, a paramilitary Zionist group which had used violence in a way that—if the group had been Palestinian—Shamir himself would have called "terror."

Still, afterward, Fatah leader Sari Nusseibeh led a march carrying olive branches through the streets of Ramallah. On his walk home, he saw those branches hanging in doorways like wishes, or talismans. When Sulaiman heard about this march, he felt something like hope. Even if the conference's launch was mostly a piece of theater, it cracked open a door. Through it, he could see what was possible. Negotiations had often worked for the prisoners, he thought, so why not on a larger scale? And maybe it was true what everyone around him was saying. If negotiations led to an agreement between Israel and the PLO, the political prisoners would be released. Sulaiman waited, watching television and studying more English. He prepared for the new world he could feel coming.

As Sulaiman waited, he was transferred from Room 4 to Room 8, where Qaddura lived. Instead of allowing the young men to watch soap operas starring Turkish models, Qaddura encouraged them to watch Israeli television and practice their Hebrew. They lay on their beds, lights off, headphones plugged into the makeshift speaker system.

Covered in darkness, Sulaiman often watched the screen without watching it. But one night, an image of a skinny little boy caught his eye, and he began to pay attention. He didn't recognize the film playing, couldn't tell what was happening. He knocked on the bunk bed above his own. His friend Abed's head peered down.

"What's this film about?"

"The Holocaust," Abed told him, eyes flicking back toward the screen. "When they killed the Jews in Europe."

Sulaiman had heard about the Holocaust from his father a long time before. They'd been in Jerusalem, leaving the shop of his father's friend, the Jewish barber with wild white hair. Either Sulaiman asked his father what the men had been talking about in Hebrew, or his father just began explaining.

"We were talking today about his family," Said said. "Most of them died."

"How did they die?" Sulaiman asked.

"The Germans killed them," Said said, pausing. "The Germans killed a lot of Jews like them. They put them in the fire."

The father of the barber with the white hair had escaped, unlike the rest of his family, and he'd come straight to Jerusalem.

"When did this happen?" Sulaiman asked his father, running his hand along the rough stone walls of the winding Musrara neighborhood.

"Not so long ago," Said said and slipped back into his usual silence.

As Sulaiman understood it, the Israelis used the Holocaust as an excuse for everything: taking his brother to prison, exiling his cousins, allowing the Lebanese Christians to kill Palestinians in Sabra and Shatila. They used it to build Pisgat Ze'ev, to take more and more of Hizma, to steal Palestine from the Palestinians.

But in the dark of Room 8, Sulaiman peered harder at the screen and didn't turn away as the black-and-white emaciated figures marched to their deaths, as bodies piled up like the Lebanese figures he'd seen on television so many years before.[2] He didn't know what to do with these pictures, didn't know where to put them. Something round and hard formed in his chest before he realized he was crying.

When the film was over and someone turned on the lights, he looked around. Many of the faces he saw had tear marks too. *Why, he heard a whisper, didn't the Jews resist? Why are they doing to us now what the Nazis did to them?*

Just before bed, Qaddura went to the door and knocked, signaling for their nightly cup of tea. When the door opened and Itamar appeared, Sulaiman paused. He thought he knew the guard's face, but now he saw it for what it was: a mask, something that covered something else.

After the initial, physical shock of the film faded, Sulaiman grew curious. He began reading more about ancient Jewish stories, Jewish life in Andalusia, Ashkenazi[3] Jewish history, and the Holocaust. He read Anne Frank's diary, along with *Yedioth Ahronoth* and other Israeli newspapers. He dedicated more time to practicing his Hebrew, as if trying to peel the words off the page to find what they covered, to see what was buried there.

What he learned didn't legitimize anything, or excuse the occupation. But it opened something, some willingness to look at his narrative from different angles. Because the Israelis he read about were not the Israelis he'd learned about before. They weren't only separate characters; they belonged to different stories entirely.

Certain foundations he'd rested on felt shaken. If the Israeli story was different than he'd thought, what would he find if he looked deeper into the story of Palestinians? He started to think in a way that frightened him. Maybe the Israelis were a little right. Maybe they were a little in need of a place. Maybe Zionism was not just colonialism *out of nowhere*.

CHAPTER 11

Many Pieces
of Paper

In 1991 the world kept changing, but not in all the ways Sulaiman hoped. The Soviet Union collapsed, and even in Jneid, a world away, the prisoners felt the impact directly. For some, faith in Marx no longer seemed like a tenable path toward freedom, and so the Communist factions lost members to Fatah and the Islamist parties. With all this around them, Sulaiman began hearing more stories about Palestinians using violence in seemingly new ways.

One day, a smiling boy from Bayt Sahur showed up in Sulaiman's cell. He introduced himself as Mu'tasim, explained that he'd stabbed a blond Israeli woman and realized only afterward that she wasn't Israeli at all, but a French tourist. There was something comic about the earnestness and silliness of his mistake, his sweet smile, and Sulaiman laughed and rolled his eyes with everyone else.

When a young man from Bethlehem arrived, it felt different. He'd stabbed children in the yeshiva where he worked. This was a person unlike anyone Sulaiman had met before. He was religious, conservative, full of certainty. Sulaiman tried to peer into him, to see something he recognized. But it didn't work. He saw only a hard person—cold, uneducated. He saw a man with a mind like a wall.

Sulaiman felt a gaping distance between what this person had done and the noble rules he'd learned in *Principles of Revolutionary Conduct*. He'd learned it was only acceptable to attack the military, not civilians. That violence and armed resistance were allowed, but only within a moral framework. He knew Fatah had not always followed these principles, and that sometimes Fatah activists had used violence against civilians. Still, what Mu'tasim and this new arrival had done, it felt different. A kind of violence that could take you, he thought, into blindness.

By his twentieth birthday, Sulaiman felt like an old man, a different creature than the boys of the new generation, especially those from Islamist parties like Hamas and Islamic Jihad, who seemed to be attacking civilians more frequently. In the past, Sulaiman had worshipped Che Guevara and his armed resistance. Now, he found himself studying frameworks for civil disobedience more closely. He'd already read Gandhi and Dr. Martin Luther King Jr. in study sessions. What he found there felt familiar, like it didn't contradict anything he knew. But their words now took on a new weight. Along with Gandhi and King, he read about Jesus, began invoking approximations of all these famous words: *Love your enemies, peace starts with me, be the change you want to see in the world* . . .

These phrases accumulated in his notebooks, scattered across the pages, as if circling a theme. Cramped between the lines, they grew larger and larger in him. One day, looking at the phrases, he found that the principle of nonviolence had overtaken his belief in a moral armed struggle. In jail, he'd seen the prisoners win so many demands through nonviolent means: organized hunger strikes, boycotts. With these strategies, they'd won. But outside, violence had won nothing. Not for him, not for Palestinians, not for anyone he could think of.

He began to wonder about certain contradictions. Some of the prisoners talked about freeing the world, but ended up fighting over who had more food on his plate. It made no sense. All the principles of justice, freedom, and democracy meant nothing if they weren't reflected in daily behaviors. He avoided the people he saw as hypocrites and stuck to Qaddura, someone who practiced the values he taught. Sulaiman watched the leader holding unsmoked cigarettes between his fingers, speaking quickly but somehow also with a slowness, holding many meetings and scribbling on paper.

In 1992, around the time Yitzhak Rabin became Israel's prime minister, Qaddura was leading negotiations with Shabas, the Israel Prison Service. Among other demands, he was fighting to return prisoners in solitary confinement back to the general prison population, and he was demanding the right of prisoners to study for university-level degrees. When negotiations stalled, Qaddura and the rest of the central council began planning for another hunger strike.

The cells of Jneid filled with scraps of paper, and not just the usual election materials, criticism, and feedback. Little slips appeared with secret directions for how to design a strike with the greatest possible impact. Everyone had pills under their tongue, ready to swallow if a guard ordered them to open their mouths. As notes were smuggled out to fellow prison leaders, Qaddura looked busier than usual, sending and receiving endless messages, scribbling in his notebook.

Sulaiman had done this before; he knew what was coming and how to prepare. While some walked around anxiously, Sulaiman felt tall, singing songs to his stomach and cracking jokes. When Waleed looked at him one day in the yard, he was bowled over. The signs of acne had scarred and faded. Sulaiman was no longer a boy. He had the look of a man.

In late September 1992, Palestinian prisoners across many Israeli jails began their strike, the biggest yet. Thousands of prisoners, though they couldn't see each other, did it together, steeling their stomachs with water and salt.

In the streets, protests broke out to support the strike. Some activists threw rocks and Israeli soldiers opened fire, killing several Palestinians and wounding hundreds. The army ordered an all-day curfew in Gaza, echoing the intifada's earlier days.

Inside the jail, Sulaiman called on his best powers of dreaming. He pretended the mixture of water and salt was something else, maybe the soup his mother used to make when he fell sick as a boy. He closed his eyes and let disparate images mix together: the soup, the hills in Hizma, playing soccer with Shimon and his enormous teeth, the sad, lovesick British people he'd met in novels.

When his dreams weren't strong enough, Sulaiman would recall stories Maher had told him about growing up in Ramallah. He'd summon the pictures Maher had painted for him: the old men sitting on stoops, the way everyone gathered together in the small streets under the open sky for days after a wedding.

He passed the time that way, until about two weeks in, when the door to Room 8 opened and Sulaiman watched Qaddura's back move away, down the hallway. He hoped this meant it would be over soon, that the violence outside would calm too. During the protests in Gaza to support the strike, one of the people killed by Israeli soldiers had been just a small boy, fourteen years old. They shot him in the chest. An Israeli visiting Gaza was found dead, too, killed by someone holding an axe or a knife or a hoe. For a moment, Sulaiman turned away from the news and toward his hunger. It seemed the easier thing.

That afternoon, he learned the prisoner leadership had nearly reached an agreement with the administration. This meant they could begin sipping on soup, though without taking in real food, the kind you could chew. If true resolution didn't come, the soup would disappear. Still, Sulaiman imagined the lovely texture and weight of bread sitting on his tongue. There was a fuzziness around the edges of the thought until something sharp moved in his belly, waking him, bringing him back to this place.

Two days later, Qaddura walked down the hallway again, dizzy from exerting himself without a real meal for strength. His mind was still foggy from hunger when an officer told him the news: they'd won. Or they'd won enough of their demands to begin eating again. The administration had decided that prisoners could now study for college degrees through a correspondence university system. Many prisoners would be released from solitary confinement.

In his office, the warden looked at Qaddura, motioned toward the phone on his desk.

"It's time to make some phone calls."

Qaddura picked up the receiver, felt the strange shape of it in his hands. It was the first time in years he'd been allowed to use a phone.

He called the other prisons, let them know the strike was over. At the direction of the guard, he also called his friend 'Ali, a newspaper reporter. Shabas was concerned about the protests outside; they were calling it a "mini-intifada." And the people in the street wouldn't stop protesting until the prisoners said the strike was over. At some point in the brief conversation, the reporter asked Qaddura if he'd like to speak to Abu Ammar (Arafat). Qaddura didn't know where the request came from, or why the Israelis allowed it. But suddenly, he heard the familiar voice crackling through.

"We are your soldiers," Qaddura told Arafat. "We won our battle for you."

After he hung up the phone in a daze, the guards brought him back to his cell. With the door closed behind him, he looked at everyone sitting and lying on their beds. Sulaiman stared at him, waiting.

"You won't believe who I've just spoken with," Qaddura said.

"Faisal Husseini?" someone asked, naming the important Fatah leader in al-Quds.

Qaddura shook his head.

"Haider Abdel-Shafi?" someone else guessed, invoking the leader of the Palestinian delegation to the Madrid Conference.

Qaddura shook his head again.

One of them smiled with a joke in his eyes. "Well, who did you talk to then? Abu Ammar?"

"Yes," Qaddura said, "that's exactly who I spoke to."

And all of them, as if pulled from above by a string, jumped off their beds.

One of the men stepped forward. He extended his hand to Qaddura, revealing a cigarette he'd saved for the end of the strike. "This is an important moment. Can I give you this gift?"

Though he'd vowed not to smoke again until he was free, Qaddura took the offering. He lit the tip and inhaled the sweetly bitter smoke. He breathed it in as deeply as he could.

The day after the strike's official end, Sulaiman got his first piece of bread, a precious and painful thing going down his throat. It was like all the other strikes he'd joined since his first in Hebron five years before, but it was also different. There had never been such effective coordination; they had never won so much. And the Israelis had let Qaddura speak to Arafat. Arafat, who was like somebody living behind the sky. Arafat, who'd so long been a red line for the Israelis. It was a historical moment. Sulaiman felt it then: things were changing—dramatically, dizzyingly.

It didn't take long for the new series of peace talks to stall. But while Abdel-Shafi struggled to gain traction at the Madrid Conference, a parallel, secret series of conversations had begun. Those talks would culminate in the Oslo process, a collection of agreements many thought would lead to a solution: a promise of security for the Israelis, and a state and system of self-determination for the Palestinians.

In September 1993, Arafat and Rabin shook hands on the White House lawn between Bill Clinton's outstretched arms. The simple physical contact of those two hands was shocking. It marked the first official, public agreement between Israel and the PLO. The paper they signed that day, called the Declaration of Principles, established a set of intentions: An interim Palestinian body would soon be established to govern in the West Bank and Gaza for a transitional period of no longer than five years. Israel would begin withdrawing troops from the Gaza Strip and Jericho area. And there would be a framework for further negotiations—leaving the most difficult questions of Jerusalem and the Palestinian refugees to the end.

When Sulaiman and his cellmates heard the news, someone started to dance and then all of them were moving their feet across the floor. The specifics of the agreement weren't immediately clear, but Sulaiman and his friends felt sure of one thing: peace was on its way, and the political prisoners would be released.

As the men twirled around the room, the Israeli prison guard Dov peered in nervously through the window in the door. Only days before, he'd thrown tear gas into their cell. But today, after staring for a while through the window, he opened the door and stood there, as if his standing were a question.

Some of the prisoners smiled at the guard. Others looked about to hug him.

Dov looked confused. "I don't know how you people will succeed with your politics," he said. "A few days ago, I threw gas into this cell. Why are you so warm with me now?"

"Everything's going to be different now," Sulaiman said. "That's why."

The Fatah prisoners were generally in favor of the agreement, even before they knew the details. Everyone had an opinion, as usual, but for most of them, there was a monumental sense that a chapter of history had finished.

It was true that Oslo meant compromise, a huge departure from the hope they'd cultivated for years. Sulaiman's dream and that of his friends matched Nelson Mandela's vision for South Africa: a democratic state, one person, one vote. Their Palestinian dream state would extend from the Jordan River to the Mediterranean Sea, a nation with room for everyone. Muslims, Christians, and Jews would all live in this Palestine: a place liberated from Zionism and colonialism.

The Oslo process pointed toward something else: at best, Israel within its pre-'67 borders—inside what was called the Green Line—and Palestine on the other side of that imaginary line, within the boundaries of the West Bank and Gaza. Just 22 percent of their home. But many of Sulaiman's friends in prison were willing to live with this enormous compromise *in order to live.* They knew, by then, that the Jews were never "going back to Poland." They felt the world had shifted, and it was time to follow.

Even before the Israeli army left an inch of Palestinian territory, before anything happened except some pen on paper and a very famous photo op, the Revolutionary University ended. Though Arafat had already pointed toward a two-state solution with the signing of the Palestinian Declaration of Independence in 1988, now it felt real. Fatah made it completely clear: it had canceled the idea of the whole of Palestine. The leadership spoke only of two states. For some of the prisoners, a state stretching from river to sea suddenly became irrelevant; it didn't apply to this reality anymore, this world they were living in.

Just like that, the biggest dreams made way for pragmatism, and in a way, Sulaiman and the prisoners around him were prepared for the shift. Jail had taught them practical principles. When they began a hunger strike, they knew they wouldn't keep going to the end—to fight to the last demand, to die. They stopped somewhere. It was the same with Oslo.

As they waited to hear what the peace process would bring next, no one could focus. They read newspapers, watched television, asked family for news about the expected release of all political prisoners. The old dream was replaced with a new one: who would be released, and when.

In February, their optimism was interrupted by news of the Hebron Massacre. Baruch Goldstein, an American-Israeli settler and religious extremist, murdered twenty-nine Palestinians in Hebron's Ibrahimi Mosque while they prayed. Sulaiman couldn't believe it when he heard, tried not to think about it—about what could have made that man believe his God wanted him to kill Muslims as they bowed to the ground. Around Sulaiman, the men cried and raised their fists, spent days in mourning.

Then, in May of 1994, not long after Sulaiman's twenty-second birthday, Rabin and Arafat signed the Gaza-Jericho agreement. Certain intentions from the Declaration of Principles were made real. The agreement formally established the Palestinian Authority (PA) to govern, temporarily and in a limited way, in the West Bank and Gaza. It triggered Israel's partial withdrawal of soldiers from the Gaza Strip and Jericho area. And it placed a new promise in writing: within five weeks, Israel would release five thousand Palestinian political prisoners.

The next time Sarah came to visit Sulaiman, she had the air of someone on her way to a wedding.

Though Sulaiman could feel hope becoming a truly physical thing, he knew freedom wouldn't come right away. The first prisoners Israel planned to release were those without "blood on their hands." If you were a Palestinian prisoner accused of an attack on Palestinian collaborators, you could still be released—at least into the jurisdiction of the PA. His friend Maher, for instance, had several life sentences for killing collaborators; he would surely be released. Though Sulaiman never killed anyone, he had attacked Israelis, a different story entirely.

Sulaiman knew he wouldn't go free in the first round, but maybe some part of him still held hope the day a guard came to the door of Room 8 and handed Qaddura a list. The names were called, one after the other.

"Ghassan."

"Asad."

"Karam. Bashir. Fareed. Azzam. Ilyas . . ."

The prisoners whose names were called had to sign a piece of paper swearing they would not "return to terrorism." Sulaiman knew that if he heard his name called, he would sign without hesitating. By then, it was only a piece of paper. In a battle between a piece of paper and the world, he would have chosen the world, without a question.

Over and over, he watched the door open and close. Eventually the last name was called and the door closed. It didn't open again.

By the end of July 1994, Israel had released 4,450 prisoners. Qaddura and Waleed were among them, and Maher was transferred to the control of the PA in Jericho. Sulaiman stayed behind.

Though this didn't surprise him at first, he kept hoping something would change at a later stage of the continuing Oslo negotiations. In a nearly empty cell, Sulaiman watched on television as Arafat arrived in Gaza—his return from exile a result of Oslo. Suddenly, he remembered Abu Ammar's departure from Beirut a decade before. After an enormous defeat in Lebanon, he left for Tunis, smiling. A reporter had asked him, "Where are you going?" And he'd said, to many people's confusion, "We are going to al-Quds." It seemed to Sulaiman now that their leader knew, that he was seeing far, far ahead in time.

Outside, such monumental shifts, and inside Jneid, only around 350 prisoners remained. The jail looked unfamiliar now with so much empty space. In Sulaiman's room, where there were once ten people, there were now only two. When he looked around in the yard, he saw something in the faces of the others still there, like him. They were trapped: leftover, forgotten.

Nothing else changed for the men in Jneid until September 1995, when Arafat and Rabin signed the Oslo II agreement, in which Israel committed to withdraw from the densely populated Palestinian cities of Jenin, Tulkarem, Qalqilya, Bethlehem, Ramallah, and Nablus. This meant Israel would hand the Jneid prison—where Sulaiman had lived for close to six years—over to the PA. Sulaiman was twenty-three years old when he and his few remaining friends prepared for transfer to a jail inside Israel.

Outside, many Palestinians were celebrating Israel's partial withdrawal. Inside, Sulaiman felt at a great distance from everything, alone in that empty room. He looked down at the stone floor and two lines of poetry, remembered imprecisely from somewhere, appeared in his mind:

> *If my homeland becomes a disaster for me, for my life,*
> *   still it is dear to my heart.*
> *If you suffer because your people are harsh with you,*
> *   still they are dear to you.*

In the evening dark, as the Israeli army prepared to leave Nablus and Ramallah, as Sulaiman watched boys on television throw roses at IDF tanks in the streets, the words stayed in him.

CHAPTER 12

Little Chance

In Israel's Kfar Yona jail, Sulaiman hardly recognized a thing. The smell was different, everything was different; he could tell Israel was outside, not Palestine. As if, overnight, he'd been thrown into diaspora.

In the brief hours of daily yard-time, he clung to the few people who'd been transferred with him—Khalil, Yasser, and members of the Tamimi family. They were the only thing that had stayed the same. Together, they spoke angrily about the Palestinian leadership, about how they had exalted the prisoners when it was convenient and then discarded them so easily.

Sulaiman only stayed in Kfar Yona for a few months before the Israelis moved him to the K'tziot military camp in the Negev/ Naqab desert. It was run by the Israeli army, not by Shabas like the other jails he'd known. There were unarmed guards, and then there were soldiers with guns behind them, avoiding eye contact with the prisoners. Sulaiman lived in a tent, where he braced himself against the heat during the day and the cold at night.

After some time, he was transferred again to a jail in Be'er Sheva/Bi'r al-Sab'. The jail was run by Shabas, familiar in some ways. But in these new times, everything felt different. By then, prisoners weren't focused on the revolution, just preparing to find a job or reunite with their family. Sulaiman spent his time studying Hebrew and English alone. He rarely read political books anymore, and it seemed no one around him did either. Instead, he read novels, and listened to Israeli Mizrahi[1] artists like Zohar Argov, like Zehava Ben singing in song what he couldn't say in prayer—*God, give me little chance* . . . He watched on television as news of the world outside unfolded without him.

Many were still expecting peace, but there was so much in the way. The Oslo Accords had divided the West Bank into three sections: Area A—big Palestinian cities with the densest population; Area B—areas just around the big cities; and Area C—everything else. Though Israel had mostly vacated the newly created Area A, the prisoners heard stories about Jewish settlers who were rebelling against the Oslo "land for peace" formula by building new settlements in Area C—which made up over 60 percent of the West Bank. And the Israeli government was often allowing—and even facilitating—this. Though this land was more sparsely populated than Area A, many Palestinians lived on in it. Even more Palestinians, including Sulaiman's family, owned plots of its agricultural land. Area C's open space allowed the olive groves and fig trees to breathe. But it seemed that space was closing.

During this time, it seemed more Palestinians began using violence. From his cell, Sulaiman watched news coverage of men, many affiliated with Hamas or Islamic Jihad, blowing themselves up in public places in Israel. He stared at the screen, jaw clenched, nearly shaking with anger. These people were using the cause of freedom he'd gone to jail for and tearing it apart, making it unrecognizably wrong.

He knew they were trying to derail Oslo. Though many Palestinians accepted the peace process, to some it still seemed a betrayal. Every other people troubled by colonialism had won their independence. Why should it be different for the Palestinians? The equivalent of Oslo in Algeria would have been the Algerians shrugging their shoulders and giving up half of their country to the French. More than half. This argument was familiar to Sulaiman, but the suicide bombings felt new. The tactic startled other prisoners around Sulaiman too, and even those Fatah activists who still supported violence grew angry with Hamas. They felt that Palestinian fighters should only target military personnel in the territory occupied after 1967.

To Sulaiman, though, there was no solution in any violence now, just a path that circled back on itself. He wanted Oslo to have a chance, and he wanted to go free. He was filled with the exhaustion of it. *Khalas*, he thought. *Enough with the struggle. Let's leave the revolution behind us. Now we have to live.*

But the reports on television kept coming in. It seemed that Hamas militants would kill anybody: army, civilians, old people, kids—it didn't matter. It seemed, suddenly, that killing had become the rule, not the exception. He watched the terrible images flash across the screen: children in stretchers, blood in the streets. Whenever he saw these things, the television camera framing a child's shoe on the sidewalk, he felt a tightening in his chest.

He knew that after every suicide bombing, the Israeli army would retaliate against the village or refugee camp where the attacker came from. Their family's home might be demolished, and a curfew might be set to punish everyone who walked down the street where that man or woman once lived. There would be protests, and Israeli soldiers would kill more Palestinians. He knew the violence would continue like this. He wanted desperately for it to stop.

One day, he heard that an old Jewish-Israeli peacenik had been killed in an attack. A few weeks later, a young prisoner showed up and said proudly that he'd done it, he'd killed the gray-haired activist. He'd spent a few weeks living in a graveyard, he told Sulaiman, preparing himself, reading the Qur'an, gathering strength. Sulaiman stared at the prisoner, confused. He didn't understand it, how his revolution had become intertwined with a version of religion that made no sense, that held such little room for other belief systems, that limited compassion instead of cultivating it.

Sulaiman searched the new prisoner's face, hoping to find something trying to break out, some uncertainty, but he found nothing.

Sulaiman's hope for Oslo shook again on November 4, 1995. Israeli prime minister Yitzhak Rabin was giving a big speech in a large square when the shots came. Rabin, a former general, had called for an end to the conflict. He'd said that if the Israeli people wanted to live in peace and without fear, they would have to give up land in the West Bank and Gaza. Yigal Amir, an Israeli religious extremist, believed this kind of compromise heretical. That morning, he had set out to kill the prime minister and the peace process along with him.

From the jail in Be'er Sheva/Bi'r al-Sab', Sulaiman heard the news or saw it on the little television. The scene played and replayed; he couldn't stop seeing it: Rabin speaking in front of an enormous crowd of people in Tel Aviv, Yigal Amir shooting his gun, the screaming. Rabin dead.

It was enormous. Sulaiman could almost feel the ground shaking beneath him.

Time seemed to slow, as if unsure what to do next. And then one day, there was a commotion in the hallway outside, the sound of a new prisoner entering the cell beside Sulaiman's.

"Who is it?" he asked the guard.

"It's the son of a bitch who killed Rabin," the guard answered.

"Fuck him," Sulaiman said, and reached a hand out to steady himself against the wall.

Yigal Amir sat in a cell just beside theirs, but Sulaiman never saw his face. He was kept alone. All of Sulaiman's friends were angry at Amir for what he'd done, for compromising the peace talks. Together with their Israeli guards, they spoke endlessly against him.

It was a little strange. During the first intifada, Rabin had given orders to break Palestinian bones. He was a tough person, and any Palestinian prisoner tortured during the first intifada connected it to him. But after Oslo began, there was an understanding that peace between enemies could only be made between people who were remarkably, almost impossibly strong. Some people believed that, without Rabin, there could never be an agreement. Arafat agreed. Sulaiman heard that after the assassination, the leader of the Palestinian people spoke it simply: "It's finished."

The confusion on the national stage echoed in every direction. During the next family visit, Fatima arrived talking quickly, as if she'd begun a conversation with Sulaiman before even entering the room. She shook her head roughly as she spoke about a conflict that had erupted in Hizma between the Farhat family and their own. Sulaiman couldn't follow it all: something about his brother Fadel upsetting someone, a physical altercation, someone—he wasn't sure who—losing a finger. It was only when time ran out, at the end of their visit, that Fatima smiled and told Sulaiman the good news, as if an afterthought. His brother Aziz had hired a Jewish-Israeli human rights lawyer named Leah Tsemel to defend him in an early release trial.

It was a moment too important to feel real. As the guards brought him back to his cell, Sulaiman's legs weakened. Everything around him—friends, bunk beds, walls—looked strange, as if he were peering through some refracting piece of glass. He kept hearing Fatima's words and his heart raced, keeping him from sleep.

Before the judge during that first trial, Tsemel argued that Sulaiman had served his time, that his sentence was too harsh, that it would have been too harsh even for a minor who'd committed murder. The prosecutor argued that Sulaiman was dangerous, a fanatic, and that the Israelis he attacked had been badly wounded. The judge asked the attorney to bring evidence at the next trial, months later.

It was as jarring as time travel, moving from the court back to his cell. He already felt miles away from this place, knew also that it was dangerous to hold the wrong kind of hope in a moment like this one. He tried to practice what he'd mastered long ago—the art of focusing on small things. He savored his cigarettes, laughed at his friends' jokes, watched television, did push-ups. When he could still find his focus, he read books in Hebrew and English. He tried not to imagine going free five years early. He could rarely think of anything else.

Near the end of those never-ending months, Fatima came home from Tsemel's office, humming to herself. She told Sarah what the Israeli lawyer had said: that since this coming week was Ramadan, there was a good chance Sulaiman would return home.

Sarah shook her head. "The lawyer's Jewish," she told Fatima. "She doesn't know what Ramadan is."

The next week, Sulaiman was in court again.

It was the very beginning of Ramadan, and right before the judge called for a break, Sulaiman took a sip from a glass of water, fumbled with the box of cigarettes in his pocket. Later, it struck him that his secularity, the fact that he was not fasting, was a very good thing in the eyes of the court.

It counted in his favor, as did the prosecutor's failure to present any evidence that the two Israelis from 'Ayn Farrah had been badly wounded. Tsemel argued the same thing she had months before: "There is no disagreement that the child was fourteen and a half years old when the offense was committed. There is no disagreement that the prisoner we encounter today is a twenty-four-year-old man. At the time of the offense he was an eighth-grade pupil. In prison he learned Hebrew very well. He also learned English and worked as a librarian. We see before us today a fully developed man who regrets the childish deeds he carried out."

The judge listened closely and responded with a question, directed at Sulaiman: "If there is a new intifada, will you sit home and watch? Or will you participate?"

Sulaiman knew this question would come. He straightened his spine and began his speech—prepared beforehand in Hebrew. It went, perhaps, like this: "I'm against violence. I'm an active person, so I can't sit and watch. But if there's violence, I will try to stop it. I'm committed to nonviolence. This is what I really believe, not something I am saying so you will release me."

Sulaiman might have said this, but what appears in the Parole Committee Protocol—in the record of his final trial on January 12, 1997—is this: "*The prisoner:* I am willing to sign that I will not do anything illegal. I agree."

Sulaiman, "the prisoner," signed a piece of paper, a bit like the confession he'd signed over ten years before. Only this time, he understood what he was doing. This time, it felt like a choice.

A long time before, Inshirah, the daughter of the refugee Fatima al-Hasan, told Sarah that if she treated Ramadan well, it would care for her sons. It turned out Inshirah was right. Karim had been released on the first day of Ramadan in 1985. And on the second day of Ramadan, twelve years later, a cousin ran into the house to tell Sarah that Sulaiman was in the Palestinian police station in al-Dhahiriya, and it was time to bring him home.

PART THREE

CHAPTER 13

'Awda (Return)

The prison administration gave Sulaiman a piece of paper as a temporary ID. In case any soldiers stopped him on the way home, he could use it to prove he'd been released legally. It was his first ID; he'd been too young for one before jail. Before he left, the Shabas officers also gave him back his belongings, some old clothes that didn't fit anymore. But what he said to himself, practicing his English, was this: *They gave me my belonging.*

The officers put him in a *posta* that drove until it stopped at a dirt intersection, deposited him, and sped away. It was evening, the sky almost dark, and since it was the second evening of Ramadan, the street was empty. Everyone was inside, filling their stomachs with a whole day's worth of food, feeling the energy flood back into their limbs. Sulaiman shivered. It was cold, and he had no coat.

After a long time, a car appeared on the horizon and he stuck his arm out. The truck slowed and a Bedouin man leaned out the window.

"*Marhaba,*" Sulaiman smiled. "Where are we?"

The man laughed. "Between Bi'r al-Sab' and al-Khalil.[1] I'm going to al-Khalil. Do you want a ride?"

Sulaiman nodded. "Will you take me to the nearest Palestinian police station?"

The man smiled a yes, and waved him in.

When Sulaiman arrived at the station in al-Dhahiriya, the police weren't surprised to see him. Every day the same thing happened: a confused man—usually a car thief—was dropped off in the middle of nowhere, just released from jail. First, they gave Sulaiman an apple and a cup of tea, then handed him a cell phone to call his family. When he held it up to his ear, the police began laughing. He was holding it upside down, trying to speak into the earpiece and hear from the mouthpiece. He'd never used a cell phone before. One of the officers gestured for him to turn it around, and he smiled, quickly did.

"How many years in jail?" one of them asked.

"Almost eleven."

"Did you steal a car?"

"No. I was a political prisoner."

"*Wallah.* Sit. Eat."

"Thank you. The apple and tea are fine."

He dialed his family house and waited, dialed and waited again. No one picked up. He'd find out later that the phone in Said's house was broken. Finally, he tried his cousin Imad, who lived just a few houses down from his family. It was Imad, or someone else, who answered the phone, and it was Imad, or someone else, who ran the three houses down the road to tell Sarah the news.

There was a pause, total stillness just for a moment, before everyone began moving. Fatima started chopping onions. Sarah and Said and siblings and nieces and nephews and cousins all jumped into the cars—three or four of them—and started the long drive to al-Dhahiriya.

Sulaiman was glad for the hours it took them to arrive. He accepted cigarettes from the police and walked outside, looked down at the dirt and up at the sky until it finished darkening. He breathed in the air so deeply he felt dizzy. He stayed like that, walking back and forth for a long time, breathing until his lungs felt sweetly sore.

He looked around and recognized nothing of the road around him. It felt like he'd lived two lifetimes, or more. But he also knew, he was sure, that the man standing on that unrecognizable road in January of 1997, on the second day of Ramadan, was not so different from the boy who'd woken to soldiers in his house over ten years before.

It was night already when he felt all the hands grabbing and squeezing him from different directions, his cheeks wet with the spit from someone's kiss or someone's tears or both. He couldn't hear himself think through the singing and the crying, those two things that somehow always went together in his family. Through the fingers and limbs nearly crushing him, he saw Sarah and Fatima, he saw the faces of relatives he'd never met or at least didn't remember from all those years before. And then the figure of his father in a *kufiya*, standing back and watching him, a stiffness about him, some wetness in his eyes he kept trying to blink back.

That slow moment between Sulaiman and his father sped up and the cars took off, headed toward Hizma, the place he'd last seen so many years before, surrounded by soldiers.

When the cars arrived at a checkpoint in Hebron, Sulaiman could make out the shapes of Israeli soldiers, their figures against the sky, black on black.

One soldier leaned into their window. "IDs?"

Sulaiman handed over his new ID, and the soldier looked at it, looked up at him, and motioned for the car to pull over. When the soldier returned, he leaned farther into the window, peering at Sulaiman, his voice like a weapon. Sarah drew back when he spoke.

"You escaped from jail, huh?"

Sulaiman spoke to him in Hebrew, tried to explain, but the soldier motioned for him to open the door and pointed him toward a nearby army vehicle.

"Where are you taking him?" Sarah was pulling her sleeves over her fingers when she asked the question.

"Kiryat Arba," the soldier said over his shoulder, naming the nearby Jewish settlement. "We're not sure about his ID."

Sulaiman looked back at his mother's face, saw the terror in it, and smiled. "Don't worry, *Yamma*, they'll check and find the truth."

He spent two hours in a cell in Kiryat Arba before someone verified that his ID was valid, that he'd been released from jail legally and hadn't run off somehow. It was almost midnight when he emerged, his family's cars still waiting for him outside, and they all began the drive home.

At the entrance to Hizma, there was a crowd of people and he was suddenly on their shoulders, the earth far beneath him. When he made it back to the ground, then back to his family house, he found himself looking at his old room—the cement and iron the army had erected to bar its entrance. He stared at it, wondering. Was the same air inside from ten years before, or had it managed to sneak in and out?

A hand was on his shoulder. Another hand reached out with clothes for him to change into. He couldn't believe how soft they were.

The next few days it was impossible to leave the house because someone was always visiting. All the family came, relatives whose names he couldn't remember, and old friends from jail.

Maher came and Sulaiman laughed, pretending it didn't feel like forever since the last time they'd been together. Maher talked about his new boss, the famous Fatah leader Marwan Barghouti; he said that Marwan was asking Arafat for a stipend to help Sulaiman organize his life after jail. Sulaiman was grateful. He knew it would be expensive and difficult to make the necessary arrangements, all the details that marked the life of a person who's free.

Everyone came and sat beside him for hours. Sadiq and Asif, who recited the names of all their children. Bassam Aramin, who'd been out of jail for five years and lived in nearby 'Anata. Omar, a friend from Hizma who was now working in the Orient House— the PLO headquarters in Jerusalem. And Omar's friend Yusuf, bodyguard and assistant to Faisal Husseini, the most important Fatah leader in al-Quds.

Later, after everyone had returned to their houses and Sulaiman had drunk too much coffee, Said led him to a house across the street. Sulaiman followed his father up the stairs and into an apartment where Said gestured in a way that told Sulaiman this place was for him. It was unfinished, just walls and a ceiling—but it was his. He opened the window wide and looked out. That night he slept in a room alone for the first time since *hafrada* in Hebron.

The quiet didn't last long enough. In the morning, people kept coming. Sulaiman's excitement rose and fell, and still there was an endless succession of tea- and coffee-drinking, of sweets, of presents, of talking and smoking and nothing else. He waited and waited for it to end, but it didn't, not for days. He wanted so badly to go walking into the hills by himself, but first, Sarah and his brothers gathered tools. They began tearing down the cement and iron the Israeli army had erected to close his old room, over ten years before. It had a certain smell, like a place that had never seen the sun.

When the stream of family and friends finally slowed, Sulaiman sat in the backyard smoking cigarettes. As Sarah brought him cup after cup of sheep's milk, drawn from the animals his family acquired while he was in another world, replacing the goats of his childhood, he could feel his body changing. There was something hard and rotting that was beginning to soften and curl and disappear.

Looking out across the field, he saw a different picture than the one he remembered. Where there used to be hills, new buildings stood in the way. Hizma was a different place, with widened paved roads and new buildings everywhere, no longer a small village.

There was something normal in this, the way things change, irrepressibly. But it was also impossible to disconnect from the occupation. Since Israel denied most applications for building permits in Area C, the natural growth of Hizma had been paralyzed, forced into a small space, while around it, the settlements had expanded.

Sulaiman took a walk in the hills, counting his steps and breathing in as much air as he could—just like he'd imagined. The earth under his feet felt better than most things he could think of. But he couldn't wander as far as he used to. To the east, he saw new red-roofed buildings. To the west, Pisgat Ze'ev had grown into a huge thing.

When he started to go on drives with his younger brothers, trips that used to take five minutes now took forty-five. The settlements were places they could only drive around, not through. They weren't allowed to use the roads that would make their trips faster; only Israelis and tourists were.

In jail, he'd held so much hope for the Oslo Accords. Now he was beginning to wonder what Arafat had actually agreed to. There seemed to be more restriction on movement than ever before, and this included access to al-Quds. Maybe this was connected to increased attacks on Israelis, maybe to something else, but either way, the result was the same. As a child, Sulaiman used to take the bus straight from Hizma. It took about fifteen minutes. Now, the Hizma-Jerusalem bus line he'd once used to visit his father and the barber was shut down. The sign still hung over the bus stop, but no matter how long you waited beneath it, no bus would come.

There were other, much longer routes to Jerusalem, but during his parole, he wasn't allowed to enter Israel at all. Instead, he walked often toward Ta'mira, through the brown hills. He stood looking at the wall of stones separating his family's plot from the surrounding land. He thought of his grandfather and lay beneath a tree, maybe the same one he'd hidden behind with Farid a long time before, as the soldiers searched for them. After all this time, he put his head down on a stone and rested, the way his grandfather had taught him.

When he returned home, he gathered all of his papers from jail. He collected the notebooks where he'd written down Arabic proverbs translated into English and notes from Freud and Rousseau; the letters from his family. He found the letters he'd sent to his mother, the ones delivered by the Red Cross, and he carried all that paper in a sack into the backyard, made a hasty fire, and held the bag open, upside down, over the heat. The papers floated down into the flames. He picked up the pieces that fell to the ground, crumpled them up, and threw them into the fire, too, as if in some ceremony of rebirth. Just like that, he burned everything.

Khalas, he thought. *Enough with jail. Now, a new life.*

CHAPTER 14

Holy Mountain

Sulaiman's house was often filled with people, but when he walked into the living room that day, he could feel this gathering was different. Karim and his father were there with other men from the family. Fatima was present, too, as she often was when a big decision was needed. Their heads were bent together, so Sulaiman bent his in too.

Their conversation tripped a memory—something about his brother Fadel, who'd been in a fight with the Farhat clan to defend the family's honor against an insult that Sulaiman couldn't get anyone to repeat. Someone threw a rock, someone lost a finger, but there were so many details, and so many phases, that if Sulaiman looked too close, it all tangled together.

After the most recent incident, Sulaiman's family had brought money—intended as a symbol of peace—to one of the Farhat elders. This offering followed the rules of the traditional Palestinian reconciliation process of *sulha*, born in the pre-Islamic Arab world. *Sulha* was still used widely throughout Palestine; it provided a complex system of mediation, with various stages. After both sides agreed to put their conflict in the hands of the *jaha* (peace council), they formalized a truce. The offending party would sometimes offer money as a symbol of remorse to protect the truce, or the victim could state that no money was needed. In the quiet that followed, the *jaha* would listen to the families, trying to understand what had occurred, what additional compensation was needed. The process would end with two hands pressed together, a public declaration of forgiveness and ceremonial meals, a way of drinking coffee and eating that meant everything was finished.

After Sulaiman's family had brought the Farhats money, they thought the fighting was over. And it was, until one of the Farhat brothers returned from Jordan and tried to ram into Sulaiman's cousin with his car. *Sulha* required a significant price for the intention to kill, and so, according to the rules, Sulaiman's family now had the right to ask for a lot of money.

There was no place for quiet in the long family meetings they held, day and night, discussing how to respond. Sulaiman and Karim agreed: though *sulha* had provided a useful framework, they would break with it now in at least one way. They would not ask for compensation. If they took the other family's money for this new offense, the cycle would only continue. And they wanted it to end.

In the room filled with smoke, the phone rang. It was the Palestinian police, calling Sulaiman, Karim, and eight other men from their family to the police station in Ramallah. When they arrived, they were invited into a room, beside which stood another room with ten men from the Farhat family. The chief of police closed the door, smiling. "Figure it out," he said, "or stay here."

The men sat in the room of the police station for two days talking, smoking, and taking visitors who brought them food and advice. One old man from the village came to visit and whispered to Sulaiman's family in low tones no one else could hear. "You will need guns," he told them. "I can sell you some. The Farhat family has already bought plenty." Then he went to the Farhat family and said the same thing.

Neither side listened to the old man. Instead, as their conversations circled, Sulaiman spoke the words that he would find himself using again, later. He said them quickly, without thinking: "There is no military solution to our conflict."

Eventually, both families grew tired of sitting in jail and agreed to set up a formal meeting—according to the rules of *sulha*—to officially mark the end of the story. The Palestinian police opened the doors and let them go. In the coming weeks, the two families met in Ramallah for hummus, in Hizma for *mansaf.* And, like that, it was finished.

There was something in the tradition of *sulha*, Sulaiman thought, in the unwritten laws of village life. But there was something in breaking with all of it, too. *Sulha* had provided a common language between the Farhat and Khatib families, but if they had blindly continued to follow the traditional practice, the conflict might have gone on without end. The more Sulaiman thought about this, and the more he tried to slip back into the world he'd spent ten years dreaming about, the more he felt the rules of that world constricting around him.

At the funeral of a distant cousin, he sat in a tent with his family, drinking thick coffee that sped his heart, listening to an elder talking. He found the man ridiculous. The elder kept speaking about how he and Arafat were very close friends, how the leader used to call him from Tunis for advice.

Sulaiman sneaked a look at his father and brothers. They were listening respectfully, seriously, even though the man was so clearly making everything up. Sulaiman didn't realize he was smiling until his brother looked at him darkly.

"Sulaiman," he said later, "don't come with us next time if you can't behave."

Sulaiman shook his head at his brother and laughed. "In jail, it wasn't like that! We all spoke and joked, there was no holy person, nothing you couldn't critique."

His family stopped bringing him to funerals after that, which was fine with him. He wanted to focus on organizing his life, on searching for ways to steal back his lost time. He wanted to live comfortably, to travel and see the world he'd dreamed about. He wanted to turn the walls and ceiling his father had given him into a place to live. But to do these things he needed money.

At the end of the '90s, many things had changed and many hadn't. Through Oslo, Israel had recognized the PLO, and allowed for the

creation of partial governing structures to emerge in Palestinian society. Two branches of Palestinian security were formed to operate
in Area A. The first was where all the ex-political prisoners seemed
to go, where most of Sulaiman's friends from jail worked.

The second branch was filled with the people Sulaiman and his
friends jokingly called *olim chadashim*, the Hebrew term for Jews
who'd just immigrated to Israel. But when Sulaiman and his friends
said *olim chadashim*, they meant the Palestinian "returnees," the tens
of thousands of Palestinian refugees Israel allowed to return to the
West Bank and Gaza after Oslo. These Palestinians came primar-
ily from the exiled PLO leadership, and they tended to arrive with
more economic privilege than the Palestinians living in the West
Bank and Gaza.

Sulaiman knew that, after Oslo, Arafat had to take care of his
people. He had to balance between these two groups—the returnees
and the prisoners. It seemed like a sort of game, and the returnees
had won. Of the thousands of prisoners, only a few were given man-
agerial positions. Most got lowly jobs in security, while the returnees received the better postings. The prisoners thought they were
the ones who'd sacrificed most, and the returnees—who'd been in
exile—thought the same. Everyone went around speaking the same
words: *We were the ones who sacrificed for Palestine.*

Several times, friends approached Sulaiman offering him a job in
security. And several times, he declined. He didn't want anything
more to do with violence, with secrets, with a complicated life. He
knew what this sort of life meant. He'd heard his friend Hisham brag
about interrogating a Hamas prisoner. Sulaiman had stared at him,
disgusted. He was against Hamas, but he wanted to fight them in a
way that modeled the world he wanted. A world in which no one
would be tortured, for any reason.

It wasn't easy to find a job other than in security, but Sulaiman
had connections from prison who tried to help. Still, as he met with
other Fatah leaders, looking for support, he was disappointed. Their
secretaries advised Sulaiman to call these important men by the most
exalted names of respect. It seemed silly, when in jail they had called
everyone—even Arafat—*brother*. Sulaiman didn't call these important men by any holy names, and he didn't receive their help.

But he would need assistance to go to university, because he'd not received any math instruction in jail, and had not been able to pass the entrance exam. He wanted very much to continue studying, so he was grateful when Marwan Barghouti offered to talk to the PA's education minister on his behalf.

The education minister assured Marwan he'd be happy to help Sulaiman. "Of course," he said. "He was in jail ten years. Just send him to me."

Sulaiman went immediately.

The minister greeted Sulaiman warmly in his office, offered him coffee, and settled down behind his desk. He seemed friendly, so it took Sulaiman a few minutes to hear what lay underneath his words: *No one told you to go to jail. You're responsible. I won't help you. Ya'ni, drink your coffee and go.*

Looking at the minister, a returnee who it seemed had sacrificed nothing, Sulaiman thought about the voices he used to hear on the radio in the cave, about the years of his life he'd given for his people. He wanted to throw his coffee cup at the wall, to hear something break, but he didn't. He turned around and left.

It wasn't only that he felt ignored, or that he'd been asked to give his life away for nothing in return. It was that the moral system, the democracy he'd learned about in jail—the notions of freedom, equality, brotherhood—now seemed completely divorced from reality. People were looking after their own interests instead of sacred things, and something felt broken.

It seemed that the style of Arafat, of Fatah, was modeled after something like dictatorship. The prisoners, Sulaiman thought, had been the free ones, because they could say anything, critique anyone. In jail they made jokes about Qaddura, Arafat, Che Guevara, themselves. There was no truly sacred person. But the ones on the outside—Arafat and his people from Tunis—it was different with them.

With few other options, Sulaiman got a job with the Orient House. But since he didn't have a permit to enter al-Quds, he began working in a satellite office in al-Ram, which felt like a little world in itself. Because it was unattached to the central mechanisms of Ramallah and al-Quds, it fell outside the structures of Fatah and the PA. It was exactly what Sulaiman needed. Though he still technically worked for Fatah, he could live and breathe, enjoy a normal civilian life. With the small salary from his job, he fixed up his apartment, painting the walls and placing pillows on the floor. His days took on a shape. He'd go to the office for an hour, work on the computer a bit, then leave. He'd visit Marwan's office in Ramallah almost every day, sitting over endless cups of coffee with Maher and Marwan's sister-in-law, laughing and talking about everyday things.

He watched as interesting people walked in and out—including the first Israeli civilians he'd met since before jail. It was strange to see an Israeli without a soldier's or guard's uniform. The leftist Israeli reporter Amira Hass visited, and with Arafat's permission, youth from Israel's Labor party came regularly to meet youth from Fatah.

Sulaiman watched them, shyly. These were the people he wanted to know, to speak with, to understand, but there was the issue of *tatbi'a* (normalization). Some Palestinians thought dialogue with Israelis did harm, distracting from the reality of continued occupation and annexation. He couldn't carry that stigma so soon after his release from jail, so he restrained himself. He decided to go in stages, carefully, bit by bit.

That's how it was, when Sulaiman heard about a pen pal program for Israelis and Palestinians, run by an Israeli-Palestinian organization called Shababik (windows). Something invisible clicked into place. He signed up for the program and wrote a letter to a Jewish Israeli living in Haifa, a place he knew only from poems. When she wrote back, he looked at the letter for a while and then put it away. He never responded. It was too frightening: what such a conversation might mean, what people might think.

Trying to forget these worries, he took little trips, driving through the limited spaces open to him—on the roads leading to Jericho or parts of the Dead Sea. At night he would go to his cousin Adnan's house, and when everyone else in the village was asleep, he'd smile. "Let's go eat *knafe*[1] in Jericho." And they would go. Sulaiman drove those long roads to Jericho in the dark, in his tiny, half-broken car, just like that, because he could.

On those drives and others, he considered the inescapable reality: the Oslo Accords were floundering. The Israelis, who had agreed to withdraw from Gaza and the West Bank, kept building settlements, essentially annexing land. And the Palestinians, who had laid out a plan for self-rule in Area A, were struggling to govern that small space. As his car crept through Palestinian city centers, Sulaiman thought about the people living there, about how much more the PA could do for them, if it tried. While the PA's capacity was limited by Israeli control, it could still do a great deal: create more opportunities for education, jobs, infrastructure. But these leaders, Sulaiman thought, didn't know how to shift from revolution to state-building. These former fighters for freedom seemed caught in a new struggle for money. The whole dream had become smaller, its borders narrowed.

While Sulaiman settled into his new routines, he waited for the peace process to continue. He waited for subsequent talks to decide the fate of Jerusalem, the Palestinian refugees, and settlements. In July of 2000, seven years after the process began, there seemed to be movement. US president Bill Clinton invited Israeli prime minister Ehud Barak and PA chairman Yasser Arafat to continue the Oslo negotiations at Camp David, in Maryland. They talked for two weeks, but left without an agreement.

In Ramallah, Sulaiman listened to different narrations of what had occurred. Clinton and Barak said Arafat refused to sign, that he was unwilling to compromise. Some of Sulaiman's friends agreed with that account; they said that Israel had offered to return most of the 1967 area, including the holy site of al-Aqsa and some parts of East Jerusalem. But in the Palestinian media, it seemed Barak had offered little, if anything: a divided version of the Palestinian West Bank, with Israel taking the best land and water. No one knew what really happened during those two weeks of secret talks, but it seemed that most Palestinians supported Arafat's approach, his unwillingness to give in. They'd given up so much already.

That September, after Arafat returned empty-handed, a report appeared all over the Palestinian news. Former Israeli defense minister Ariel Sharon was planning to visit the al-Aqsa mosque. Leaders of

Fatah in Jerusalem received a notice from Arafat himself: they were to visit him in Ramallah that night, immediately. Sulaiman heard about the meeting later, how Arafat said something like, "If Sharon comes to al-Aqsa, I want blood there."

Their leader was over seventy years old. He was a revolutionary, not a state-builder, and maybe he thought a small intifada might improve the conditions of his negotiations. Or, maybe, he didn't plan for what came next, didn't know the situation would travel entirely out of his control.

On September 28, Sharon visited the Temple Mount in East Jerusalem. This site, the Jews taught, was where Abraham almost sacrificed his son to God, a very long time ago. Where the first and second Jewish temples once stood, where Jews walked long days to pray, or to bury someone they loved, close to the presence of a God whose name they couldn't speak. Some considered this mountaintop the holiest site in Judaism. And it was also the Haram al-Sharif, the third holiest site in Islam. This was the place where Islam taught that, one night, the Prophet Muhammad ascended. Where, hundreds of years after the second temple was destroyed, the caliph 'Abd al-Malik built the Qubbat al-Sakhra (Dome of the Rock). Where Muslims had since come, looking to pray somewhere close to the sacred, close to heaven. A place symbolic of Palestinian identity, not just for Muslims, but for Palestinians of all (and no) faiths who knew what it meant to have land and life taken away.

This was the place where Sharon arrived, accompanied by one thousand Israeli police wearing helmets, carrying clubs and shields. He told reporters that this was a simple tourist visit, that he was carrying a message of peace. That Jews and Arabs (he did not use the word *Palestinians*) could live together. That Arabs had the right to visit wherever they wanted in Israel, and that Israelis should have the same privilege.

It was a controversial statement, and Sharon was a controversial figure. Israel's Kahan Commission had found him indirectly responsible for the massacre at Sabra and Shatila. He owned a house in a Muslim neighborhood of Jerusalem's Old City—on land that many Palestinians saw as part of their future capital. So to many, his visit to the Temple Mount said something different than his words. To many, it seemed he was pandering to the right-wing base that could make him leader of the Likud party, and prime minister in the next election. It seemed that, like Arafat, he knew what it meant for him to set foot on this mountain.

Whatever his intentions, Sharon arrived in sunglasses, hedged in by a garrison of police dressed as soldiers. Palestinians protested. They yelled and began to throw things: stones, metal, chairs. Israeli police pushed them back, beat them with sticks, shot rubber-coated metal bullets. Both sides met with injuries.

The protests moved from East Jerusalem to Ramallah, where Israeli soldiers again shot rubber bullets into the crowd. Some Palestinian protesters threw rocks and firebombs. On September 29, a Palestinian policeman killed an Israeli soldier, and that same day, Israeli police killed several Palestinians on the Temple Mount/Haram al-Sharif. Sulaiman took in all the news from Hizma, and an old sick feeling rose in his stomach. From this moment on, the violence would spread everywhere.

CHAPTER 15

Helicopters

In the early days of the second intifada, protests continued, and soldiers responded with force—tear gas and rubber bullets. Many Israelis felt this was justified, that they were living in a world of threat, protecting themselves against a long accumulation of violence. But one Israeli border guard noted that if the protesters had been Jewish, the soldiers would have used only gas, not rubber bullets, as a first line of defense.

The reports were endless, varying. Forty-seven Palestinians were killed that first week, or fifty-three, or seventy-six. Three Israeli officers and one Israeli civilian. The numbers felt separate from reality, entirely failing to represent the individuals lost, the whole world within each of them.

As the death count rose, Marwan began appearing on television to call for armed resistance—though only within the '67 borders, targeting the army and settlers. Sulaiman didn't agree with Marwan. He wanted to see his people using exclusively nonviolent methods of resistance, but some days he felt lonely in this.

Everything was building and building on itself. Israeli police and soldiers used live ammunition to disperse rock-throwing protesters. Some Palestinians also opened fire, and in the early second week of the intifada, an Israeli settler was shot and killed in the West Bank. The Israeli army brought greater force. It seemed that every morning, at least ten more Palestinians were dead—most killed by rubber-coated or plain steel bullets shot into protesting crowds. Sulaiman knew some of the protesters were throwing Molotov cocktails as well as stones. He knew some had firearms. And he knew many were unarmed, like Muhammad al-Durra—a twelve-year-old boy shot and killed in Gaza as his father tried to shield him. Later, he would learn the Israeli narrative: that the stray bullet of a Palestinian combatant, not that of an Israeli soldier, had killed al-Durra. Whatever was true, the image of the little boy hiding behind his father was everywhere, behind Sulaiman's eyes when he closed them.

In those first weeks, Sulaiman sat with the families of the dead in their homes, drinking coffee. He attended demonstrations in Hizma and in Ramallah where he saw protesters throw stones. He almost grew accustomed to the wind the rubber bullets created, flying by his shins.

Almost immediately, it became difficult to leave Hizma, to move from place to place. The Israeli army was using a strategy of siege and block, choking off the entrances to Palestinian villages and camps. Checkpoints were everywhere, roads closed. A five-minute drive took a full day, and the soldiers at the checkpoints and intersections looked tense, their fingers quick. Sulaiman thought he could see the fear in their shoulders. Maybe when they closed their eyes they saw the image of Yosef Tabeja, the twenty-seven-year-old Israeli soldier shot by Palestinian police in the West Bank town of Qalqilya. He had died the day before Muhammad al-Durra.

When it became difficult to keep track of the Palestinian dead, Sulaiman stopped attending the funerals. There were too many living rooms to sit in, too many crying mothers. Instead, he kept finding new ways to get to Ramallah. He wanted to visit his friends in Marwan Barghouti's office, to pretend things were normal. But this sort of pretending became impossible.

In Marwan's office, he stopped seeing Israelis and students. A new military wing of Fatah—the Aqsa brigades—was forming. Many of Sulaiman's friends joined, and started carrying guns. It was strange. From the magazines he'd read in secret as a boy, from the lessons he'd learned from the elders in jail, he'd gathered that resistance was something to do quietly, carefully. This was different. There was a lot of *shufuni*,[1] a lot of show.

It seemed everything was like that now, out in the open. He saw guns in cafés worn proudly, just as the soldiers did in Israel; teenagers sipping espresso with rifles slung casually over their shoulders. In the presence of these guns, he felt the people around him competing for positions of power. It wouldn't free anything, he thought, or anyone.

Sulaiman knew he wouldn't carry a gun. After everything, he'd never even touched one. Instead, he spent his time with Maher in cafés on Ramallah's Rukab Street, arguing and laughing. He sat across from acquaintances from jail like Jamal, who had joined the Aqsa brigades.

One day, Jamal sat there with the gun leaning up against his chair, telling a story, but Sulaiman wasn't listening.

"Jamal," he said. "You look just like the Israeli soldiers, swinging their guns around like children with toys. What are you doing?"

"Sulaiman, you think if they shoot at children, we shouldn't shoot back? International law justifies resistance against an occupying force, remember? Why do you think Israel left Lebanon? Or the French left Algeria? Because of nonviolence? No, because of armed struggle. And besides, we're not talking about bombing inside Israel. With Hamas it's different. But we're shooting only inside the '67 borders."

"Come on," Sulaiman said. "It won't work. The world isn't the same as it was with Algeria and Vietnam. If we want things to stay the way they are, we should use violence. If we want something different, we have to try something different."

Jamal rolled his eyes. "*Khalas*, Sulaiman. The first intifada was nonviolent. We tried dialogue and peace with Oslo. They only understand force."

Sulaiman shook his head, waved his hand, thought they would continue the argument later. But things around them could change so quickly; no one knew what would happen, if conversations dropped could be picked up again.

This danger was everywhere, so close. Sulaiman was walking out of a Ramallah office one day with a Fatah official, side by side. In the street, they said goodbye, and Sulaiman turned right while his colleague headed in the other direction, toward his car. A sound, a

light, something quick. Sulaiman looked back. There was a hole in
the street, the place where a man used to be.

After he got home, after his heart slowed a bit and he sat
chain-smoking next to the young trees he'd brought his mother
from Bayt 'Ummar, Sulaiman shook his head, hoping to dislodge
the images collecting there. He called on his old practice of wiping
things from his mind and tried to act as though the world wasn't
the way it was. He kept traveling to Ramallah, until the day the sky
turned black with helicopters.

When it happened, no one understood what was going on. In
al-Manara Square, there was the sound of screaming, then the sound
of missiles, then smoke so thick that people didn't know which
direction was which. Everyone was running back and forth asking *which way for Jerusalem, for the bus station*; they couldn't tell. The
number of people normally on that busy street multiplied, with bodies now shuffling everywhere, bumping blindly into one another.
Sulaiman's shoulder caught the arm of a young woman whose face
had the look of an animal running for its life. His legs kept moving
in the direction of the shared taxis to take him back to Hizma, but
they weren't there. He couldn't see anything, couldn't breathe in all
the smoke and fire, so he kept running until he got away from the
city center and found someone who would drive him toward home.

He found out later that the helicopters belonged to the Israeli
Air Force, the bombs a response to what had happened after Israeli reservists ended up in the Ramallah police station.[2] A crowd
of Palestinians had attacked, beat and stabbed two soldiers, flung
one of their bodies from the upstairs window. That's when the air
force came to drop missiles on the Palestinian police station, and fire
rained from the sky.

The numbers of dead kept growing. Sulaiman heard about a road-
side bombing in Gaza that tore into an armored Israeli school bus
of settler children. Something in his stomach fell. Two adults were
killed in the attack, several children wounded. At first, this felt new.
It didn't stay that way for long.

The day after the school bus attack, Sulaiman watched as Israel
bombed Gaza, as Hamas and Islamic Jihad began organizing more

suicide bombings inside Israel. A bomb would go off near a bus, in a mall, in a gas station, each instance taking several lives. On Israeli TV, the cameras sped past a hysterical woman with blood on her face, zoomed in on a child's toy. Sulaiman wanted to be as far from these acts as possible. He watched, though he wanted so much to look away.

Israel continued using live ammunition to disperse protests, and the number of Palestinian dead rose dizzyingly, thousands of people marching in the streets behind the bodies of martyrs. After attending one of the first marches, Sulaiman didn't join again. He understood the collective mourning, but couldn't stop thinking that some people, the ones competing for positions and power, were benefiting from all this. It was a game for them, the martyrs only numbers. But it was also impossible to avoid the numbers. By December 2, 2000, more than twenty Israelis and two hundred Palestinians were dead.

One afternoon, Sulaiman found himself rushing his youngest brother, Nabil, to the hospital. A rubber bullet had struck his head. When the doctor said Nabil would be fine, Sulaiman let out a breath, thinking how easily it could have been different, a miracle of centimeters. But it seemed impossible to let a full breath out, to escape what was happening. In Hizma, the sounds of helicopters became so familiar that Sulaiman only noticed their absence. During his village's demonstrations—filled with shouting, tears, stones, and, occasionally, Molotov cocktails—the soldiers often used live bullets. Sometimes, villagers would die. Often they were not the people at the front throwing stones but the ones in the back or, once, someone sitting on his balcony, reading a book. Every day people were taken to jail, sometimes for planning the violence, but often for throwing stones or nothing at all.

The first time that his brother Karim's oldest son, Khalid, went to jail during the second intifada, it was for throwing stones. After his second arrest, this time accused of inciting other children to throw stones, Sulaiman's sister-in-law asked him to speak to the boy, urge him to be careful. The rest of the family had already tried to keep Khalid away from the demonstrations, to focus on studying, but he wasn't listening. Sulaiman agreed to try.

When Sulaiman came face-to-face with his nephew, he raised his voice, told him he was throwing his life away. "You want to die?" he scoffed. "It's easy to die. It's much harder to live."

Afterward, the boy's mother pulled him aside. "*Shwayya*, slow down. You were too harsh on him. You did the same thing when you were young. How can you yell like that?"

Sulaiman shrugged, laughed at how quickly his sister-in-law had changed her mind.

But Khalid was arrested again, along with Sulaiman's brother Nabil, who'd thrown a stone. Sarah cried and cried, but as the violence outside continued, Sulaiman thought of his nephew and brother inside those walls, found himself thinking: *Maybe it's safer for them in jail than outside it.* As those long months passed, Sarah was not allowed to visit her boys. *Not one day*, she would remember later, *not one night.*

After a suicide bombing at a Jerusalem pizza restaurant killed fifteen people, the army closed the Orient House; the important center of leadership became just another prohibited place. Stuck in his apartment, or Fatima's house, or his parents' house, Sulaiman listened to news of more and more Palestinians dead. To feel alive, he continued going out, heading to work in al-Ram, walking around town or visiting friends in Ramallah, where Arafat would soon come under siege in al-Muqata'a—the building where Sulaiman had once been interrogated by Israelis, many years before.

Within that nightmare, he was walking home from the barber one night when a bright searchlight surrounded him, bleached and sharp, a perfect circle at his feet. He knew that if he ran, they'd kill him. He wouldn't run. And they would probably kill him anyway.

He began walking, putting one foot in front of the other, in the way people do, and with the sound of the beating propellers above him, he moved through the excruciating seven minutes it took to get home. There were no streetlamps, just his personal search beam from above, following him all the way. He didn't look up, just stared at the feet below him. When he walked into his parents' house, the sound of the helicopter stayed above, hovering. He moved up the stairs, through the kitchen, where he looked out the window at Ta'mira during the daytime. Sarah and Said were there. They stared at his dry, white face and asked him what was wrong. He couldn't say anything until the helicopter moved away. When it did, when his parents gave him water and his voice came back, when they understood what had happened, Sarah began shaking her head and praying with her beads.

Said looked at his son. "It's time to leave your work in Fatah." And he did.

Sulaiman had grown up in love with the idea of sacrifice, of ignoring fear, of telling himself he was ready to die at any moment. But he wasn't ready.

For a year after, as Israel re-occupied Palestinian cities in the West Bank, he barely left Hizma. After settlers shot his neighbor Reza while he was on his way back from work in the Jewish settlement of Ma'aleh Adumim, Sulaiman sat for a month in what used to be Reza's living room with his wife and small daughter.

It was a lost year of Sulaiman doing things some would call irrelevant: getting hit by a car and almost dying in a senseless apolitical way, marrying a girl who came to sit with him in the hospital, divorcing her to the despair of everyone around him. During that time, he dreamed at night about living far away, marrying a European woman, tall and blond, with blue eyes and cool skin. He dreamed about walking easily at night without an ID in a soldier-less place.

Too often in his sleep, great black machines flew over his head, dropping bombs on his friends, leaving their coffee cold, until he woke up in the morning, always with the same thought. *I want to live.*

CHAPTER 16

Properties of Snow

It was a series of letters that interrupted his time of dreaming and hiding, what he would later call his "mountain time" in Hizma. Looking down at the first of the letters, he saw something earth-shattering. A group of Israeli soldiers were refusing to serve in the West Bank and Gaza. Their letter had a gravitational force to it, it pulled him in, though he wasn't sure what its pull meant. The second letter had a beautiful, different kind of force. It was signed by a group of prominent Palestinians, including Sari Nusseibeh and Hanan Ashrawi, advocating for a nonviolent intifada. This letter asked anyone who agreed to add their name. When the letter was republished in the daily al-Quds paper, it carried many more names. Sulaiman's was one of them.

It was as if, suddenly, he felt ready to be in the world again. But as he peered out, away from the hills of Hizma and cups of coffee with his mother, he knew he wanted to return to something different, pursue some other way. The images circled in him: the spring of 'Ayn Farrah, the chair he'd been tied to, the gun on Jamal's shoulder, the light of the helicopter surrounding his feet. He remembered the beginning of the intifada—not long before but such a distance away. How he'd walked with crowds of people, shouting with grief and anger, carrying bodies through the street.

It wasn't working, he thought.

Like many other Palestinians, he'd become certain that violence couldn't solve the conflict. It felt like violence—not just the violence directed against them, but the violence they'd used against Israelis—had caused his society, what he loved best about it, to unravel from the inside. This is why, he realized, nonviolence had become more than a tactic. It was now the only way for him—even if he wasn't entirely sure what it was made of, what exactly it meant. But he knew one thing: it wasn't just an absence of violence. There was an undeniable presence in it: an interruption, an exit to a circle that seemed to have none.

Trying to envision the most significant interruption possible, he kept coming back to the idea of dialogue. He wanted to meet *the other side*, to see what magic could happen through this. He hadn't been ready right after jail, but something was different now. He began speaking all his questions in conversations with friends: Bassam Aramin, his friend from the Hebron jail, and Yusuf, bodyguard of the late Faisal Husseini.

As he dreamed ahead, Israel announced its plan to build a wall between Israel and the West Bank. The announcement came after a string of suicide bombings in Israel, the same series of attacks that had prompted the letter calling for a nonviolent intifada. The wall's stated purpose was to decrease suicide bombings, but the proposed route cut wide swaths into the West Bank, going far past the Green Line.

As Palestinian villages along the barrier's proposed route steeled themselves for what would come next, Sulaiman received an invitation. A contact of Yusuf's asked if Sulaiman would travel to Cyprus with the Peres Center: a huge organization, founded by Israeli politician Shimon Peres, who'd worked closely with Rabin and Arafat on Oslo. The center hosted a wide variety of dialogue projects, including this one, which brought Israeli and Palestinian kids together to play football. The organization worked everywhere, mostly in underserved communities—in Palestinian villages, in the Israeli south. Sometimes, they would take their soccer balls and travel the world. Sulaiman accepted the invitation without a second thought and soon found himself looking out a window at the small earth beneath him. It was his first time on an airplane, and when he arrived in Cyprus, he took a breath. It felt like the first he'd managed since the intifada began.

For five days, he stayed on that bit of land at a nice hotel on the sea. Watching kids on the street playing soccer, he thought about Shimon, the Israeli boy he'd played with growing up. How soccer seemed to make strange things possible. When he got home, inspired, he co-founded a center with Yusuf and Bassam for ex-prisoners committed to dialogue and nonviolence. And more opportunities kept coming. After a trip with another NGO to Malta—where he listened dreamily to all the songs about fishermen, all the traces of Arabic in the language—he picked up the phone and heard Yusuf's voice.

"Sulaiman," Yusuf said, "it's time to buy clothes for some very cold weather."

Israeli businessman Heskel Nathaniel was living in Berlin, watching the second intifada unfold on television, when he had the idea. He wanted to send a boat of Israelis and Palestinians to the bottom of the world, have them climb an empty mountain. He wanted to put it on television so that Israelis and Palestinians—and people all over the world—could see a different kind of story than the one on television: endless Israeli army invasions and Palestinian suicide bombings.

When Yusuf called Sulaiman and invited him to Antarctica, Arafat was still under siege. The intifada was still the reality, would stay so for some time. At the end of the first four and a half years, the death count would rise to over 3,000 Palestinians and 950 Israelis.

Yusuf didn't have to tell Souli: this was an enormous decision. The delegation would appear on television; all his friends and family would see him there, with Israelis on a mountain while Palestinians were dying. People would be very angry. Sulaiman looked inward and saw the fear there. He turned from it, gave Yusuf a quick yes, and started making phone calls. They would have to make sure Arafat was on their side.

From a room in the Muqata'a, not long before his death, Arafat signed a letter of support for the Palestinian Antarctic delegation: a blessing from the siege. Still, many people told Sulaiman and Yusuf not to go. Some denounced them harshly in the newspapers; one critic threatened Yusuf's life.

As Sulaiman waited to leave, as he listened to news of the growing number of dead and bought his jacket, scarf, and gloves, he hoped this choice would point him toward the thing he was searching for but could not quite name. Something different, an exit, something outside history. He tried on his new clothes and looked in the mirror, imagined how others would see him, a little figure on the television. Waiting to leave, he dreamt of the strange properties of snow.

On his way to the bottom of the world, Sulaiman met the other Palestinian members of the "Breaking the Ice" expedition: the leader, Ziad Darwish, cousin of the famous poet, and Sahar, a Palestinian citizen of Israel and member of the Israeli national volleyball team. He met the Israelis, two of them from the center-left Labor party, and two right-wing Likudniks: an Ethiopian-Israeli woman named Hadar who'd walked through the desert from Ethiopia to Israel at fourteen years old, and Noam, a former soldier in one of the Israeli army's elite units.

After several stops in Chile—marked by smog, mountains, a party in an old boat docked in a very southern city—they left land behind. Their two boats set into a sea that stayed calm—until it began rocking so hard, Sulaiman spent days rolling in his bed and clutching his stomach, calling out half-crying, half-laughing to his mother, *Yamma Yamma*, thinking this was the end, after everything. But the rocking stopped and the delegation reached land, practiced finding their feet on the ice, getting ready for their big climb.

Speaking to the Israelis as they walked against the blinding white, he grew friendly with some of them. Even with Hadar, the Ethiopian-Israeli who pointed to his *kufiya* one day, and said, as if joking: "You guys have twenty-two Arab countries. This is our only home."

"*Habibti*," Sulaiman said, pretending to joke, too. "You're from fucking Ethiopia. You hardly even speak Hebrew. I'm *from there*." He pointed in the general, distant direction of home.

It was more difficult with Noam, the man's seemingly never-ending arguments about how Israelis wanted peace, how it was the Palestinians who wanted violence. It was more difficult the evening before the biggest climb, as they argued about the joint resolution they would read at the expedition's end. Sulaiman said they should call for an end to the separation wall. One of the Israelis shook his head, saying they should avoid politics. Sulaiman tried to explain that such a thing was impossible. In this way, they kept arguing about what to name their mountain, until they woke early the next day to climb, to tie themselves together with rope. If someone fell off an icy edge, the others would have to pull the person back, or they'd all go down together.

Sulaiman blinked out at the world. Everything was cloudy. As they climbed through the ice and up the mountain, their limbs freezing, he sang songs to himself, sometimes revolutionary songs, sometimes the songs Fatima used to sing during the wheat harvest—*Wayn? Al-Ramallah!*[1] And when it hurt to walk or his breath wouldn't come, he called on the skill he'd learned in jail, a way of leaving his body. He barely felt it at all.

On the peak four days later, someone pulled out Israeli and Palestinian flags, and Heskel read the statement they'd finally agreed upon, proclaiming their mountain "The Mountain of Israeli-Palestinian Friendship."

Sulaiman reentered his body, felt the huge feeling of ice and mountain under his feet, and thought, *This is the quietest place on earth. We as humans are so small, little nothings.* The quiet had a holiness to it. He let his thoughts turn toward home, and from here, on a high peak at the bottom of the world, everything looked different.

When it was time for a photo op, Sulaiman stayed distant while Noam and Yusuf argued about flags and Ziad wept. He was also thinking of home, remembering his brother who'd died in Lebanon in 1982. Somehow, the group managed to plant both flags on their mountain. They drank their champagne and took a picture. Sulaiman lifted his two fingers into a *v*—like he had years before as the army dragged him from his house—but this time the *v* meant something else.

On his way home, he couldn't stop thinking about the picture someone had taken on the mountain. In it, he was kneeling, holding a Palestinian flag from the bottom, his whole arm stretched along it.

But, in the fingers of his other hand, much farther from his body, he held the tiny corner of an Israeli flag.

People would already be angry with him, and this picture of him touching the Israeli flag, even just a bit, could only make it worse. Even with Arafat's support, the Antarctica trip had been a dramatic and controversial move. It was among Sulaiman's first, most public acts that anyone might call *tatbi'a*—normalizing the occupation. For some, the delegation—its attempt to show the world how the two sides could work together with mutual respect—dangerously missed the point. This was not a conflict between two equal sides; it was a situation of occupier and occupied. Talking, becoming friends, and climbing cold mountains wouldn't do anything to change that. Not when it now seemed Israel had used negotiations and dialogue as a stalling tactic to build more settlements, to take more land.

Back in Hizma, Sulaiman found a look of pride on his father's face, but it was something else with his brothers. Karim was running for a spot on the village council, and after watching Sulaiman in all that snow on television, some people had come to ask him, what exactly was his brother doing? Why was he posing for pictures with Israelis, pretending everything was all right, as Israeli soldiers continued to kill and jail their children?

Karim and Aziz poured Sulaiman endless coffees on their family's checkered patio, asking him to pursue another path, or at least to take this one more cautiously. They asked him to think about what people were saying, the *fadiha*, the shame it was causing their family. Sulaiman argued back until he got tired of arguing. He told them he'd be careful.

Sipping coffee on those long days, Sulaiman felt the space between himself and his brothers growing, as if peering at them from some distance. He knew he wouldn't be as careful as they wanted. He was already looking for more opportunities to meet Israelis, searching for ways to travel and get perspective on this place, to win a moment of breath away from the home that sometimes had a choking feeling to it. He was the only one among his immediate family to go so far from home, and Sarah hated him leaving. It would be so easy for him to disappear, like their distant cousin who had traveled to South America before the Nakba; the family didn't know what happened, but they never heard from him again. Or war could erupt while Sulaiman was away, and like his uncle and cousins in Jordan, Israel wouldn't let him return.

So far, every time he'd left—for Cyprus, Malta, Antarctica— Sarah had grabbed him, crying, trying to stop him from leaving. She'd already lost ten years with him. Too many people had gone and never come back.

During the next years, everything felt new. Sulaiman threw himself into whatever opportunities for peace work arose, trying to find his place within it, even as reality kept tugging at him. The separation wall was growing steadily and, one day during this time of shifting ground, Karim sat the family down to tell them the news. The wall was coming to Hizma. Despite complaints about Sulaiman's dialogue work, Karim had won an election. He was head of Hizma's village council, and the army had come to him with the news: they would build a piece of the wall, several kilometers of it, through Hizma. It would further the work Pisgat Ze'ev had started, cutting Hizma off from al-Quds, *al-medina*, the city that was theirs. The place where Sulaiman's grandfather used to travel every Friday, riding his donkey through the hills.

And there was more. The wall's planners had drawn a line placing Ta'mira on the Jerusalem side. Or not the Jerusalem side exactly, but in the "buffer zone" where no Palestinians from the West Bank could visit. In the family living room, Karim looked at everyone steadily, delivering the news with his almost-but-not-quite-perfect composure, the anger controlled but boiling underneath. As he spoke, Said, who'd worked for the Jerusalem municipality much of his life, listened quietly at first. Sarah wrung her hands. Fatima raised her voice and pointed her chin toward the ceiling. And then Karim shared the last piece of news. "They told me that if Hizma doesn't take them to court, they will make sure Ta'mira is left on our side."

Sulaiman felt the pause between the end of that sentence and the beginning of the next one: a strange, gaping space. And then, through that seemingly endless moment of quiet, Karim said simply: "I told them no, of course. We can't legitimize the occupation wall in that way."

Something in Sulaiman's stomach, some bottom he didn't know was there, dropped away. He was both listening and not listening as Karim continued speaking, as Said argued back. Looking at his brother, Sulaiman felt both anger and admiration. The decision was too revolutionary, he thought; it wasn't pragmatic, and yet, it made sense. Karim could save their land, but then they'd have to watch the wall built on someone else's precious space; they'd have to live knowing that Ta'mira was only theirs because someone else's Ta'mira had been taken. Because they'd said yes to something no one should say yes to.

As he listened to the raised voices around him, he noticed a strange, almost parallel, narration. It was like he could hear the voice of an Israeli—any Israeli, no particular person, maybe one of the Israelis from the Antarctica trip. Someone who seemed to stand for a whole people, explaining the need for the wall, for security. It seemed a strange excuse to build the barrier so far over the Green Line. But he heard the arguments in his head anyway. He felt the connection between the imagined and the physical. As the wall rose, the words playing in his head were made real.

CHAPTER 17

Shared Words

The reality of the wall was impossible to ignore, everywhere in the house. Nearby, the sounds of construction were immense. Sulaiman managed to stay far away somehow, though his body stayed where it was. He found ways to summon the memory of the Antarctic cold on his skin. He sat in the al-Ram office smoking, laughing, wondering how to *exit the circle*, until Halim called Bassam with a proposal.

Halim worked in one of the PA's security branches, and both Bassam and Sulaiman knew him from jail and Fatah circles. In their tiny shared office one day, Bassam told Sulaiman what Halim had called to say.

"His cousin Haitham is starting a new project, and he's looking for people."

"What is it?"

"He wants to hold meetings for ex-prisoners like us, and Israeli soldiers who've refused to serve in the army."

Sulaiman looked at the mess of papers on his desk, looked into his cup of coffee and remembered the letter he'd seen in the newspaper, the first that had helped pull him from hiding in Hizma. It had given him an unnameable sort of hope, knowing that elite army soldiers and officers, by publicly refusing to serve in the West Bank and Gaza, were trying to draw Israeli society's attention to what occupation was, what it meant. As the refuseniks searched for their next step, a member of the Israeli anti-occupation group Ta'ayush[1]

had introduced them to Fatah contacts in Ramallah. One or two
meetings had already occurred, and now Haitham was looking for
Palestinian ex-prisoners to join the next one.

"He's looking for people like us," Bassam said to Sulaiman.
"Ex-prisoners who speak Hebrew. People he can trust to meet with
Israelis." Sulaiman took a deep drag of his cigarette and looked back
at his friend. He didn't have to give an answer. They both knew
they would do it; it was a huge sort of knowing.

Many years later, people would remember different things about
this time. Each person had their own version of the first meeting:
whether it was in Haitham's house in Bethlehem, with the Israelis
stepping into cars whose drivers they didn't recognize. Or in nearby
Bayt Jala, in the Everest Hotel. One of the first meetings Sulaiman
would later remember was there, at Everest, which fell in Area C.
Israelis were prohibited from entering Area A and Israel had made it
difficult for the West Bank's Palestinian residents to get the permits
needed to travel into Israel. Everest felt like one of their few options,
but it wasn't an easy one.

Though the intifada had cooled, it was still an intifada. Within
the walls of Bethlehem's main church, not far from Bayt Jala, Sulaiman's friend Murad was still armed and hiding with the al-Aqsa
brigades. The wall was growing longer and taller. Bullets were still
flying between Bayt Jala and the Israeli settlement of Gilo.

These stories were everywhere, surrounding the men as they
discussed how to bring the Israelis to the Everest Hotel, zigzagging
back and forth through safer areas so no one would hurt them. Sulaiman knew it would be the first time some of these Israelis would
visit the West Bank without uniforms, without guns. Picturing them
on the path to the meeting, he saw two versions of them: the civilian
clothes they would wear, but also the army uniforms they had worn
before. In the image of these men, as with so much here, if you
looked closely you could see the past beneath the present. And in
the not-so-distant past, these Israelis had stood at checkpoints, turning Sulaiman's family away from al-Quds. Some of these men might
have trained in prisons, like the men who wore gas masks from the
time of *qam'* (repression) in Hebron. Some had been pilots in the air

force, flying terrible machines through the sky like the ones that had dropped fire on al-Manara Square. Whether from the sky or on the ground, some of these men must have killed.

Now, Sulaiman was responsible for their safety. He peered at the strangeness of this feeling, then quickly turned to planning the Israelis' route to Bayt Jala.

When the day came, the Israelis followed the path planned for them, still unsure of what would happen next: if they would be kidnapped and thrown from a window, like the soldiers they'd heard about on Israeli news, who'd gotten lost in Ramallah. As happens in moments like these, time moved strangely. And suddenly—or not suddenly at all—they were all sitting in the Everest Hotel, looking at one another.

Outside, a garden. Inside, fluorescent-lit, hospital-like hallways. Sulaiman had been to the Everest Hotel so many times, but now, in this new context, it was almost unrecognizable. Everyone sat around a long table. In what felt like an almost comic gesture, they wore name tags.

Sulaiman stared across the room at the Israelis, at one man with the name Zohar printed on his chest. Zohar Shapira had served in the IDF's Sayeret Matkal—an elite intelligence, counterterrorism, and hostage rescue unit. When he spoke, his voice sounded like that of any Israeli army leader. Avner Wishnitzer, who'd also fought in the Sayeret Matkal, spoke with similar tones of authority. Listening to them, Sulaiman could hear Captain Tzahi's voice, just as it sounded when the soldier stood on his family's patio so long ago, asking after his brother. It seemed likely that at least one of these refuseniks was actually an undercover officer from Shabak, Israeli intelligence, looking to gather information, or something worse.

He forced himself to turn away from Zohar and Avner and looked at another Israeli. "Yoav," his name tag read. He had long hair and looked strangely familiar. But it wasn't strange, Sulaiman realized; he knew exactly where he'd seen this man. He used to work at the crowded, painfully slow-moving Qalandiya checkpoint, presiding over the line of Palestinians trying to get to work, or to the hospital, or to al-Aqsa to pray, turning away anyone without the proper permit. Sulaiman had only seen this man standing, never sitting. And now he was here in Bayt Jala, bent forward in a folding chair.

Sulaiman looked and kept looking. This was different than anything he'd done before: different from the soccer project, different than speaking to the Israelis in Antarctica. It was not an academic, theoretical conversation. These men were from the *real enemy*, not just Israelis, but men who'd served in the army very recently. It was heavy; he found he couldn't look into their eyes. He survived his first meeting by practicing something he'd learned long before: shutting some part of himself that usually stayed open. He couldn't remember the last time it felt so important to be careful about what he said, about what he left out.

When Yoav finished talking about his work at the checkpoint, his service in Gaza and Jenin, Bassam looked at him and said, "You know that everything you did was a crime?"

"Absolutely, yes," Yoav said. "For that, I'm here."

There was little argument that day. Most of the Israelis at the meeting had already refused to serve in the West Bank, East Jerusalem, and Gaza. The Palestinians present were from Fatah, not Hamas. So at the end of the meeting, they all signed their names on a piece of paper supporting the two-state solution. They didn't discuss some of the most difficult issues, like the Palestinian right of return.

To Ta'ayush activist Hillel Cohen,[2] who served as translator so all attendees could speak the language they were born into,[3] the meeting seemed ordinary. But there was one moment, one he would remember years later, when the group walked out into the stone streets of Bayt Jala. The muezzin began the call to prayer, and Hillel watched as the arms of the Israelis reached, as if pulled invisibly and mechanically, for the guns they no longer carried. They heard the call to prayer and immediately thought they were under attack. It was the first time most of them had been around Palestinians without metal between them.

Afterward, Sulaiman began the trip home. Though geographically close, Hizma had been made far by the intifada's multiplied roadblocks—some permanent and some temporary. The temporary ones, known as "flying" checkpoints, appeared according to a logic Sulaiman couldn't discern.

Waiting in long lines, he looked at the soldiers with their helmets and guns and clothes that made them look bigger than they actually were. It was easy to imagine Yoav still standing there before the line of cars with his long hair and the power to tell Sulaiman where he could and could not go. It's what he'd done not long before. Sulaiman felt heavy, like his body was an anchor, pulling him toward the earth. For a moment, he imagined giving in to gravity, sitting on the ground in the checkpoint line, refusing to get up. He smiled at the thought, then stopped smiling when he pictured how the soldiers might react.

In the days that followed—as Sulaiman pored over newspapers, checking the stories the Israelis had shared, making sure they told the truth—his thoughts traveled such different places. In certain moments, he felt willing to do almost anything to protect this work, whatever would come of it. In others, he wondered if it was all a trap the Israelis had set for him. If these meetings amounted to an unforgivable act, a way of cheating, of selling the cause he'd given years of his life to.

He didn't know what to do with the immensity of the question: What did it mean to continue talking with these men? He imagined their path back into Israel after the first meeting. How they could go straight back to their homes, where they could move through space freely. How he had to struggle on the road home to Hizma, where his family was watching their land disappear.

This difference seemed uncrossable. They had all used violence, he and the Israelis at that long table. This made them similar, and still pointed toward difference. Sulaiman had been punished for his use of violence. Because he wasn't a citizen anywhere, he was judged in the military court of another people. But these Israelis might have been responsible for many deaths. Still, they'd never been to jail for this, not even to court. Waves of heat and anger rose in him, and then, as if suddenly, he felt calm, found something in his body that wanted to forgive these men. Though they had not asked him to.

As the meetings continued, these shifts happened in him every day and night, also in dreams. He dreamt of his family exiled in Jordan, all the stories of death and exile he'd grown up with. And then something else would appear; he'd remember a particular word or phrase the Israeli refusenik Zohar had used. He'd think about how much language he shared with these ex-soldiers. The language of armed struggle, of violence, and how it was lifted up. Some part of him wanted to keep the fact of these shared words secret, but they were there, wherever he put them. And some things could not be hidden.

One day, Sulaiman received a call from a Palestinian security officer asking him to come for a visit. It didn't feel at all like a question.

He thought he knew what this was about: not the secret meetings with the Israeli ex-soldiers, but something else. After the first secret meetings, he had attended a camp run by Kabbalists (Jewish mystics) in the Israeli city of Tzfat, a place with a long history of Jewish mysticism, which had also once been the Palestinian city of Safad.

There, during the Jewish holiday of Lag BaOmer, he'd watched as mystics danced around a fire. Though it bothered him that these Jews didn't speak of the occupation, he liked their spirituality, their habit of wearing white and promising that the magic of the *Zohar*[4] would protect him. They made him smile, reminded him a bit of Fatima singing songs or Sarah burying her hair under the ground.

He liked them so much that, afterward, he began working with the camp's organizers to create a summer camp for Palestinian kids. From all over the West Bank, he brought Palestinian children to visit the zoo in the Israeli city of Ramat Gan. He couldn't stop smiling that day, watching Karim's daughter and Bassam Aramin's daughter Abir, all peering at the hippos and chimpanzees.

He had a feeling the call from Palestinian security was about the Kabbala camp. And when he finally sat in the chair across from the security officer, Sulaiman could see the anger in the man's face. He felt it even before raising his head to look across the desk. When the questions began, they didn't stop. They focused on the Kabbala camp but they moved across all sorts of topics and kept coming, one after the other, as if the officer were delivering a speech, not conducting an interrogation:

"Who are you? How did you join this kind of work? When did you first meet Israelis? How much are you being paid?"

Sulaiman knew this feeling, exactly. It was just like interrogation in jail, without the physical force, but with a great deal of force all the same. He did understand why the officer was concerned. The Israelis had cultivated many Palestinian informants, sometimes from a young age. The man looking across the desk at Sulaiman was wondering if he'd been recruited in jail, brainwashed when he was just a child. But the part of Sulaiman that understood was overtaken. He was trembling. He couldn't remember the last time he'd been so angry.

"Look," he said, cutting the man off, "Shabak interrogated me when I was fourteen. I investigated people in jail. I'm not afraid of you. These are my beliefs. This is the kind of work I think will save us. And who are you to talk about collaboration? You collaborate with Israeli security; this is how your job exists. You take money from America to do this. So why are you asking me about collaboration?" The officer stopped for a moment, looked at him hard, and kept delivering his speech made of questions.

Not long after Sulaiman left the office, still shaking, he cut ties with the Kabbala camp. He'd been dreaming of using Kabbala in peace work, with its emphasis on love and spirituality and inscrutable stories. It reminded him of Sufism. But the suspicions around Kabbala in Palestinian society were too great; it wouldn't work. He wasn't quite ready to articulate it, but this suspicion bothered him enormously. It felt like the occupation had seeded a suspicion among Palestinians—not just of the army, settlers, and Israel, but of Judaism itself. He knew it used to be different. He remembered Fatima talking about how villagers in Hizma used to be friendly with the Jews in Jerusalem and Neve Ya'aqub, how people from Hizma would sell them eggs, almonds, milk. How before Israel, the Jews in Palestine were Palestinians.

Now, he heard that when tour guides took Jews into Palestinian villages in the West Bank, they advised them to remove their *kippot*. How sad it was, to ask someone to remove a thing meant for remembering God. But in the West Bank, the *kippa* had become associated with settlers. And some Palestinians were used to seeing

settlers with guns, objects that couldn't be further from God, glinting at their hips or in their hands.

Still, Sulaiman felt this suspicion of Jewish symbols was leading
his people toward something dangerous. Even after he cut ties with
the Kabbala center, Palestinian intelligence continued to call him in
for questioning until one day, waiting in the lobby for another interview, he saw Tariq. His friend from jail walked easily into the room
and greeted Sulaiman warmly. When the officer emerged, Tariq
smiled back at him. "Sulaiman's one of us, one of the good ones,"
he said. "Take care of him."

As the security officer looked at him, accusing him of *tatbi'a*
and worse, Sulaiman understood what was happening. They wanted
him to be afraid. They wanted him to be born one thing, to stay
that thing forever, without searching and getting lost. It made him
worried that in this system his people had constructed, in the small
space Israel allowed them, there wasn't any freedom, and it made
him want to run. To put more distance between anyone—family,
friends, Israelis, Palestinians—who kept him from feeling free. To
travel further from his old self, to search more resolutely for something new.

He would keep searching through meetings with the Israeli refuseniks, exploring what seemed to be the immeasurable power they
held together. As people who'd fought, who could never be called
cowards, the men who showed up to these meetings had credibility in their societies. The kind of credibility that could change
everything.

That whole first year, they kept their meetings a secret. Because
while their histories lent them power in their respective communities, they also marked a danger. Sulaiman thought, and tried not to
think, of the real risk they faced: that people might not just express
anger, but turn that anger into force, into violence. He tried to turn
from the images when they arose, but they kept rising. He imagined
shooting, killing, a big, big thing.

This is maybe why, when Sulaiman told American activists Len
and Libby Traubman about the secret meetings the following summer, they worried for him. "It was clear," Len would say later, "that
he was risking his life."

CHAPTER 18

Trees

Ｗhen Len and Libby called Sulaiman for the first time, they invited him to the woods of Northern California. He didn't know them. They'd been offering unexpected invitations for many years. In the 1980s, they'd founded a dialogue project between citizens of the US and the Soviet Union, using pen and paper and an old shortwave radio. After the Berlin Wall fell, they set their sights on transforming the Israeli-Palestinian conflict, especially as it arose in US communities. In the intervening years, they'd launched a living room dialogue project to bring Palestinians and Jews together; they'd created a peace camp in California's redwood forest.

While Len was recruiting camp participants for the summer of 2005, someone told him about a Palestinian who'd attended a Kabbala camp in Tzfat. When Len heard the name Sulaiman Khatib, it sounded familiar. He and Libby had carefully followed the Breaking the Ice expedition in its planning stages. They'd helped organize a meeting between Santiago's Jewish and Palestinian communities before the delegation set off to sea.

When Len and Libby re-watched a short video about Breaking the Ice, they saw Sulaiman there on the mountain against all that white, and they set to work finding his phone number. When they called for the first time, they had to ask him to repeat himself. His English was unpracticed; it was from books still.

Though he also had to strain a bit to understand what they were saying, Sulaiman quickly agreed to join them. It felt theoretical at first; he doubted the US State Department would issue an ex-prisoner like him a visa. So when the visa did arrive, he was shocked. He stared down disbelievingly at the paper in his hands, as if waiting for it to disappear.

At camp, Sulaiman fell in love with the redwood trees, the smell of wet earth. He was welcomed by Len, a retired dentist, a short man who made joyful, large movements with his eyes and mouth. And he was quickly embraced by Libby, a remarkably warm person who wore a small white pin in the shape of a dove on her collar. He listened to them and tried to understand the things they said. Sometimes understanding was difficult, like when Len told him to speak of the Israeli-Palestinian *relationship*, not the Israeli-Palestinian conflict. It didn't make sense to him then, but maybe he felt somewhere how much their words would change him, get lodged inside his body and fill him with new ways of seeing.

But at that moment, Sulaiman was busy taking so much in. When they introduced him to the others at camp, he found that while there were a few Palestinian Americans, many of the campers were American Jews—a group he'd never encountered in person.

He studied them closely, surprised by what he saw: they were so polite compared to Israelis. And they seemed to know little about the conflict he'd been born into. He struggled to see the connection between these Jews and the Israelis he knew—the ones at the checkpoints, even the ones he'd begun meeting in secret.

When an interviewer asked him to stand under an impossibly tall tree and talk to the camera, Sulaiman spoke about what he expected from camp, from the other participants. "Some of them have not heard Palestinian stories before," he said. "I think some of them are going to be changing."

Sulaiman spoke until he got to a point where he couldn't find the right word in English to name what it made him feel—the thought that his own story might make someone change. He paused, not for long, just until the interviewer behind the camera said: "Emotional, it makes you feel emotional?"

Sulaiman said yes, though it wasn't clear the word covered enough ground at all. What could describe it, the sense that through telling his story he could transform the people who determined so many components of his life? There was no word for it, but he was here, and he'd have to find certain words. He wanted these American Jews to hear something. He wanted to tell them—to tell the whole world through these people before him—how much Palestinians had suffered. This meant a certain kind of telling, and a certain kind of withholding, too. It was not the right place, he thought, to show people his frustration with the PA, or with the Palestinians who had proudly worn their guns in cafés during the second intifada. He was in an outside space here, and it was his job to protect his people.

But Reem, one of the few other Palestinians at camp, kept saying things that seemed to undo all his protective efforts. She came from a Palestinian Christian family, and it seemed her favorite activity was criticizing Palestinian Muslims. Sometimes when she spoke, Sulaiman could barely sit still. He wished she'd stop talking, quit revealing their faults in front of these strangers. The people around them paid taxes that bought Israel's guns and bombs and metal gates and bulldozers. Palestinians needed these people as allies and Sulaiman feared they wouldn't support Palestinian freedom if they understood the struggles within Palestinian society.

There at camp, he kept witnessing Len and Libby's language of love and listening; he learned that dialogue was full of theater. In one exercise, facilitators asked the participants to speak in the voice of "the other." An Israeli participant named Esther stood, and when she spoke, Sulaiman couldn't believe she wasn't Palestinian. She sounded just like Fatima, lamenting the loss of the sea.

And when a facilitator asked for a volunteer to play the role of Ariel Sharon, as if without thinking, Sulaiman raised his hand. He had seen all of Sharon's speeches on television—in jail and after his release. This was the man who'd been defense minister at the time of the Sabra and Shatila massacre, the man who'd visited al-Aqsa with one thousand armed guards; this was Israel's prime minister. So when he heard Sharon's name, it was like a tape began playing in Sulaiman's head. He knew the words and inflections Sharon had long used to justify Israel's actions.

Sulaiman began to speak, and Sharon's voice came out.

"We came back to the ancient homeland of our ancestors after almost two thousand years," Sulaiman said. He made a face as if joking, but his body shook. It hurt in an almost physical way, letting the words come through his mouth. "After two thousand years in diaspora," he continued, "now we have so many enemies. The Arabs want to kill us. The security of the state of Israel is the most important thing, and we have terrorists all around."

When his turn was over, he was relieved, but still glad to have spoken. Though he would never respect Sharon, never accept his justifications, speaking in his voice opened something. It helped him understand in some way he couldn't name, in a way he hoped to use.

Later that day, his new friend Hilit came up to him, eyes wide. "How did you do that so well? You sounded like an Israeli."

"*Habibti*," Sulaiman winked at her, "I know alllll his speeches from jail."

It's not clear, he couldn't remember how and when, but it might have been there in California—a place Indigenous peoples call by other names—that Sulaiman first received the nickname Souli. Maybe someone called him Souli and he smiled and took the name and brought it home with him. Either way, before long, Souli would become his name in English and Hebrew, sometimes in Arabic too. So much so, that when certain people called him Sulaiman, it sounded wrong and he would tell them: "Call me by my name."

Back home, everything kept moving. By September 2005, Israel had unilaterally withdrawn from Gaza, but kept control over the strip's borders, sea and air space, population registry, tax system, and access to resources like fuel, electricity, and water. Late that month, Souli heard that Gazan militants had fired a series of Qassam rockets into Israel, wounding five civilians. Though the continuing rockets would kill few Israelis, those deaths broke whole communities open. And they would terrify residents of towns like Sderot, where it seemed sirens were always blaring. Gaza's residents would also continue living with fear, on an entirely different scale. Israel escalated strikes and raids on Gaza, and in the last half of 2006, the army would kill more than four hundred Palestinians in Gaza, including over two hundred civilians. The numbers—both connected and detached from the people they represented—would keep rising.

In January of 2006, when Hamas won a significant majority of seats in the Palestinian parliamentary election, Souli couldn't sleep. He kept thinking of the televised aftermath of Hamas suicide bombings he'd watched in jail and after. He knew that in Hamas's 1988 charter, the movement had called for violence against Jews and the destruction of Israel. Though some people felt its positions had become more nuanced and pragmatic, it had never officially amended its stance. Souli felt sure Hamas's victory had little to do with its position toward Israel; it was about people's gratitude for the strong social services the party provided, and their exhaustion with Fatah's corruption. Still, he worried over what would come next: how Hamas would govern, how Fatah would respond, and how Israel would react.

As it all unfolded, Souli kept attending the meetings with Israeli refuseniks. He started to invite some new people, including Khaled, one of his teachers from Jneid. His friend arrived older, but seemingly unchanged.

In jail, Khaled used to sit on his bed, twirling his impressive mustache, saying funny things to Sulaiman like, "*Shibl*, when I was your age, I used to have breakfast in al-Quds, lunch in Beirut, and dinner in Damascus. I left the country all the time—I'd go to Amman just to use the bathroom!"

In the meetings Khaled attended, he spoke just the way he always had, twirling his mustache, his mind traveling a path that didn't reveal itself to anyone but him; his words were so strong and strange, it was as if he'd invented them himself. When Souli tried to translate him into Hebrew, he couldn't do it; he'd end up bent over, slapping his knee, laughing.

Souli listened to all the stories, hearing the Palestinian participants speak of familiar things. There was Imran,[1] whose family land the Israeli army had taken to build a base, who'd been held in jail at sixteen years old for two days when falsely accused of throwing stones. Later, after an Israeli officer killed seven unarmed Palestinians at a bus stop, Imran had constructed a bomb. He'd gone to blow up an Israeli police station but was caught and sent to jail. Watching Palestinian children throw flowers at Israeli tanks during Oslo, something shifted for him. He knew it then: using violence meant more and more sacrifice; it was time for something new.

And there was Nour Shehada, who'd joined Fatah after witnessing two young men killed right in front of him in the Tulkarem refugee camp. He'd met his future wife at a demonstration—and noticed her because of how beautiful she looked throwing stones. He'd escaped his own wedding when IDF soldiers came to arrest him, then he married his wife secretly in the hills, and slept in hidden places where he hoped he wouldn't be found. He was found though, and went to jail for some years. Afterward, after losing too many friends to the second intifada's violence, he'd become committed to nonviolence and found himself here, sitting around this long table, having unlikely conversations with Israeli ex-soldiers.

The stories of the Israelis revealed themselves to Souli more slowly. There were the three Shapira brothers, whose father was a career air force pilot. There was the oldest brother Zohar, with his textbook soldier face. During the second intifada, he'd found himself just down the road from a suicide bombing in Jerusalem. After the blast, he held a religious boy with a screw lodged in his head, overpowered by the smell of burnt organs. Zohar couldn't forget the sight of a small Palestinian girl running toward him in a village near Nablus. He couldn't forget that unbearable moment after he ordered her to stop, how she kept running with her small feet in his direction. He shot above her head, saw her stop, looked into her eyes, and knew that—though she was not physically hurt—he had done something unforgiveable, and changed her forever.

There was Zohar's brother Yonatan. He'd grown up, his friends joked, as a "Zionist poster boy." He'd led memorial songs for the Jewish dead every Yom HaZikaron, Memorial Day. And he'd been a rescue pilot in the army for many years, learning later what other pilots had done: dropping bombs on Gaza, killing entire families at once.

There was the youngest Shapira brother, Itamar, who'd played a role in a famous incident, when the Israeli army killed three

Palestinian police officers in the West Bank. Itamar had been standing outside a village in the north, where the IDF was conducting
raids to arrest Palestinian fighters. His job was to stand there and
prevent anyone from entering the village. That day, he watched as
three Palestinian police drove up in a jeep. It seemed they wanted
to confront the soldiers, to stop the continuous raids. Itamar saw a
gun appear in the jeep's window, pointing at him. Everyone, suddenly, was shooting—Itamar, his friends beside him, then the police
in the windows—until the jeep came to a stop. The officers inside
were gone.

There was Avner Wishnitzer, who'd also been in an elite unit,
who'd witnessed an activist in the West Bank using nonviolent tactics to confront soldiers. Who'd surprised himself by realizing this
activist was the brave one, not the soldiers facing him with their
helmets and weapons. Avner, whose words carried a slow and particular weight, who spoke Arabic warmly, making Sulaiman think
he might serve as a bridge.

And there was Elik Elhanan, who'd lost his little sister Smadar.
The family had chosen her name from the Song of Solomon—Smadar, "the grape of the vine"—and they watched her grow and smile
often until a September day in 1997, when Smadar and some friends
went to buy books on Ben Yehuda Street. The school year was
beginning when young Palestinian men near Smadar hit a button
or pulled a switch. They killed themselves that day, along with five
people passing by. Smadar, not quite fourteen years old, and her
two friends were among them.[2] Elik belonged to a family of leftists;
sometimes, his father would look at an old picture of Smadar, four
years old, holding a little sign that read "Stop the Occupation." Still,
Elik entered the army, where he did many things, until he found he
couldn't anymore.

All the stories, unsurprising but dizzying, unfolded as the group
continued meeting. Some people came to one meeting and never
again. But the ones who stayed seemed to want something similar:
a movement of ex-combatants from both sides who would work
together, through principles of nonviolence, to end the occupation.
And they wanted to build something new. In most organizations
that worked with Palestinians and Israelis, the Jews seemed to make

the decisions. From these meetings, though, they wanted to attempt a start on more equal terms. So they set parameters.

To join, the Israelis had to refuse to serve in the West Bank, East Jerusalem, and Gaza. The Palestinians had to oppose armed struggle. And the two sides had to make all their decisions together, on equal ground, or as equal as possible given their political reality. They chose Haitham as the Palestinian coordinator, and Zohar as his Israeli counterpart. They set everything up through this model of co-leadership—one Palestinian and one Israeli sharing each position.

They also knew they didn't want to just talk; they wanted to *do* something. But it seemed that, in order to act, so much talking had to come first. And their ways of talking rarely lined up.

The Israelis wanted to make decisions according to the principle of "one man, one vote," to discuss everything all together. But the Palestinians wanted to decide on their position uninationally, before presenting it to the Israelis. For some of the Israelis, this difference triggered a deep anxiety, a sense that the Palestinians dealt behind closed doors, a fear that they weren't sincere about their reasons for showing up—particularly that some of them might have adopted nonviolence as a practical strategy rather than a moral principle.

And since most of the Palestinians joining were members of Fatah, and Haitham was a Fatah official, some Israelis felt that the work of the Palestinians was being sanctioned, and therefore monitored, by one of the dominant Palestinian political parties. They were right. After Arafat's death, and the enormous grief that accompanied his absence, Mahmoud Abbas had become president of the PA. He'd given his permission and encouragement to the Palestinians in these secret meetings. Some of the Israelis wondered if this made their partners beholden to, and limited by, Fatah. And it all felt uneven: there was no parallel sanction on the Israeli side.

As the Israelis worried over this, Souli and Bassam spoke endlessly about what could make this project different from other peace projects—not just something to make the Israelis feel better, but a tool for genuine, transformative change.

In the midst of it all, each group struggling to understand the motivations of the other, they decided to bring their experiment to the next level: to hold a bigger, semi-public meeting to recruit more people. Each side would bring twenty-five people who might join this movement they were building, whatever it was. But when they agreed that one Palestinian and one Israeli should tell their stories at the meeting, no one volunteered.

No one wanted to do it. It was scary; they didn't know exactly who would be at this meeting, but Souli and others on the Palestinian side were certain a Shabak officer would be there. And it wasn't clear how to tell a story of your life, to tell it briefly. To tell it both as a call to action, and something true. Souli had never done it—not in Arabic, not in Hebrew, and not in English. To narrate it on that stage would mean going further: not just knowing how to tell it, but how to tell it to your enemy.

When no one raised their hand, offering to take on the role, the other Palestinians in the room turned to Souli. One after the other, they said versions of the same thing: "Souli, your story's the strongest. You were in jail when you were fourteen, you should speak."

By the end, he felt he had no choice. He would have to find a way to do it, to tell the story to a room of people who had been in jail with him, and Israelis too.

The Israeli group chose Chen Alon as the first storyteller because he'd been, as he'd laughingly say later, "the Forrest Gump of the intifada." Like Gump, he'd been present and clueless (as people always are inside history) at so many important moments. He'd been an unlucky firsthand witness of a series of famous, horrific events he couldn't stop remembering.

Years into their friendship, Souli would invoke Chen's story often. But that day, as Chen stood on stage for the first public meeting and all the new faces gathered before him, Souli didn't really know what he would say. As Souli waited, legs crossed, Chen didn't quite know what to say either, what version of the story to lay out. He couldn't possibly tell the whole thing.

Before World War II, Chen's paternal grandparents had left Poland for Palestine, pursuing their desire for a Jewish nation-state. No one else in the family would survive the European years that followed. Chen grew up knowing this: Zionism was a necessity, a life raft.

When it was Chen's time to join the army, he was proud to sign up for a tank unit, to defend his country—the one that had made his life possible. He pictured himself standing at his nation's edges, facing out toward all the Arab armies that wanted to throw him and everyone he loved into the sea. But when his army service began in 1988, he found himself in Gaza, fighting a different kind of war than he'd imagined. On that tiny strip of land, he imposed curfews, he stood with weapons in front of crowds of children throwing stones, before mass demonstrations in the streets. After all his training with guns, he found himself mostly using a baton to push away children who looked at him with an anger he didn't understand. "Why," he wondered, "do they hate us so much?"

One of his primary jobs was to contain protest, but as an officer, he often spoke with his soldiers about how to conduct their missions with as much empathy as possible. He tried to hold on to this in a world where he stood guard over a nightmare: checkpoints, roadblocks, arrests of sleepy-eyed children in the middle of the night, beatings and house demolitions.

After his release from active duty in 1992, he served forty-five days a year in the reserves. As the peace process unfolded, his presence all over the West Bank and Gaza seemed temporary. Soon, he was sure, they'd be done with all this. Soon, Israel would withdraw from the West Bank and Gaza; Palestinians would declare an independent state. But year after year, he served and watched—in Gaza, in Jenin, in the areas around Nablus and Bethlehem—as more settlements, more roadblocks, more checkpoints were built. He and his unit would visit the Palestinian police, shake hands, have coffee, smoke, make small talk. Before they left, his commander would stand and count the Palestinians' guns, making sure everything was in its place. It wasn't until later that this would strike him for what it was: a ritual of domination, of colonialism.

In 2000, Ehud Barak came back from Camp David with nothing, saying it was impossible to make peace with the Palestinians. Chen was outraged. It was as if Barak were speaking directly to him, giving him the news: he should plan on serving as an officer of the occupation for the rest of his life. And after his years of reserve duty in the West Bank and Gaza, he knew what Barak said wasn't true; it wasn't that Israel's hand was stretched out for peace while the Palestinians were demanding the impossible. For years, while Barak had recited his mantra of peace, Chen had watched the settlements grow.

And then, the second intifada. At home in Tel Aviv, it seemed the explosions of Palestinian suicide bombings were everywhere: buses and restaurants, dance clubs and private weddings, hotels and sidewalks. There was no place that felt safe. Sitting on his scooter behind a bus at a red light, he'd wait for a bright burst, the kind of unbearable sound that would seem to happen more inside your body than out. When the light turned green, he would let go of the breath he didn't know he'd been holding. When his mother and young daughter took the bus, he'd count the minutes until he heard from them again. During his next reserve duty, he found himself standing at a roadblock in the West Bank, a choked and smoking place, a horror film.

Looking back, he saw many moments of breaking, a dissonance that would eventually lead to refusal. There was the time a man drove up to the checkpoint Chen was guarding with a backseat full of children. They were ill; they needed to get to the hospital. Chen shook his head at the man. The children didn't have proper permits, and he didn't know if they were really sick. What if there was a terrorist in the trunk? Or a weapon hidden?

As the man in the car argued, Chen stepped away to take a phone call from his wife. She needed help with his daughter. He reassured her, said he would call his mother for help. Turning around, he saw the children in the backseat as the man finally gave up and went back the way he'd come. The children's faces were pale, they looked very small. It was a moment of breaking, a feeling that the two figures in him—father and officer of the occupation—could no longer fit in one place.

The last day of his reserve duty that year, his mind was already home with his family when his commanding officer announced an operation, unfurled some maps, pointed at the houses.

"We need to demolish these houses tonight."

They'd gone so many days without losing any soldiers and were almost home.

"Why now, why here?" another officer asked.

The officer tried to avoid the question, but when the questions kept coming, he answered cautiously. "We have to aerate this region a bit. The settlers have put a lot of pressure on us."

Chen looked at him. "But we don't take orders from the settlers."

"Yeah, but it comes from the minister of defense. You know how it is. The settlers put a lot of pressure on us and we have to do something."

Chen argued with the officer, said they should refuse the order. But they didn't. They went to demolish the homes and it turned into an all-night battle.

When the sun came up and Chen looked around at the rubble, he knew. It was so clear. He was done; he couldn't do this anymore.

As Souli stood to take his place at the front of the room, something Chen said echoed in him, somewhere hidden in his body. Chen had said, standing on that stage, "We are not here to ask forgiveness. We are here to take responsibility for what we've done."

Souli thought about it, what had been done. How he'd just arrived in jail around the time Chen was learning to use his baton. As Chen held back protesters in the streets of Gaza, soldiers just like him were visiting the jail in Hebron for their "practice," marching Sulaiman and his friends naked through the halls.

Souli shook the thought away, began to speak some version of his story. He hadn't told the whole thing before, and now he stood in front of these people, searching for the cringes in Israeli faces when he spoke of the attack in 'Ayn Farrah, looking for anger in Palestinian eyes when he talked about rejecting violence, about wanting to work the rest of his life for peace.

He wouldn't remember later what he said, if he'd mentioned the choking feeling of Pisgat Ze'ev, the fact of his torture, how long he spent on hunger strike, how often he interrupted himself with jokes. In the coming years, he would learn to tell the story easily.

But that day it was different. He traced the lines of the story, played on its surface. He cut things, he broke things; he still doesn't know how he made it.

With the energy of that semi-public meeting behind them, the group began planning an *intilaqa*, a launch. An event to officially begin this movement, which they'd finally given a name: Combatants for Peace.

Amid the talking and planning, Souli grew more and more convinced that these Israeli partners were committed to fighting for freedom beside him. There was often more fire in their words than in his own. This felt enormous: to see sympathy and solidarity from your supposed enemy, from the ones you thought once wanted to kill you. It broke something.

He wished he could have known these people before jail, before everything. And this wish made him want to bring more and more people into the work, to support dialogue and meetings, to protect this common ground, to keep it and strengthen it. He started to feel they could do something big together, something historical. He protected this certainty, with its immeasurable weight, like gravity, or prophecy.

But as he dreamed outward, something kept pulling him back to Hizma, where the army had kept its promise. Soon, Souli's family would only be allowed to visit Ta'mira during the olive harvest, once a year—if they got the proper permits. And though Ta'mira was the most important piece of land that would end up in the buffer zone, there were other pieces, too.

One plot held two old *rumani* olive trees someone in the family had planted a very long time before. The army told Karim that, before the land disappeared behind the wall, the family could dig up these trees and take them away. To a place where they could keep seeing them, watering them, allowing them to continue growing their sweetly sour green fruit.

When it was time, the family drove big trucks up to the ancient trees and prepared to dig. They would plant the trees in the backyard, near the *tabun* (outdoor oven) and the sheep, near the slight, young fruit trees Souli had brought from Bayt 'Ummar after jail.

Souli was glad they could keep the old olive trees, but it wasn't just the trees that mattered. It was the fact of their belonging here, in this specific place, for so long. These *rumani* trees were older than any human could understand. And now they had to remove the ground beneath them, tear them out by their roots.

Souli stood there looking, a shovel in his hand. He thought about how Sarah and Fatima could still tell, no matter what happened, when it was going to rain. It had to do with a knowledge that arose in the body, with something that could not be taught. How could he explain this to the Ashkenazi American Jews he'd met in California, to his new Israeli partners? They had not watched his mother tend the trees on Saturdays, had not grown up so close to the land that the olives, the za'atar, the jasmine, the air and the birds—all of it—seemed a part of the family itself. That's how it was: the land was not outside them. So taking these trees from the ground, it was like taking the spirit from someone's body.

They all stood looking, and then finally, someone put the first shovel into the ground. But as the digging began, as the first roots came up out of the soil, something essential in Said's heart stopped working and he fell into the dirt he loved, clutching his arm.

Said didn't die that day, but he became weak in a way he would never recover from. In the days after his heart attack, Souli's father lay in bed, under a doctor's orders to stay still. As his family replanted the trees in the backyard where they looked wrong, as the cement wall grew up tall around Hizma, Souli stayed home, sitting by his father's bed.

But he couldn't bear the stillness for long. When it became clear his father would survive, he gave his mother some money and got back to work. In the mornings and evenings, he'd say hello to his father and the ancient olive trees replanted beside the sheep's pen. During the long days, he prepared for the public launch of Combatants for Peace.

The date of the event, April 10, 2006, came just before Palestinian Prisoners' Day and Passover. While preparing for an occasion when both peoples would obsess over water and salt, several hundred people showed up for the launch in 'Anata.

It was beautiful to begin this way—in concert with two holidays all about freedom. In the school where the event was held, many words were spoken. But the most important thing was a shared feeling, an enormous hope. A feeling that was interrupted, momentarily, when a frightening sound came from nearby. Israeli soldiers had thrown stun grenades not far from the school. It was a reminder of why these ex-combatants had gathered, and only made Souli feel stronger. After the boom and rushing of air faded, standing beside his friends, he looked out at the crowd. He felt in the presence of something being born.

PART FOUR

CHAPTER 19

Bullets & Theater

In the months after the *intilaqa*, the new movement's members got to work exploring what exactly they had made, what they would do. They told their personal stories—one Israeli and one Palestinian—at house meetings and even at *mekhinot*, pre-army courses for youth. They spoke about how they changed, how they became committed to nonviolence. They attended protests organized by others, and as they began planning their own, they looked inward and noticed something: their new movement was made only of men. So Itamar was glad, around this time, when he managed to bring his friend Reut to a meeting.

They knew each other from growing up in the city of Ramat HaSharon, and Reut had served in an army tank unit, as what was called "a secretary." She did what women were expected to do in such roles, as she explained it later, laughing: resolve conflicts and make birthday cake.

After Reut's first Combatants meeting, she looked at Itamar, shook her head. "How can I be a part of this? This group of men, of *milu'imnikim*, reservists?" she asked. She'd been the only woman in the room. She felt they had little in common, though that wasn't precisely true.

In her tank unit, Reut had served near the border of Lebanon, fighting enemies she couldn't see. It was surreal. She saw only the beautiful natural landscapes around her and rockets, falling from the sky. But in the last four months of her service, during the second intifada, her unit was called to Gaza. And in those four months, seeing what occupation meant, it was like losing her mind. In just one of those months, she lost six friends. At night, she couldn't sleep. She felt she could hear the screams of Gazan mothers who'd lost children. And they began to mix with the screams of her friends' mothers, when they learned their sons were gone. Afterward, she couldn't stop asking herself: *What are we doing? Are we doing everything in our power to stop this pain?*

It was this recurring question that brought her to a second Combatants meeting. But she agreed only after Itamar told her that Sima Umbus, a Palestinian woman from Tulkarem, would attend too. Sima had lost many relatives to the conflict, including her husband—taken from her during the second intifada. Left with four small children, she'd joined the armed struggle, and went to jail for several years. Later, she would tell Reut what had happened there, how she would never forget how the Shabak interrogated her, how she would never be the same.

Sima and Reut both joined the movement, and as the two sides met to tell their stories—both to one another, and to their communities in house meetings—they began taking action too.

Later, Reut and many others would remember one particular action from the years that followed, an action that captured something. That day, they gathered before a roadblock the army had erected between the connected villages of Shufa and 'Izbat Shufa.

At the front of the group, a line of women stood shoulder to shoulder as the soldiers approached and began shooting stun grenades and tear gas, very close. Reut and Sima held hands, looked at each other. Sima had health problems from jail, difficulty breathing. Inhaling gas was dangerous for her. And so just a second before the gas hit, they jumped together, high into the air, and off to the side. Somehow, someone took a photo at that moment—of Reut and Sima with their feet off the ground, hands intertwined, jumping to something like safety.

Sulaiman loved actions like this one, as they began to occur. He loved the work of storytelling and conversation that made such things possible, that made them work. But during the meetings where the Palestinians met separately, he felt frustrated. Some of

the participants had a rigid approach, entirely unfriendly to the revolutionary values of self-critique he'd learned on Saturdays in jail,
eating some precious replacement for cake, taking responsibility for
every unwashed cup—even the imaginary ones. The conversations
seemed to circle the question of how to mobilize their Israeli partners, convince them, change them. Souli heard little about the need
to change themselves. It surprised him at first, that he felt more patience for the movement's Israeli members.

He paid attention to all of it, and grew curious about another
dynamic, one he noticed in Elik, Reut, Chen, and Yonatan. He
never heard them criticize Palestinians, only Israelis. He learned
that, though his Israeli friends sometimes felt frustration with their
Palestinian partners, they were careful not to criticize. They came
from a position of more power, and so it seemed a huge aspect of
joint nonviolent work for them: to accept difference, and move
forward. Souli knew this approach the Israelis took made some Palestinians feel safe, but he wondered how it might affect his new
partners' ability to speak to the Israeli mainstream.

Something was moving in him then, some impulse to run away,
to leave all of it. He couldn't wait for summer, when he'd go back
to Len and Libby's camp, when he'd stand again in the sharp air under the trees. That year, the Traubmans hired him as a recruiter, so,
as he counted the days until summer, he invited other Palestinians
to join him at camp. They left together for America as everything
erupted behind them.

In June 2006, Hamas militants entered Israel through a tunnel, killing two soldiers and capturing Gilad Shalit. Through land and air,
Israel responded.

Souli was in the US as the Israeli army entered Gaza and dropped
bombs from above, killing over two hundred Palestinians in the
course of two months. He was still away when another war in Lebanon began, listening to the news, the dizzying recitation of events
that seemed so separate from the events themselves.

Hezbollah, a militant group backed by Syria and Iran, injured
five Israeli civilians in an attack on the town of Shlomi and, in a
separate raid, killed three soldiers and captured two.[1] On the day of

fighting that followed, the Israeli army named Hezbollah as its target, but killed at least thirty-five Lebanese civilians.

And then Souli heard. Hezbollah had fired rockets into Israel's northern towns and cities, killing two civilians, and the first draft orders had arrived. Israeli members of Combatants for Peace were being called to fight.

To join the movement, Israeli members had agreed to refuse army service in the West Bank, Gaza, and East Jerusalem. Some of the Israeli activists still believed in fighting for their army, to defend their borders. Their refusal had been specific, not total. But as conversations unfolded, it became clear that many members—Palestinian and Israeli both—felt this an unnecessary war. It was true that Hezbollah was firing rockets into northern Israel, that many families were hiding in shelters, that the group's weapons kept improving, reaching further. But it seemed the Israeli response would kill scores of Lebanese civilians and Palestinian refugees—just as it did during the last Lebanon war, when a young Sulaiman watched the bodies pile up on his aunt Shamsiya's television.

One Israeli general announced the army's strategy, making it very clear: "This affair is between Israel and the state of Lebanon. Where to attack? Once it is inside Lebanon, everything is legitimate—not just southern Lebanon, not just the line of Hezbollah posts."

And so Itamar, Chen, and a number of other movement members refused. In the end, it seemed the two things—fighting in the war and fighting for the movement—couldn't share the same space.

Through all of it, Souli stayed in America, imagining he lived in a different world. Yonatan Shapira joined him for a speaking tour and, after so many speeches, they began to lose their voices. Toward the end, they would meet backstage before every lecture, and Yonatan would take out a lozenge for each of them to soothe their sore throats. As they unwrapped the candies, they told versions of the same joke:

"These lozenges are our ammunition now. They allow our mouths to open; they allow us to speak. Who needs guns when you have cough drops?"

Souli loved speaking with Yonatan, talking about how they'd been born so close together—just a few miles and weeks apart—how their lives had been so different, but also shared various shapes and patterns. And he began noticing certain dynamics that collected around his friend. As they stood on stage again and again, Souli watched as Jews and Israelis became angry the moment Yonatan opened his mouth. It was different when they heard Souli. As he watched them listening to the soft way he joked through his story, he felt he could see them changing, asking new questions.

None of it surprised Yonatan. It made sense that American Jews would feel moved by a Palestinian who refused to kill Israelis, but would feel uncomfortable with an Israeli who refused to kill Palestinians. In this way, it felt powerful what they could do together: with Souli's softening, and Yonatan's challenge to face the reality of the occupation's violence. And the dynamic reversed, Souli noticed, when they visited Muslim and Palestinian communities. In Texas, as they traveled between various mosques, their Muslim hosts warmed immediately to Yonatan, but seemed to look at Souli as if from a distance.

After Yonatan left, Souli flew to Minnesota to speak at an event organized by Rabbi Amy Eilberg, the first woman ordained by the Jewish Conservative movement. It was on this trip that he sat in my mother's living room, that I first shook his hand, that I became angry about him sleeping under the Israeli flag in my stepbrother's bedroom. It was on this trip that, for the first time, he laughed at me and told me to calm down.

He wandered until Philadelphia, where he stayed for several months, working on his English and exploring what it meant to live in an apartment with an American girl. Drinking daily espresso in the Green Line Cafe, which sat on the border between very different neighborhoods, he knew what he was doing: trying to disconnect from home, search, see the world differently, from new angles. He wasn't sure he wanted to return to Hizma anytime soon.

He was still in Philadelphia months later when I called and asked him to speak on my college campus in Ohio. I left him a message, and soon after he left one for me. His voice was bright as usual. *I'm going back home*, he said. He didn't tell me until much later what had tipped the scales, what had brought him back to Hizma.

He'd been looking out the window into the streets of Philadelphia the day his phone rang. He picked it up to hear the voice of his younger brother Nabil.

"*Immi*, mother, is here," he said. "She's angry with you."

"Can I talk to her?"

"No, she says she doesn't want to speak with you anymore."

"Why?"

"She says . . ." Nabil paused as Sarah cried in the background. "She says, 'Your father is going to die, and you don't care.'"

Souli hung up without speaking to his mother. He left me a message and bought his ticket home.

After the long flight, the hours of standing in lines, he found himself back in Hizma, looking down at his father. A man lying in the same bed as always, but in a changed body. Said had always seemed so tough, made of some material that couldn't be molded; now he was a soft thing.

Something turned over near Souli's ribs. Here was his father, his roots pulled from the ground, and Souli had been away for months. Even when he was here, he hadn't really been here. Over the last few years, busy with his new peace work, he hadn't helped as his brother Aziz had, always emptying buckets of water and refilling them, looking useful and upright, doing the things expected of a son.

He'd supported the family with money instead of time. But looking down at his father, he felt money was nothing, and in the coming weeks, he stayed close. He held his father's feet in his hands. He massaged Said's tired arches and soles. He hoped it was enough.

He stayed at his father's side until he couldn't sit in Hizma any longer. Once back to work with Combatants for Peace, he found everything in motion. The movement was trying to understand itself, what exactly it was doing.

In house meetings and lectures, Souli began telling his story more and more, feeling how the words moved in his mouth. And as a group, they tried to find some understanding of when to talk—with one another, with the public—and when to face the occupation

directly. Sometimes, it was clear. Like the November day they sat
for hours in a sterile room, listening to corporate psychologists from
a big NGO who seemed to understand nothing. At some point,
they learned that Israel had fired on Gaza that morning. The army
said it had missed its target, but whatever the intention, the result
was the same. Nearly twenty Palestinians in Bayt Hanun were dead:
sleeping people and children in pajamas. That day, the movement
members knew what to do. They left what Elik liked to call the
"liberal corporate democracy bullshit." They headed for the streets.

Outside of the dramatic, remarkable disasters, there were the
slow-growing ones. Souli often joined Elik, the new Israeli coordinator, at the demonstrations in Bil'in. Palestinian villagers there and
elsewhere were protesting the route of the lengthening wall, which
was confiscating their land far beyond the Green Line. But whenever the children began to throw stones, Souli would leave.

Some of his friends—Israeli as well as Palestinian—felt that stone-
throwing was nonviolence. But it wasn't the nonviolence he
dreamed of. He was more excited by the concept of the Theater of
the Oppressed and the magic it brought: the puppets, the different
way of relating.[2] He loved how they could use this strategy to name
and process power dynamics within Combatants, to rehearse a new
reality. Led by Chen and Nour, Combatants activists also started
bringing this theater practice to checkpoints, using puppets and balloons and skits to reflect the soldiers' actions back to them. To show
the soldiers in their strange uniform-costumes how they might act
differently.

Watching this theater unfold, Souli began to see the helmeted
soldiers as lost children. He began to feel that stone-throwing only
pushed them into more lostness, deeper into the roles they'd been
given. And he wanted the soldiers to feel invited to join peace
work; he wanted to welcome everyone who might one day choose
freedom.

Combatants for Peace was trying to think about how to welcome more people, to widen the movement. Though they began
with only ex-combatants and ex-prisoners, they quickly changed
the framework to allow anyone to join. Because after their lectures,
people were always coming up, moved, saying they had never been

in combat, but wanted to be a part of this work. No one wanted to turn these people away, because in this place, it was often unclear what it meant to be a combatant. In the end, everyone here had been touched by—or implicated in—the work violence and occupation had done.

Souli was proud of this decision, of this movement he'd helped make. And looking at his Israeli partners one day, he realized it. It was like love, what he now felt for these people. Itamar and Yonatan and Elik and Avner. They gave him the sense of strength that love gives. But still, along with the Palestinian members of Combatants for Peace, they represented only a small number of people. He was curious about the others. About whether, like the Jews in America, they might hear his story and be changed somehow.

CHAPTER 20

The Year
of Long Drives

It was around then, perfectly, that Souli received a note from Gadi, a very different kind of Israeli. Gadi had grown up in Tzahala, a Tel Aviv neighborhood populated by many who'd helped bring Israel to life. His father was among the founders of the Israeli Air Force; his elementary school teacher was David Ben-Gurion's[1] daughter; Yitzhak Rabin was a family friend and neighbor.

Gadi's mother was a modern dancer and a liberal, a kind person who understood many things. After the 1967 war, when Gadi was still a child, she told Rabin that Israel should unconditionally withdraw from the occupied territories. Gadi didn't understand it. During those six days of war, he'd listened to the sounds of Jordanian shells whistling over his head, and one day saw his older brother come home with something black in his hand. It was a piece of shrapnel from a bomb that had exploded just one kilometer away, taking an entire house to the ground.

He felt then, and would always feel, that the state of Israel was— and should always stay—a moral project. That his country hadn't wanted the occupation of the West Bank, Gaza, and East Jerusalem. That it happened only after his people defended themselves from the attacks of Arab armies. But now that they'd won this land, he didn't understand why they would surrender it to a group of people who didn't recognize them, who wanted them to disappear.

When Gadi was about the same age as Sulaiman would be that day in 'Ayn Farrah with his small red knife, another war came. In the wake of the 1973 war, feeling how it had threatened the existence of his home, Gadi felt a vision come over him. He saw it then: that the main challenge of his life would be bringing peace to Israel. He kept living, as one has to. He joined the air force's pilot course, and was relieved to be released a year later. Grateful to be free from the airplanes and cockpits, the levers and buttons, from everything they could do.

In 2003, trying to escape the pressures of the second intifada, he enrolled in a master's program at American University. There in DC, he spent the year fleeing conversations about home. But the conversations managed to follow him, and after meeting a Gazan intellectual at a Chanukah event, he suddenly found himself involved in dialogue workshops, taking tours of the West Bank and Israel. The experiences were enormous, entirely shifting his understandings of reality and history. Each side had such different stories of the past and present, stories that lived in disparate worlds. If you were born on one side, you had no idea where the story of the other came from, what it truly meant. Only through meeting and discovering the roots of these stories, he thought, could the two sides maybe live together peacefully.

At American University in the summer of 2006, Gadi was sitting in a room when Souli and Yonatan stood to speak. Later, he would remember Yonatan saying, with the authority of a former pilot, that the IDF was dropping bombs on Gaza without regard for the lives of innocent people. That they had no problem bombing a huge crowd to take out one wanted person hidden among many. Yonatan's descriptions seemed exaggerated; they filled Gadi with anger. Gadi had to leave the lecture early for his volunteer job with a peace project, so he heard Souli speak for just a few minutes.

That summer, Gadi heard others speak too, listening as representatives from the organization OneVoice presented results from a survey in Palestine and Israel. Through the survey, which gathered responses from people in many different places, they'd learned that most Palestinians and Israelis agreed on the central aspects of a two-state solution. Though neither side believed the other felt the same.

Gadi couldn't stop thinking about it, and about how a OneVoice presenter had suggested someone organize a big event to mark the fortieth anniversary of the 1967 war. If neither side believed the other ready for peace, he thought, a huge event on June 5, 2007, could change everything. Through this commemoration, each side could tell the other, and the whole world, that they were ready. Far more ready than anyone thought.

On his way home in 2006, at a peace conference in Turkey with many Palestinians and Israelis, he raised the June 5 idea with the Israeli and Palestinian co-directors of the prominent peace organization IPCRI (Israel/Palestine Center for Research and Information). He asked Gershon Baskin and Hanna Siniora why someone hadn't yet done a joint public event, something to mark the desire of peace on both sides. Gershon smiled and told him they'd love to do it, but it was a matter of money.

Gadi looked at him. "I'll bring the money," he said. So they began working together to plan two big events for June 5, 2007: a gathering of Palestinians and another of Israelis—all under the principle of "two states for two peoples." Together, they would mark forty years since the 1967 war—the war many Israelis felt their country had not wanted, a war they felt surrounding Arab countries had caused, creating an occupation that showed no signs of waning. With Gershon and Hanna, Gadi poured himself into the work of bringing these big events to life, the work of making them real.

Still learning, Gadi listened carefully to Gershon and Hanna, and when Hanna suggested Gadi meet Ghassan Sistani, he did. Ghassan, who'd been in jail for many years, was now a former staffer at a big dialogue organization. He said he could bring thousands of people to the event, but that they could not use the word *peace*—the word was a broken one in Palestinian society, and would draw no one.

Gadi kept working through his confusion. And when a mentor gave him Souli's email address, the two men began sending each other emails about everything they knew to be true.

Souli couldn't always find his way through Gadi's words. But while they often made him angry, he sensed a crucial challenge in them, one he wanted to see up close. He knew someone like Gadi would be difficult for his friends in Combatants for Peace—both Palestinian and Israeli. But he wanted to push through that challenge somehow. If they wanted to grow their movement, they'd have to make inclusivity more than a word they used; it had to be practiced.

Souli invited Gadi to meet in the basement of East Jerusalem's American Colony Hotel, and on that day, Gadi arrived first. He stood there, watching Souli approach, taking in what he saw: a tall and lanky man, a solemn face with a chipped front tooth. Sitting down in the dark room, at a small table by the fireplace, Gadi thought the man before him looked just like a pirate from a film.

When Souli put his backpack on the ground and began unzipping it, Gadi felt a fear rising. The intifada had calmed some, and he'd met many Palestinians before, even ex-prisoners. But the fear was still there. So many bombs had gone off in Israel in buses, pizza parlors, nightclubs, killing too many innocent people. Israelis were taught to look for unknown packages, for "suspicious people." So Gadi stayed frozen in place as Souli pulled out his laptop, poised his fingers over the keyboard, and smiled impishly at Gadi. "So what's the idea you wanted to discuss?"

Gadi took a deep breath, and explained his vision for the June 5 events.

"Who are you working with?" Souli asked.

"Hanna Siniora and Gershon Baskin are helping. And Ghassan Sistani. But he told me we can't use the word *peace* in our campaign for peace. I don't understand it."

Souli clapped his hands together and tipped his head back, laughing.

"I'm in Combatants for Peace! What does he mean you can't use the word? What else are we fighting for?"

They were unclear what would happen next. They didn't yet feel all the warmth that would later exist between them. But some time after, they would realize they'd each felt something similar there in the basement, that they were talking to someone not just from the other side, but rooted in it. Someone distant enough from the mainstream to see it clearly, yet close enough to change it. They spoke and they listened from this place, wanting to understand what they heard, and what it might mean.

In the days and weeks that followed, as Gadi invited Souli to meetings about June 5, it became clear Souli would take a leading role in the initiative. There was a sense, slow-growing at first, that some new work was coming to life. So they began to drive, spending many long hours in Gadi's car, moving between Tel Aviv, Jerusalem, Hizma, and Ramallah, showing each other their versions of things.

On their first trip down road 443 in the West Bank, Gadi found himself staring up at some newly erected watchtowers. He looked in horror at their enormous height, small windows, grayness, and concrete; they reminded him of pictures from Nazi concentration camps. "How could it be," he thought, "that these were here, and I didn't know about them? How terrible they look!"

As if in another world, they also visited Gadi's northern Tel Aviv neighborhood, Souli peering around like a tall, thin child. In those streets, he felt that everyone must have known he was Palestinian, that they were staring at him, waiting for something to explode. He knew their fear could be dangerous and he clutched tightly at the straps of his backpack, as if invoking some protective magic. Walking through those streets, Gadi looked over at Souli, saw his hands turning a little white from the gripping.

"You're safe," he said. "I'll make sure of it."

That night, when Souli slept on Gadi's couch for the first time, he realized something. Though he had built close relationships with the Israelis in Combatants, this was only the second time he'd slept in an Israeli home.

Souli began to grow fond of Gadi, of how committed he was to building peace, of how much he wanted to learn about Palestinian cultures and experiences. There was something common slowly revealing itself between them, in the way they both liked to explore, to understand and peer beneath what they found. In the way they hated all the cement growing around them, wanting to protect the trees and the soil that fed them.

Soon, it seemed they were together all the time. Talking about how important the June events could be, saying to each other the same words over and over, driving with the windows open: *We are here on a mission.* As they drove and talked, Souli studied Gadi as much as he could, poring over this man's words like one of the foreign texts he'd read in jail. He was interested in the things Gadi repeated over and over, in the things that made him cry.

He listened to Gadi talk about his grandparents who had come from Eastern Europe to Palestine in the early 1900s. How many early European Zionists used Arabic to communicate with their Arabic-speaking neighbors—Muslim, Christian, and Jewish alike.[2] But his grandparents settled in urban centers and knew virtually no Arabic. They spoke Yiddish among themselves, and focused on reviving Hebrew. There were so many gaps between them and the people already living on this land: huge spaces of language and culture. And Gadi knew their attempts to purchase land had alarmed Palestinians.

"I can understand that fear," he told Souli. "For the Palestinian leadership, it was like an invasion, another colonial power coming." It was tragic, he thought, because while the Palestinians saw these European Jewish immigrants as colonists, they were something else. They were a people who needed a place, a people coming home after centuries of displacement, ghettos, and terrible violence. Gadi wished the Zionists had made this clearer to Palestinians, done more to connect and show respect, to include Palestinians in their decision-making. He wished the Palestinians had understood that his grandparents were not outsiders at all, but people returning after a long, long time away. If both sides had made these efforts more fully, he told Souli, maybe everything could have been different.

As Souli listened, Gadi drove him through his childhood neighborhood of Tzahala, pointing at things as if revealing secrets he'd never shared. He stopped in front of many different houses to turn to Souli and say, "Rabin used to live there, and Sharon over there, and there, that's where Moshe Dayan lived."

Souli looked up at the homes with their white walls, tall trees, and lush green plants pouring over iron railings. He'd grown up hearing about the people in these houses, representatives of Zionism.

They were killers, colonizers, the worst people on the earth. Everything terrible that had happened since 1948 came from them.

But here was Gadi beside him, looking up at these houses with tears in his eyes, talking about studying with the children of these people in school, occasionally spending an afternoon at Sharon's house with his kind wife, who was always baking cakes for children. It wasn't easy for Souli to listen, but he did. He tried to put himself in the shoes of someone who'd grown up hearing the stories Gadi had. And Souli felt Gadi listening too, even when it challenged him. He felt how much Gadi wanted him and his family to be free.

One day in January 2007, when Gadi called Souli to make plans, Souli didn't answer. He'd just received another phone call. Bassam's ten-year-old daughter Abir was in the hospital.

After a math test, she'd left her school in 'Anata, heading to a nearby store with her sister and friends to buy candy. She was standing on the street near some Israeli border police when an officer shot a bullet, and then Abir wasn't standing anymore. She was lying on the ground.

Before Bassam could get to Hadassah hospital in Jerusalem, Elik's parents, Rami and Nurit, arrived. They'd grown close with Bassam and his wife, Salwa, and now stood beside their friends, looking down at Abir, thinking of her and also of their daughter Smadar, who'd died in a suicide bombing just before she turned fourteen, looking for school supplies.

As Abir lay unmoving in the ICU for days, both Palestinian and Israeli members of Combatants for Peace gathered at the hospital, standing and pacing and praying. After two or three endless days, Abir was gone.

Preparing for the funeral, Souli kept thinking of how Abir looked when he'd brought her, along with other Palestinian children, to the Ramat Gan zoo. He pictured her staring at the animals—maybe the hippos or chimpanzees, he couldn't remember. But he remembered her looking.

In the silence and sound of Abir's death, the members of Combatants for Peace did what they could. They sat with Bassam and his family. They held protests outside Israeli police headquarters, demanding someone properly investigate the killing. An autopsy showed Abir was killed by a rubber-coated bullet, but the police emphasized claims that someone had been throwing stones nearby. The police quickly closed the case, stating insufficient evidence.[3] As if they wanted to erase what was true, bury Abir where she would be forgotten.

After Abir's death, everything tipped forward and, around the same time, Souli became the movement's Palestinian coordinator. When he reached out to Gadi to explain his absence, they got back to work—Souli balancing his responsibilities with Combatants for Peace, continuing to protest, and building gardens in Abir's name as he and Gadi moved forward.

During those full days, Souli went to meet with Qaddura, who'd taught him so much in jail. Gadi went too and, watching Souli speak in many rooms, realized that Souli understood something: the way feelings moved between people. Listening to Souli's disorganized, dreamy way of speaking, Gadi felt there was so much he didn't know of this man, some rare wisdom he wanted to understand, and help protect.

Souli felt the intifada had ended, if only recently. But Gadi felt it continued raging—Palestinian suicide bombings, shootings, and stabbings still so present. You could never know when or how this violence might appear. And there was Hamas. After the Islamist party won the 2006 elections, there had been violent clashes between Hamas and Fatah supporters. Rockets had been flying into Israel. So Gadi didn't want to imagine what it would mean if Hamas took full control in the West Bank. Already, he felt his friend was in danger.

During those crazy months, Souli sometimes felt frightened for Gadi, too. That's how it had been the first day they drove through the Hizma checkpoint together, not long before Abir died. Souli was allowed to travel in this direction, from Jerusalem into Hizma. But only Israelis and internationals were allowed to use the checkpoint going in the opposite direction—heading from Hizma back into Jerusalem. Palestinians with permits to enter Israel had to take a long, circuitous route, funneled through one of the few, often traffic-clogged checkpoints allowed them.

Beside Souli, driving through the gap in the wall toward Hizma for the first time, Gadi looked up. The nearly finished wall rose up on either side of them, gray and tall, and just ahead, through the tall narrow opening, they could see the white houses of Souli's village. As they turned onto Hizma's main road, Souli laid a *kufiya* on the dashboard. He knew people were still living in the mindset of the intifada. The army frequently closed the village, saying they were responding to some recent violence. But to the villagers, it seemed the army was often punishing them for something that had not yet occurred. People were angry, and Souli was nervous about what could happen when the villagers saw a car with Israeli license plates driving through the small streets.

The checkered scarf stayed in plain sight, a clear marker as they approached Souli's family house. Children peeked out from around corners, and Sarah came out with a perfectly timed tray of tea. That night, they slept in Souli's room, mattresses on the floor, the smell of sheep coming through the window. Before lying down, they talked and ate whatever Sarah brought: olive oil and *khubz tabun*, bread she'd baked that morning in the stone oven outside, before the sun rose. With the window open that night, Gadi spoke and Souli listened.

"You, the Palestinians," Gadi said, "your problem is with us. But we have an issue with you and the Egyptians and the Lebanese and the Jordanians and all Arab states. The whole picture is complex. Let's say you have a state . . . you think it's going to be suddenly peaceful?"

"Wait," Souli said, tearing off a piece of bread while still chewing. "You think I want just another Arab dictatorship? No, I didn't go to jail for that, and I'm not fighting for that. I want a democratic state. With equality for everybody, for all people." He held the piece of bread in his hand as he kept speaking for a long time.

Gadi stared at Souli. He couldn't believe a Palestinian ex-fighter and ex-prisoner would dream in this way. He'd often felt frustrated when Palestinians didn't speak openly about the undemocratic tendencies in their society. And here was Souli, doing just that: not talking only about fighting occupation, but about working for something bigger, something it would take much longer to win.

It was a captured moment, one that exists so you can remember it. Suddenly, sitting there on the mattress, Gadi felt he had a true partner in his work. That he wanted to act in service of this man, his vision. That he would do anything to lift him up.

Time slowed that night but moved very fast during the days and months that followed—Souli driving all over the West Bank, meeting more and more people to win support. He wasn't always sure Gadi would be welcome, so he left his new friend behind as he spoke with Marwan Barghouti's wife, as he won Mahmoud Abbas's blessing.

When it grew dark, Gadi would come meet him in Hizma to talk about everything that had happened. One night in March 2007, after Hamas formed a unity government with Fatah, Gadi wondered aloud if it was really safe to continue. Souli tried to calm his friend, but it was difficult when apparent disasters seemed to occur around them all the time. Like the day Gadi heard there'd been a violent conflict between two families in Hizma, houses burnt all the way to the ground, triggering a huge *sulha* process to find resolution. Again, over endless coffees and cakes and dishes of Sarah's *maqluba*, Souli reassured his friend, said he could manage it, that they would be safe.

Though they'd usually meet in Souli's apartment, sometimes they crossed the road to sit in his parents' house, to exchange brief words with Souli's father, who was still unwell, lying on a mat on the ground beside an open window. One day Said was lying there, or had stood for a moment to peer out the kitchen window at Ta'mira, at the stone wall Said's father had built a long time before, at the other stones that had been around long before that. They had just received a final notice: the wall was nearly complete. Ta'mira was about to disappear fully into the wall's buffer zone.

That day, Said, who'd often been too angry with his sons to visit them in jail, who'd worked for the West Jerusalem municipality most of his adult life, looked at Gadi.

"If they take Ta'mira from us," he said, "I'll die."

It was a promise he kept. A month before the June events, Ta'mira was closed to the family permanently. And on May 8, 2007, Said's heart stopped for good.

At first Souli held himself straight, feeling proud of his strength. But when they carried Said from the house, the one he'd cared for and built, something in Souli crumbled and he fell to the floor, making a sound he didn't know he could make.

Still, he took only a few days off to gather with his family and bury his father. They stood together in the graveyard next to the mosque and the well, on the hill above Najla's cave where Sulaiman, Sadiq, and Asif had once huddled around the old radio Sulaiman stole from Said's secret room of old things.

Soon after Said's death, Souli and Gadi's big events arrived. It was June 5, forty years since the world-shaking first day of the '67 war. In 'Anata, some three thousand Palestinians gathered, linked by satellite to a parallel event in Tel Aviv. Banners, scarfs, and flags flew around in the hot wind as Knesset member Dov Khenin spoke, and as Sima Umbus stood to speak. Her words carried the strength of someone who had seen too many things. "I lost my husband Ibrahim, my brother Mustafa, and my cousin Ahmad to the bullets of the occupiers," she said. "This has been the fate of the religious Jew, Yehuda Waxman, who lost his son Nachshon. But I don't want to conclude that in order to reach the moment of truth, we must lose our beloved. Never! I call all those who still haven't lost their loved ones, to lift their heads to the sunshine so as not to lose their loved ones. Say yes to two states for two peoples: the Israeli people, and the Palestinian people."

Two days later, outside Tulkarem, one bus arrived and then another and another. When the buses stopped, around seven thousand Palestinians were sitting under the hot sun and a banner that read "Two Peoples, Two States, One Peace." At the head of the crowd, Fatah leader Jibril Rajoub read a message from President Mahmoud Abbas.

When it was over, Gadi and Souli embraced and felt something together, as if standing somehow before and inside history. This was the first time Palestinians had gathered officially, and in such large numbers, in support of a peace based on two states. Israelis had gathered to show their support for the same wish. Maybe this could push their leaders back into negotiations, convince them that peace was truly, unequivocally what their people wanted. There wasn't much media coverage of the events, but still they felt like prophets who'd summoned something momentous, even with Hamas holding roles in the unity government.

Souli couldn't remember, looking back, when he knew he would continue working with Gadi, when he realized that he'd found a partner, too. But something was created between them to make this happen. This thing between them was invisible and deep, impossible to break. They were linked now, married.

As with any true marriage, it was a complicated one, full of confusions. Like the night, several weeks after June 5, that Souli told Gadi he didn't believe in the two-state solution. He would accept it if it meant peace, but it was not what he dreamed of. He wanted a reality in which he, and other Palestinians, could live by the sea.

Though the trust that Gadi had felt days before was shaken, they kept moving.

In Combatants, Elik had grown tired and left for school in America, and Itamar had become the Israeli coordinator. Souli loved helping Itamar implement his vision for an infrastructure of regional groups: each with Israeli members in one city and Palestinian members in another. Like mirror towns. As more groups formed, Souli would meet Itamar in the little corner of Y Cafe in West Jerusalem, where Itamar would pass him a joint, laughing. In those moments, Souli couldn't believe that this man—that Chen, Avner, and many of his close Israeli partners—had once carried and fired a gun.

He felt he could never stay far from these men, but he'd known for some time: he needed space to think differently. In the coming months, after a year and some spent as Palestinian coordinator of Combatants for Peace, he would pass the role to his friend Osama. He'd keep talking with Gadi, gesturing wildly, dreaming of the next steps they'd take together.

But dreaming had become difficult in Hizma, his father's death a breaking. Souli no longer knew how to keep living there while continuing this work. When he and Gadi founded the People's Peace Fund to support activists with advice and financial support, with Gadi investing the initial funds, something shifted. The People's Peace Fund paid Souli a stipend, and though he received money from only a few of his projects, though he worked often as a volunteer, he had finally saved a bit of money.

He found a small apartment in Ramallah, his own place, with no one commenting on his failure to marry, or naming the *fadiha* (shame) his work was causing the family. The first time he entered his apartment alone, he walked over the carpeted living room, through the kitchen, to the small cement balcony. He smoked a cigarette next to the washing machine, inhaling deeper than usual and looking out at the sky as it purpled. It was perfect then, this distance from home. For some time, he would cling to it.

The distance he made was a place with many stories in it, stories that came and went in the years that followed, as Souli and Gadi began a new project.

Like others before, it was a project born in cafés. One, near Jerusalem's Biblical Zoo, where animals of the biblical past ran about in the present. Another café, in a slightly otherworldly desert junction of the Palestinian West Bank, between Jericho and the Dead Sea, beside the settlement of Almog, in a restaurant whose sign spelled out, between big Coca-Cola bottles, "The Last Chance."

There, at various tables, Souli and Gadi sat with Dudu, an Israeli Jew of Iraqi descent and a relative of their friend Gershon Baskin.

Dudu, they learned, wanted to meet Palestinians who'd been wounded in the conflict, like him. And he was right-leaning on the political spectrum, quite different from the Israelis who usually arrived to dialogue. When they met for the first time, at a tiny table pushed against a wall, Souli understood. Dudu's story was very different from those of most Israelis in Combatants for Peace.

In 1951, his parents had escaped Iraq for Israel: a new country in an old place they'd always known as holy. The government of Iraq didn't allow them to bring anything. So, leaving with nothing, dreaming of a return to their homeland, they imagined a warm welcome. Instead, they found themselves in a refugee camp. With other Jewish arrivals to this brand-new state, many from Arabic-speaking countries, Dudu's parents crowded together in tents with their fellow *olim chadashim*. They found they couldn't breathe.

One day, soon after Dudu was born, his parents woke up and walked to the sea. They didn't have enough to eat, and it wasn't clear what would happen to them. Their feet were already wet when Dudu's mother turned to his father. "What about the baby?" she asked. His response, whatever it was, didn't satisfy her, so they stopped walking into the water; they turned back toward land.

Dudu's father lived to raise his children; he occasionally saved up to buy a mango, like the ones that were everywhere in Baghdad. The fruit was expensive here, and he didn't have the money, but he wanted his children to know its taste. He always cut the single fruit into small pieces so each child could get one bite.

Dudu had fought in the Yom Kippur War, served for many years as an officer in Israeli jails, watching over Palestinian prisoners. He didn't trust them when he arrived, and he didn't trust them when he left, decades later. Like everyone around him, he attended too many funerals for young Israelis during the second intifada. And after his wife's nephew was killed, something shifted. He decided to meet Palestinians, to search for some alternative way out of the mess—something like peace. But he didn't see where he and his friends fit.

It seemed that most Israeli participants in dialogue were like the refuseniks from Combatants for Peace. He disliked the air of apology about them; he thought they were erasing their identities, making themselves small, meeting Palestinians from a place of weakness rather than strength. He didn't want to cut any part of himself out for peace. He didn't think it would work, anyway.

When Dudu stopped speaking that first day, Gadi and Souli looked at one another. With this new player, they wondered if they could create something different, connect with the mainstreams of both societies in a way Combatants for Peace never could. They wondered if this kind of connection, if it grew big enough, might generate mutual understanding on a wider level, even allow their leaders to reach a peace agreement.

That first day, Gadi stayed quiet and watched as Dudu and Souli—a former prison officer and ex-prisoner—kept talking. The atmosphere at the little table was tense, but somehow they spoke as equals, talked about creating a group for many people wounded in the conflict from both sides. It was not a surprise, when they ultimately launched the dialogue project Wounded Crossing Borders, how difficult it was. To create something between Dudu's friends—mostly Israeli Mizrahim, mostly right-wingers—and Palestinians who had to worry about the accusations of *tatbi'a* (normalization) that would likely come.

But Souli loved the Palestinians he recruited: Abu Muhammad, who'd been a prisoner in the Hebron jail when Dudu was a prison officer, who often brought the sweet grapes of al-Khalil to their meetings. Nasrin, who as a teenager had fetched a knife from her kitchen. She took that knife to a checkpoint and held it in front of her, facing the soldiers. They told her to stop, to drop her weapon. She refused and kept holding the knife before her until the soldiers fired; she waited for the sky to open for her, but it didn't. Her mother would tell Gadi later about how Nasrin ended up in an Israeli hospital, how the Jewish doctors saved her life. How she would always be grateful to them.

And he recruited Ahmed Helou, whose story had stayed with Souli when they met a short time before. Ahmed was born in Jericho to a family of refugees originally from Gaza. His parents were born in Bi'r al-Sab'/Be'er Sheva, and displaced to Jericho in 1948. As a child, he'd heard the stories of his family walking along the roads during that war, and again in '67, looking for safety. About all the bodies they found on the way, lying about the ground.

Looking for a place to resist occupation, Ahmed had become involved with Hamas through his local mosque, began throwing stones with them, painting notices of protests and strikes on the walls during the intifada. He went to jail for seven months, where he became a negotiator for Hamas, helping to manage conflicts that arose between Hamas and Fatah prisoners.

One day, he got word that young Hamas prisoners had cursed at a Fatah leader. He brought them together, thinking the youth would apologize. But just before the meeting, Hamas leadership notified him that never, under any circumstances, would a Hamas prisoner apologize to a Fatah prisoner. Whatever part of him believed in Hamas broke then. He didn't say it out loud, but he wondered, "What? Are we God? Are we so sure we never make mistakes?"

When he left jail, he disconnected from Hamas and founded an organization that worked with the Palestine Red Crescent in Jericho. Volunteering with their ambulance service one day, he heard that people were out in the street, protesting and throwing stones beside a nearby settlement. He headed in that direction, in case help was needed. It was.

Looking out at the settlement fence that day, he saw a man fall beside the wire. No one moved, and so Ahmed moved. He ran until he reached the fence, then he looked down and saw the face of his friend Wahid, a law student. He lifted him up and began to run toward the ambulance. He started running but realized he'd stopped; he'd fallen to the ground. He tried to get up, couldn't, and didn't understand why. He heard people crying, felt hands lifting him from the ground. There was a numbness taking over his back. He understood, for a moment, before everything went black.

He awoke from a coma after three days to the face of a doctor, staring at him as at a miracle. The bullet was still in Ahmed's neck, and it would stay there. But he was alive.

Over many years, the two sides of Wounded Crossing Borders met, telling stories like these. Both the Palestinian and Israeli members had been wounded in the conflict and now they traveled together: to Bosnia, where they stood in cemeteries, and to Switzerland, where they played in the snow. Through all of it, they talked and talked. They believed each other and didn't.

Later, Souli would remember how unfamiliar the Israelis seemed to him then. He would often think back to certain stories, especially the words of Israeli participant Shlomo Zagman. He'd moved to a city in Israel only a few years before, but he had lived most of his life in the settlement of Alon Shvut. He loved the West Bank, felt deeply connected to its Jewish religious history. Despite this love for his home, he gave it up; he didn't want to continue living under the occupation's sponsorship.

Souli was interested in Shlomo, the way he spoke about crossing the red lines he grew up with, about the pain that came with understanding things in a new way. But sometimes his words didn't go down smoothly. Like when Shlomo spoke about how he didn't see peace coming anytime soon, not when Palestinians didn't recognize his right to be here, didn't acknowledge his right to have a home at all.

It seemed like such a strange idea. Palestinians were the ones under occupation; Palestinians were the ones who had died in the greatest numbers throughout this conflict. Why ask for recognition of your connection to this place, Souli wondered, when you were denying another people's right to move and live?

And Souli wasn't quite sure what he thought about Jewish connection to this place. Of course, Palestinian Jews had always lived here. But to say that all Jews—from Europe, from North Africa, from other Arabic-speaking countries—belonged here felt impossible. To say this, it seemed, would be to forgive everything: the Nakba, and all the pain and loss Palestinians had experienced over this long century. *I can't do it*, he thought. *I won't.*

CHAPTER 21

If I Forget

Over the next years, it wasn't any particular event that mattered to Souli, but something rearranging itself in him, a thread winding and unwinding, and winding again. These shifts were confrontations with the unfamiliar, like when the Israelis in Wounded Crossing Borders spoke of things like the Farhud—the massacre of Baghdadi Jews in 1941, on the Jewish holiday of Shavuot.

It was difficult to take the stories of these Israelis in, especially when they seemed constructed as weapons to challenge Palestinian narratives. Listening to them, Souli often felt a nearly uncontainable anger rising—though he could usually cover it with jokes. The day they watched *The Forgotten Refugees*, though, jokes felt impossible. The documentary told the stories of hundreds of thousands of Middle Eastern and North African Jews who were expelled or fled their homes in Arab countries after the founding of Israel. It shared how deepening discrimination and anti-Jewish violence caused so many Jews to leave their countries. How they found the home they needed in the Jewish state.

Watching the movie, Souli could barely sit still. It left so many things out, how Israel advocated for the mass exodus of Jews from Arab and Muslim lands. How, as those hundreds of thousands of Jews were arriving, Israel was preventing the same number of Palestinian refugees from returning home.

When the film finally ended, Souli felt for his cigarettes and eyed the door as Huda Abuarquob, a Palestinian dialogue activist, began to speak. Gadi had invited her to facilitate the conversation, and it was a difficult one.

Soon after the lights came on, Dudu echoed the words of the film's interviewees. "Palestinians think they are the only ones who lost their homes!" Souli looked around the room and saw other Israeli members of Wounded nodding. Their families had come from Lebanon, Iraq, Yemen, Oman, Egypt, and Morocco. Many of them had traumatic stories of rupture and escape.

"Plus, the Arab leaders *told* the Palestinians to leave in '48," another Israeli Mizrahi participant said. "They left on their own. Our parents were forced out."

Souli shook his head. "There's no comparing! These refugees from Iraq and Syria—the Zionist movement brought them here on purpose, to displace Palestinians. They convinced them to leave the places they came from!"

He was about to leave, cigarette between his fingers, when Huda spoke. "Some left on their own and some were forced to leave," she said. "It doesn't matter the reason. Every refugee is a refugee."

Sulaiman had to hear those words many times before they felt really true. Before he found himself thinking one day: *Khalas, it happened. All of it, both the Nakba and the Jewish refugees from Arab countries.* But Huda's words were maybe circling there, hidden in him, as a soldier waved him over one day. Right near the settlement of Modi'in Ilit, his taxi stopped, and the soldier's white face appeared. In Russian-accented Hebrew, unsmiling, he ordered Souli to step out of the car. He took Souli's ID, walked away, and didn't come back for a long time.

When the soldier returned, he told Souli they were still checking his permit, that he'd have to wait. And then, as if someone, somewhere, had cut a string holding him back, Souli spoke, his voice shaking, and loud.

"Why are you checking me? I've been standing here watching Jewish settlers go by—some of them don't even speak Hebrew—without being checked. This is what apartheid looks like. You are occupiers, colonizers. You are not even from here. You come here and stop us, Indigenous people? You are not Israeli even; you are Russian!"

The soldier froze, his face transformed completely, a total red, as he yelled at Souli. "I'M. NOT. RUSSIAN. I'm from Chechnya. Russians are the occupiers."

The young soldier was breathing heavily as Souli looked, stunned, at his flushed face. Another string cut, and he began to laugh. "I'm sorry; I didn't know." When he spoke again, his voice was softer. "I didn't mean to assume you were Russian. But maybe as a Chechen, you can understand me a bit, what I'm saying—what it's like for someone to come from outside. To come and tell you what to do with your own land."

That day at the checkpoint, Souli was asking for many things. Some of them were concrete: the ability to move freely, to determine the elements of his own life, to be safe from harm. But at least one request pointed to something invisible. He wanted that soldier to see him, to know that he was here, and belonged here. To offer him recognition.

The soldier, he thought later, was maybe asking for something similar. Souli kept wondering about recognition: why people asked for it, and what offering it could do. It did seem to hold some magic, working as a chemical reaction—introducing an element that changed the substances you started with, causing everything to entirely rearrange.

Souli had watched it happen in Gadi. When Gadi met a Palestinian who offered recognition of his family's experience, of his grandparents' desire to return home, something softened in him. When he didn't have so much to defend, he appeared more ready to work for peace, for both Palestinian and Israeli self-determination.

Souli found himself wanting to practice it more, this art of offering recognition. He sensed how the Israeli need for recognition marked an opportunity. Because when a person—or people— needed something from you, it gave you power. Palestinians could choose to extend recognition to Israelis, or withhold it.

But the precious thing Israelis needed most, he understood, was recognition of their connection to this place. And it was unclear what it would mean to offer this. To believe in Jewish connection, it seemed, would mean recognizing Zionism, saying it was okay somehow. Though he knew that Palestinians had made grave mistakes, it was Zionism that initiated everything. Zionism, with its dreams of a modern nation-state built from a Jewish majority.

He listened, over years, as Gadi spoke about Zionism, all this moving through him. There were no sharp reversals, just a series of sometimes jarring questions. One question appeared while they were on a flight somewhere, and Gadi said something that felt new. "If I learn that Zionism is a colonialist movement," he said, "I'll leave."

It struck Souli the way true things do, reminded him of something, a phrase he'd heard at an Israeli friend's wedding. Standing there during the ceremony, he'd heard the rabbi recite Psalm 137. He recognized it from a book of Jewish history he read in jail. The psalm contained just a few words that leapt out:

"If I forget Jerusalem, may my right hand forget its skill."

In jail, he'd learned that Zionists invented Jewish connection to this land as a way to bring Jews here, to colonize his home. In jail, the psalm had arisen like a question. At the wedding, it felt like an echo. Both times, he'd turned away.

But now with Gadi, many miles above any land, the words came through very loud. Their reverberation stayed with Souli long after the plane landed. He kept thinking about this old line, used by Jewish writers even under Islamic rule in Andalusia. It gave him the idea, one that felt harder to turn from now, that Jewish connection to his land was real. That it was not invented by Theodor Herzl.

The thought troubled him, but in some ways, he thought, it didn't contradict what he'd learned. The issue wasn't Jewish history; it was Jewish peoplehood. Growing up, he learned that Zionism had justified everything with the notion that Jews were not just a religious group. They were a distinct people. Armed with this notion, Israel's founders had caused hundreds of thousands of Palestinians to lose their homes in 1948, to lose much more since. That's why, in jail, Sulaiman's teachers had stressed that Judaism is a religion, only. Nothing else.

As he heard Israelis speak about Jewish peoplehood more and more, he kept hitting against their words like a wall. Many of the

Jews he'd met were not religious. Still, he couldn't see what connected Dudu and the American Jews he'd met in California, other than religion. They had no single race or culture. And what was a people without those things? When he thought of the people he belonged to, it was clear. He was Palestinian, simply.

Something shifted again after another flight with Gadi, this time headed to an Amsterdam cultural center, where people saw Souli and Gadi speak as brothers. Another day on that trip,[1] Souli wandered alone through the cobblestoned streets, dodging bicycles. He stopped in front of the Anne Frank House, went in as if without thinking, and found himself there, alone on the creaky floorboards of the attic where Anne Frank had once kept a diary.

He stayed for hours, standing for the longest time in front of a quote, printed on cloth or paper and hung on the wooden wall. It was something Anne Frank had written about how Jews would never really belong to another nation—English, German, not any of them. She had not been religious, but she'd been a Jew and died for it, in a nation that rejected her.

Staring at the quote, smelling the dust, and reading Anne Frank's words, he thought—for the first time—that the idea of Jewish peoplehood might make some sense. It didn't justify what had happened to Palestinians, but he understood it somehow. In the old attic, he stayed there thinking, losing all sense of time.

When he was finally ready to leave the museum, he stopped to sign the electronic guest book. All visitors were invited to write their name, the date of their visit, their age, where they came from, and any words they wanted to share in the historic attic. He logged the date, his name, his age. But looking through the list of countries in the drop-down menu, he stopped. He didn't know which to pick.

There was no option to select Palestine—not even the "Occupied Territories" or the "West Bank." The only choice was Israel.

The changing questions of this time were painful. Sometimes they made Souli want to run, and sometimes he did.

In the last days of 2008, as Israel launched a war in Gaza—stating its intent to target Hamas infrastructure and respond to the organization's rocket attacks—Souli had kept his distance. During those endless days, he went outside only briefly, to do a television interview with Yonatan in the hills of al-Tur in East Jerusalem. When some Palestinian boys heard them speaking Hebrew, they pointed their chests at Souli; they raised their voices.

"Don't do this," they said, "don't tell them there's no war, that everything is fine and we're living peacefully together."

Souli smiled at them, though he felt his heart speeding. It was a dangerous situation, and his body knew it as he called each boy *habibi*, trying to calm them down. He told them Yonatan was a re-fusenik, that they were actually speaking against the war. The boys grew quiet and stepped away, but for a moment, Souli felt it could have gone another way. He let out a long breath. All he wanted then was to hide in his apartment, and that's what he did.

In Bosnia, he'd fallen in love with a woman who insisted on carrying his suitcase. So during that terrible war, which would end with more than 10 Israeli and nearly 1,400 Palestinian deaths, he stayed inside with his Bosnian love when she came to visit. In the mornings, he went out to buy falafel and hummus. He spent the rest of the winter days inside with her, smoking on the balcony, listening to love songs, and trying not to watch the news.

It was one time among many that he would try to escape, to find a little space, and it left Gadi feeling very alone.

Years later, one day when Gadi felt he couldn't stand another disappearance, he turned to his friend. "I feel like I've lost my part-ner," he said.

He told Souli, had been telling him for some time, that Wounded Crossing Borders wasn't really working. Though there'd been suc-cesses over the past three and a half years, it was a heartbreak. The Israelis and many of the Palestinians seemed unchanged—at least not transformed into activists, as he'd hoped. He left to attend a peace camp in the US and didn't come back for years. Wounded Crossing Borders wouldn't last much longer.

In Gadi's absence, Souli looked back and saw how much change had actually occurred, at least in him. After years in Wounded Crossing Borders, he found he had more space for certain stories. And after years with Gadi, he'd become more accustomed to his friend's version of things. They had listened to each other over so many hours. It felt impossible to name all the ways they had each been changed. But he knew that Gadi's words no longer angered him as they once had. Now, when he met people from the Palestinian mainstream, he heard his friend's voice. Gadi had created a problem for him in this.

Souli knew others might look at this dynamic and see the subtle and not-so-subtle power dynamics of a colonial story. But that wasn't right. They existed now in each other. And so he looked at this dynamic and called it love: the thing that happens when someone gets in your head and creates problems, changing your mind forever.

CHAPTER 22

If I Remember

Over the next few years, Souli felt as a person falling, slowly and from a great height. Everything with his Bosnian love was over. And he suddenly found himself with little to hold himself up, to survive with.

In this strange suspended space, he kept changing.

Though he rarely visited Hizma, he found himself thinking often about its hills. He imagined walking through them the way he used to, easily, before Pisgat Ze'ev, before the wall started carving everything away.

He thought about his grandfather who, drawing on the wisdom of their culture and all their ancestors, used to say that land doesn't belong to people, that it's the other way around. About his father who'd died when Ta'mira became impossible to reach.

But he also found himself wondering more and more about the history of the place where his family had always lived, as far back as anyone could remember. It was a place where history stayed very close. Even when he was little, he'd felt this. You didn't have to dig very far, or at all, to find it. His cousins were always showing him things they'd discovered: old, old things, from Canaanite times, Jewish times, Roman times, Islamic times. The ancient grape press some person, now long gone, had once used to make wine. Rusty swords and coins that his cousins would sell to tourists in al-Quds.

As he'd listened to the stories of people like Gadi and Shlomo, Israeli Jews who spoke passionately about ancient Jewish history, he began looking more closely at the names of things near his village. Like the two caves called the *yehudiat* (Jewish women). Like the old graveyard, just to the north, called Qubur Bani Isra'il (Graves of the Sons of Israel).

That graveyard was where the oldest ghosts lived, not far from Najla's cave where he and Asif and Sadiq used to dream of revolution and girls. He thought about the ancient cemetery's name, its reference to Jewish history. He started reading about it on the internet in Hebrew, English, and Arabic.

Though one archaeologist had found no conclusive evidence, Souli learned that others believed present-day Hizma lay on the site of Azmaveth, a biblical Israelite town in territory once home to the tribe of Benjamin.

It felt dangerous to think about. That was why no one in Hizma talked much about what came up from the ground. Of course people knew there was Jewish history here. Palestinian culture included many traditions—Canaanite, Philistine, Christian, Muslim, and Jewish—among many others. The danger came because archaeology was no neutral instrument; it had been a powerful tool for displacement. Not far from Hizma, within the Palestinian village of Silwan, foreign archeologists had long been excavating a site they believed was the City of David. Israel picked up the project in 1978, and though some archaeologists would question whether the site was ever in fact the City of David, the digging continued.

Now the City of David National Park was a tourist destination, managed by the settler-run Elad Foundation—a group famous for removing Palestinians from their houses and replacing them with Jewish settlers. The people in Silwan were facing more evictions and home demolitions, all making space for Israel's continuous archaeological projects. A sort of digging that seemed to say the Jewish dead mattered more than the Palestinian living.

Because of their deep closeness to their land, Souli's family lived inside this danger, the sense that their place was being taken. Disappearing around them, step by step. He learned that years prior, not long before the founding of Pisgat Ze'ev, the Archaeological Survey of Israel had sponsored a dig in Hizma. Ta'mira was already lost. If Israelis kept thinking of his village as an archaeological site, Souli thought, his family would eventually have no home left.

For some time, this sense of danger kept Souli from saying certain things aloud. But a belief was forming in him then, even if it felt impossible to speak. *Some Jews*, he thought one day, *have a huge historical, religious, spiritual motivation to live here. This is a deep thing. It's hard for me to say I respect them. But I want to understand it. It's not because of the Holocaust the Jews are here. There is a fucking story here.*

As these sentences took shape in him like a shock, he thought of Gadi and Shlomo, how much they wanted Palestinians to recognize Jewish historical connection to this land. While Souli heard Palestinians acknowledge this, it was usually within the context of Palestinian identity itself. Jewish history here belonged to Palestinians, including Palestinian Jews, but had little to do with Jews from other places.

Many Israelis, though, were looking for a different kind of recognition, and Souli saw how offering it could calm them, gain their trust, open something, ease their fear that Palestinians wanted them to disappear. It could allow Israelis to change, commit further to ending the occupation. To fight beside Palestinians, for a freedom they could share.

But recognition as strategy was different than this, what Souli was considering as he dreamed about Hizma's hills. Offering recognition of Jewish connection in order to transform your Israeli partners was one thing. It was different to believe it—to feel that belief in your body. To hold it while knowing Jewish history had been used, was still being used, as a weapon against your people, your family.

He'd refused the thought of it, but found he believed it now: Jewish connection to this place was natural, not invented. Not every Jew around the world felt it, of course, but he understood why many did. The more he thought about Psalm 137, the longing it held, the more it made him think of the Abu Arab songs he'd loved growing up. Both were about *hanin*, yearning, dreaming for a way home. Refusing to forget.

------•------

All of this led Souli to a meeting he'd been avoiding. Some time
before, a friend suggested he sit down with Yehuda HaKohen, and
he'd made excuses. Yehuda lived on a mountain just past Beit El,
the Jewish settlement not far from Ramallah, not far from the busy
Civil Administration office that determined whether or not Souli's
mother, and many other Palestinians, could receive a travel permit.

Souli had met settlers before—the children of Neve Ya'aqub
who used to play soccer in the grove near Hizma's center; a few
through Wounded Crossing Borders. With his brother and with
Gadi, he'd stopped to help settlers stalled by the side of the road. But
this felt different, this sitting down with someone alone.

Somehow he was ready as he listened to Yehuda explain that he
was a *mitnachel*. The usual English translation for *mitnachel* was "settler," but Yehuda objected to the English term's tones of colonialism. The word in Hebrew made more sense to him; it came from
the word *nachala*, which meant tribal inheritance, and pointed to a
deep connection to the land. He believed that Jews were indigenous
to this land, but after long histories of exile and persecution, had experienced colonization and lost the deepest aspects of their identity.
For him, this loss explained the motives of Israelis who were willing
to give up land. And it also explained the military occupation: a result of the Israeli need to imitate European and American systems of
control. "Israel's military occupation of the West Bank undermines
the Jewish people's belonging to Judea and Samaria," he would tell
Souli later. "The Jews in Judea are not the Americans in Afghani-
stan. The problem is that we sometimes act like we are."

Yehuda argued that the army's actions—the checkpoints, the
wall, restrictions on freedom of movement—were expressions of a
Jewish identity crisis. But to surrender portions of *Eretz Yisrael*, he
told Souli, would be a symptom of that same crisis. That's why he
would never leave his home in the West Bank, would never support
a two-state solution. And he saw no contradiction in this. If Jews
came home to themselves—understanding that they belonged here,
and were not occupiers—he could one day live in his home beside
Palestinians living safely and freely in theirs.

Souli found he liked Yehuda a great deal. Before they parted that first time, Souli glanced down at the gun glinting at Yehuda's hip. "Oh, *habibi?*" he smiled. "Next time, maybe leave the gun at home!" Their friendship would continue, through both alignments and disagreements, and that first meeting was the last time Souli saw Yehuda with a gun.

This unusual encounter signaled an emerging process for Souli: dreaming ahead, moving forward, exploring new possibilities. But he also felt stuck, frightened, unsure where to find his place within all the ways he'd changed, in this work, in love. He kept dreaming of escape, and after years without a visa, his application came through. He packed a bag and ran for Canada, where he stayed wandering for months.

He thought often of Gadi: his friend out there somewhere in the world, traveling all around South and North America. Though they hadn't spoken for some time, Souli heard from mutual friends that Gadi was thinking about healing trauma—personal and collective. He was diving in headfirst, with the belief that he would find answers there. It was the opposite of what Souli had always done, and seemed like almost a foolish, privileged thing: to enter a place of such danger by choice.

Souli reached out to Gadi after this long silence, and Gadi came to Vancouver for a healing workshop with a facilitator named Little Woo. At Gadi's invitation, Souli agreed to join, unsure what he would find, what he was looking for.

At the workshop, he found himself again in foreign territory: in the space of what Little Woo called "group soul work." He listened to her speak about how they could look inward to find their true purpose, express the beauty and meaning that belonged to them, that they belonged to. There was a safe distance for him, until Little Woo asked each participant to find a place alone in that room full of pillows, in the dark.

The course had focused on beauty and light, but for this exercise, Little Woo spoke briefly of fear. She told a story about a time when she was a child, locked in a dark room, frightened. About the little crack of light she saw under the doorway. Little Woo invited the participants, from their corners in the dark, to understand this

fear that can arrive, to practice knowing how there is always at least
a crack for the light to come through.

In Souli's corner of the living room, he closed his eyes and the
dark wasn't dark. Red and green and gold shapes moved across his
field of vision. He waited, unsure what for. And then, something
happened, a feeling in his stomach, like when you wake from a
dream in the middle of the night with the sensation of falling.

He wasn't in the room filled with pillows anymore. His hands
were tied behind his back, a chair beneath him forcing his body into
strange, unbearable shapes. A hood over his head, making it impossible to breathe. He was in the Ramallah jail, in those first days of
interrogation.

He forgot to look for the crack of light, and couldn't stay with it:
the shock, the sudden transport. He opened his eyes and saw where
he was. He whispered to himself: *You are here, you are safe.* But in the
days that followed, the feeling of danger didn't leave him.

It was clear: this was why many Palestinians chose not to talk
about trauma. Once you opened these memories, they wouldn't
close again. Memories was the wrong word, anyway. What he was
experiencing now were visitations, or nightmares. He'd survived by
forgetting, and now he couldn't. For a moment, it seemed his only
path, his only escape, was to stay away from home.

During one of those endless days in which the visions refused to
leave him—that freezing room, his knees buckling, a strike to the
head—he told Gadi, "I don't want to go back."

He was searching and hoping for distance from so many things:
those early traumas, occupation, the obligations of family and traditional culture, fear that he could not continue safely in his work, that
some Palestinians would continue to critique him, even harm him.

Searching and hoping for distance, he applied for an extended visa,
but he wasn't successful. Instead of running, he came home to Ramallah, where he lay on a mattress on his living room floor. He closed
his eyes and remembered words Little Woo had used, sentences about
reconnecting with your dreams, with your ancestors. Understanding
you are part of a line, and at the same time, could always begin again.
Through the open window, to the sounds of boys shouting and playing outside, he fell asleep and didn't wake for a long time.

When he opened his eyes, there was light outside, and something felt clean. Little Woo's words stayed with him that morning as he stood up, made coffee, smoked on the balcony looking out at all the cement growing around him, listening to the early sounds of birds. That morning, he knew: something was pointing him toward Combatants for Peace, pulling him back, though it wasn't entirely clear what he was being pulled back to. But he thought it might have to do with the fact that he'd started close to home, gone far away somehow, and was now trying to return. Attempting to find something in the middle—a place made of home, but changed somehow, like him. But he knew the middle was a very difficult place to find. It's rarely marked on maps, you have to follow invisible signs to get there, and it's nearly impossible to know when you've arrived.

PART FIVE

CHAPTER 23

Balloons

Before long, Souli did rejoin Combatants for Peace, first doing some lectures and fundraising, and eventually becoming Palestinian codirector. He was still glad he'd left, found a little freedom, new perspectives and experiences he could bring to this joint Palestinian-Israeli project that practiced both dialogue *and* direct action against the occupation. A movement built around an honest attempt at equal partnership—an attempt that could serve as a map for the future. As a way to create a new narrative, piece by piece.

That spring, with the arrival of Yom HaZikaron, he knew he was in the right place. The holiday, which commemorated Jewish losses in war, was central in Israel. Every year, on that day around dusk, a siren would fill everything. Cars would pull to the side of the road and people would step out, standing with their arms straight against their bodies, remembering all the people they'd lost—in wars, in bombings, and before Israel existed. They stood and kept standing, waiting for the sound to fade away.

In the early days of the movement, they'd started holding an Alternative Memorial Day ceremony, mourning Palestinian and Israeli losses together. The idea had come from Israeli activist Buma Inbar, who'd lost his son in Lebanon, and a small number of other bereaved parents. The first ceremony began in a black box theater in Tel Aviv, a big idea unfolding with just a small audience sitting before the stage. So when Souli arrived at this year's ceremony, he thought his heart might stop in his chest. Thousands of people filled the huge Tel Aviv auditorium. He listened as Palestinian and Israeli members of Combatants for Peace and the Parents Circle–Families Forum spoke of people they had lost in the conflict: brothers, sisters, parents, children. They shared the stage. They spoke of a different, shared future. And maybe, Souli thought, looking around, that future was already here in certain ways.

It wasn't perfect; there were far more Israelis in the audience than Palestinians. The ceremony was in Tel Aviv; few Palestinians outside Israel could get permits. But Palestinian members organized watching parties in the West Bank and Gaza, and the Israelis who entered that wide room hardly ever returned to the normal Yom HaZikaron spaces. They stayed in an alternative space, in a third narrative that didn't speak for just one side. A narrative that showed the truth: both peoples were caught in this conflict, and they would have to find a way out together.

Still, the idea of Alternative Memorial Day wasn't only to bring people to the ceremony this one night, to speak in Hebrew and Arabic together to show solidarity. That was important, but Combatants for Peace wanted to take it further. To transform passive observers into activists. And Souli felt it happening. After the ceremony, he watched as more people joined the work of the movement's regional groups.

In addition to house meetings and storytelling workshops, each group planned and performed their own direct actions. Some stood by Palestinian farmers who were facing harassment from settlers and the army. Others held protests at checkpoints. Souli's favorite actions were always those that folded in some element of dialogue. Like the time the theater group gathered in front of a checkpoint outside Tulkarem and performed that checkpoint back to itself, inviting the soldiers to look hard into the mirror that theater held up. One soldier had looked and seen. He later contacted the movement, joined, and refused further service in the West Bank and Gaza.

Souli thought about this man again and again. Maybe he'd been among the soldiers who sometimes threw tear gas at Palestinian movement members. Maybe he'd heard the words Chen Alon sometimes spoke into the loudspeaker: "Take off your uniforms, and join us."

He began pushing the movement to do more of this—to deeply embed dialogue principles in every action. To work toward an activism that always functioned as invitation rather than accusation. And Souli knew that to be successful, invitations required recognition. This realization was linked to the notion that had taken clearer shape in him over the past years. The idea he now began speaking aloud in his lectures: "Our two peoples belong to the same place. I believe it's important to start there. I don't see another way."

In Combatants for Peace, Souli felt he'd found one of the best frames that existed for building a just future, but not everyone agreed.

At some Combatants actions, right-wing Israeli counter-protesters waved angry flags. At Alternative Memorial Day every year, a group of protesters gathered outside shouting "Arab lover" and "traitor" at the Israelis walking in. The faces of some protesters turned red. Sometimes they spit; sometimes they threw stones and urine.

These attacks from the Right were focused on Souli's Israeli partners, but he faced his own set of challenges. The charges of normalization that came from the Left and from Palestinian society were mostly manageable, but there was a danger in them, a fear that he could go too far, or draw the attention of someone who could cause him real harm. And this critique didn't just belong to Palestinian society or international circles. Even some of Combatants' Israeli founders had left the movement, believing its work came too close to normalizing the occupation.

In one interview Yonatan, a founding member, shared his thoughts on Combatants for Peace years after its launch. "It was a very important thing for us, for the Palestinians and for the Israelis. But later, nevertheless, I realized that the framework was problematic because it's not a conflict of equal parties. It's not that you have two countries fighting each other. It's a colonial struggle—colonizer and colonized. So there is a conceptual problem when you come to create something that is based on equal power balance, which it's totally not."

Yonatan still believed in dialogue as a tool of transformation. But he felt it had to include an approach of total solidarity with the occupied side. This meant, among other things, support for the Boycott, Divestment, and Sanctions (BDS) movement—on which Combatants for Peace did not take a position. And when Yonatan looked at the movement's website, he found an absence calling out. To join this movement, Israelis had to refuse to serve as soldiers in the West Bank and Gaza. But on the movement's website, Yonatan looked and looked for the word *refuse*. It was nowhere.

Souli knew Yonatan was right; there could be no equality between the movement's two sides given the external reality of occupation. As for BDS, Combatants for Peace did support the boycott of settlement products, and some Combatants activists supported BDS as individuals. While Souli spoke about the legitimacy of BDS as a nonviolent method of resistance, it was not the method he chose for himself. He didn't see how they could reach new Israelis if their language was too strong, and he wanted to welcome as many people as possible into the movement, to facilitate wider and wider circles of change.

Because there were so many stories of transformation that came through meeting, when you allowed it to occur. There was the soldier who'd removed his uniform and refused to serve any longer in the West Bank, the hundreds of Jews who'd approached Souli after lectures to say he'd changed their minds. Who'd appeared later, at Combatants for Peace actions in the West Bank, eager to stand in front of soldiers, singing freedom songs.

For Souli, this movement was the best place to practice values of equal partnership—even if such a thing couldn't yet be reached. The outside reality was, of course, always seeping in; the two sides came from different positions, disparate realities. The majority of Israelis in the movement came from privilege. They were largely Ashkenazi Jews from north Tel Aviv and the kibbutzim. The Palestinian members were mostly from smaller villages, from refugee camps. Not privileged Ramallah people. He tried to stand between these realities somehow, to translate one for the other, noticing that Avner—who spoke Arabic and always seemed to understand what ran beneath a conversation—did the same.

But translation could only bridge so much of the divide, and there was no doubt: all Palestinians in the group faced greater risk than their Israeli partners. When they went to demonstrations, the Israelis could have problems, but mostly soft ones. The Palestinians could lose so much facing the Israeli army: their remaining freedom of movement, their life. This was a microcosm of the wider reality in which Israel held more outward power. And because of this, many of Souli's Israeli partners, even those committed to fighting the occupation beside Palestinians, arrived with what he called a "colonial mindset." When Souli saw this in his friends, he tried to fight it in his own particular way. He gave it a name.

It happened sometimes with his good friend Eyal. Souli loved Eyal's care for people, his incredible commitment to the movement. And he also found himself offering his friend occasional reminders. As he did one night, after a workshop in Bayt Jala, when a group of Palestinian participants drove into the dark to buy cookies in Bethlehem. Eyal stayed behind, giving a long speech about strategy. He referenced Bayt Sahur's tax refusal during the first intifada, spoke about how successful nonviolence strategically sought out unjust law in order to break it. How it forced violence in the system to reveal itself more clearly.

Eyal mentioned a town where the army was currently blocking a road and said Combatants should go there to teach the villagers nonviolent resistance. Souli made a dismissive noise. "*Shwayya* with the teaching stuff, Eyal," he said, simultaneously amused and annoyed. "Your Ashkenazi good intentions are coming out!"[1]

Still, none of this bothered him as much as the "victimhood mindset" he perceived among some of the Palestinians—another product of the outside reality. Many Palestinians inside the movement and out thought the change had to come from the Israelis. Because they had the power. With the Palestinian experience of colonialism and occupation, it was deeply complicated to criticize their own side, even here in Souli's political home. While Souli understood, he felt this aversion to self-critique wasn't just about occupation. It was also about culture, one that condemned airing out the dirty laundry.

But some days, he felt occupation had become an excuse for everything: for competing over leadership positions, for failing to create a democratic atmosphere, for not lifting up the voices of women.

They were trying to remedy some of these things; they had formed a women's group to address the male-dominated nature of the movement. There was resistance to this work on all sides, but when he encountered it among Palestinians, it angered him more than he could handle.

He knew he was not perfect in this; he'd had relationships with women in activist circles, been asked to consider the power he held and how he used it. But he wanted to change; he didn't want the occupation to serve as his excuse.

An idea he'd encountered in jail kept arising in him: the notion that "peace starts with me." He'd read about it and it took years to truly believe it, because it seemed so difficult at first to find the power he held. He saw the walls, the guards, the army outside, and he felt, *They are the strong ones.* This is why the hunger strikes were so sacred; they had showed him his strength.

Now, he carried this knowledge around, speaking it in all his lectures. He'd point to his chest, saying, "Now I believe change has to happen in here." And he'd point to different corners of the conference rooms and restaurants and parks and homes where he spoke, saying: "And there and there and there and there."

This belief in self-transformation was part of a difference in him, one that showed itself often. It appeared in the way he maintained hope and lightness during impossibly difficult times. In 2014, during the next war on Gaza, when over 2,200 Palestinians died—more than half of whom were civilians—along with close to seventy Israelis (including several civilians). And when his friend Ahmed Helou lost fifteen members of his extended family, thirteen of them civilians, eleven of them from the same immediate family.

Souli somehow held hope during all this. When in the 2015 election for Israeli prime minister, after promising more settlements, vowing that he'd never allow the establishment of a Palestinian state, and warning that "the Arabs" would be voting "in droves," Benjamin Netanyahu won again.

The difference in Souli showed itself again some months later, when someone proposed the idea for the Freedom March. Every month, Combatants for Peace would bring Palestinians and Israelis to walk beside the separation wall on the West Bank side, in Area C, where both Palestinians and Israelis could attend. The march could do more than react to the latest injustice. It could offer the first word in a new sentence.

This is what Souli wanted: to change the movement, to change history, to change the conversation. To do something different than what he saw as the typical Palestinian demonstration. At these protests, the Israeli soldiers would show up in their big green helmets with guns pointed at the ground or sky; maybe the children threw stones first or maybe the soldiers began with their tear gas and bullets, rubber and steel. However it began, the activists would run, holding kerchiefs over their faces and trying to breathe. Sometimes Palestinians were killed. And the next time, it would begin again. It seemed like a play with a circular script, an end that led right back to the beginning. Souli wanted to rewrite it. But it was hard for people to imagine a different kind of demonstration, to accept that something new was needed.

As Combatants leaders Eyal and Jamil planned the first march alongside activists from other organizations, Souli invited other players to generate ideas. He invited Sami Awad, a Palestinian activist and kindred thinker: someone who spoke differently than others, a man with deep knowledge of and commitment to nonviolence. This knowledge ran in Sami's family. His uncle, Mubarak Awad, had famously spoken about and taught practices of nonviolence that profoundly influenced the tactics of the first intifada. For one action, he proposed that children should visit the homes their grandparents owned before 1948, houses now inhabited by Israelis. They would show up to the doors holding flowers and other things to plant in the ground. Charged with overstaying his visa in Israel, Awad was deported from Palestine, the country of his birth. Souli and others felt his deportation had less to do with visas, and more to do with his acts of nonviolence, his flower-related crimes.

Sami had said something once that stuck with Souli, an articulation of what he felt but didn't know how to say. Palestinians had practiced many principles of nonviolence, but in many instances, one principle was missing: the importance of recognizing and understanding the presence of Jewish fear, of devising actions that could transform it. Sami was working with this concept and was also engaging in dialogue with settlers—not just for its own sake—but because he believed it was an essential tool for ending the occupation. Though Souli loved Sami's contributions to the conversation, he also wanted to welcome more traditional voices into the room. So he brought Bassem Tamimi, a friend and prominent Palestinian activist who was suspicious of joint work.

During these conversations, Souli argued often about the Palestinian flag. He wanted to leave it out of the march, and his friends in the movement argued back. It was funny. As a little boy, he'd drawn Palestinian flags in his notebooks, thrown all those little Palestinian flags over the electrical wires in Hizma. He'd done it before jail, before the intifada, when the Palestinian flag was still illegal. Now that his flag was legal, he couldn't stand it, or any flag. He wanted other things, images that didn't belong, gestures that would surprise people into listening and watching. He wanted puppets and music and balloons.

With all the different perspectives in the room, those planning meetings were difficult. But Bassem said something that Souli kept repeating: "We don't have to be the same." The typical demonstration with its flags was important, and so were new, strange ideas. The different strategies could help each other somehow.

At one of the first Freedom Marches, Souli didn't see any flags. He met the others in a hot parking lot not far from Bayt Jala, where nearly ten years before, he'd attended one of the first secret meetings, not knowing what would come next. As the activists began walking, Souli thought about how it felt to wait at Checkpoint 300, not far away, how it felt to walk through a cage. He looked over at Chen walking next to him, holding an enormous handmade puppet. They smiled and kept walking until marchers entered a crosswalk to interrupt the fast-moving Route 60.

They stood in the middle of the road, blocking traffic, holding up enormous cardboard slabs, painted gray to match the separation wall. They stood there for a minute, holding up the cardboard wall against the noise of cars trying to get through. As someone spoke words about freedom into the loudspeaker, they let the cardboard pieces fall, and let the cars continue.

Souli hoped some of the drivers understood what they meant by holding cardboard and letting it fall. That they were here to show another way, another future for all of them, one in which everyone could be safe and everyone could move freely, without exception. Souli looked around him and saw his friends Ahmed and Maya, Jamil and Avner, each holding a small gathering of balloons.[2]

With the slender strings in his own palms, he waited until someone shouted into the loudspeaker that it was time, cuing Souli and his friends to let go of the strings. Along with everyone around him, he tipped his head back, saw so many hands do the same, and they all laughed and yelped as their balloons floated into the sky—some over the wall into Israel, some straight up in a line toward who knows where.

During one Freedom March, Souli was standing onstage when a man in a *kippa* approached. He put his hand out for the microphone, and Souli handed it to him. The man began to speak. He was a settler who felt his home was in the West Bank, but who spoke about Palestinian rights and wanted the army to take down the checkpoints and halt the home demolitions and violence.

Souli knew that a few settlers had started coming to the march. They belonged to the lineage of Menachem Froman, the Jewish settler who'd built relationships with PLO and Hamas leaders. His followers advocated for peace, and also felt deeply religiously connected to the West Bank. They wanted to stay there, and said they'd be happy to live there under Palestinian rule—whatever was needed for peace.

While Souli was glad to see these newcomers to the march—wanting to welcome anyone committed to freedom and justice—many activists in the movement disagreed. Combatants for Peace was an anti-occupation movement, and settlers seemed integral to the occupation. It was hard to see what role settlers could play in a march aimed at freedom and dignity for Palestinians as well as Israelis—even if this was the language they used. But Souli felt open to these settlers' presence, in part because they supported the Two States, One Homeland proposal. It was an interesting alternative to the only other recognized solutions: two states or one.

In principle, Souli had always liked the democratic one-state solution, in which each person living between the Jordan River and the Mediterranean Sea would get one vote. He felt a deep connection to places like Haifa and Jaffa. Given the historical Palestinian claim to those cities, he felt he should be able to live there as a Palestinian.

But he also understood the limitations of the one-state solution. After so much violence, it seemed unlikely that the two peoples could build a state together right away. And he also understood the Jewish fear that, without any structure of Jewish leadership, the one-state solution could strip Jews of the self-determination they sought.

For a while, it seemed the only alternative was the beleaguered two-state solution: a Palestinian state beside an Israeli one, based on pre-'67 borders. Some felt this solution was impossible now. When you took a trip from Ramallah to Nablus or Hebron, you saw a settlement on almost every mountain.

In the space between these two old ideas, Souli grew more interested in Two States, One Homeland. He loved the proposal of a confederation that would allow people to become citizens of either Israel or Palestine. How each government would be accountable for the safety and civil rights of its citizens, but the borders would be porous. People could live where they wanted. He loved how this acknowledged both peoples' desires for self-determination, the fact that so many saw this land as one thing, not something easily divided in two.

Because if you asked many Palestinians about Haifa, they called it Palestine. And if you asked many Israelis about Hebron, they called it Israel. Souli wanted his family in Jordan to have the choice to come home, to live where their ancestors had tended trees. And theoretically, he wouldn't mind fighting for a Jewish person's right to pray—or maybe even live—in Hebron. It's just that he wanted that Jewish person to fight for him to be here too. He wanted that Jewish person to wait to fulfill their connection to this land, until he and his people could do the same.

But some of Souli's friends were suspicious of Two States, One Homeland. If everyone could live where they wanted, what of the settlers on privately owned Palestinian land in the West Bank? How could a truly just and shared future be built on them staying put as Israel kept expanding the settlements further and further?

When Souli passed the settler the microphone at the Freedom March, he knew these arguments by heart. Afterward, some friends were angry. He shrugged and told them he didn't have a choice, though that wasn't quite right. His action was tied to an increasing belief that the movement should widen its view.

In focusing only on ending the occupation, Souli thought, a person or a movement could get lost. It seemed that his friends in Combatants for Peace should shift their focus from what they were fighting *against* to what they were fighting *for*. To work from a civil rights framework: not just a battle against the occupation, but a struggle for shared values of democracy, human rights, and freedom. To build coalitions across organizational lines in service of love, forgiveness, dignity, and self-determination. To keep weaving a third narrative, something that would help them build both peoples a safe place, which was here.

He knew his story, and those of many others, had a part in this work. He'd been thinking about it years before, on a trip to Spain with Gadi, as they stood atop an old gray tower, peering at the far-off ground. After watching the magic of flamenco dancers, they'd climbed the tower and Souli had said to his friend: *I need a place to put my story.*

Now, driving back to Ramallah after the Freedom March, he rolled the windows down. The wind blew as if he were still standing on some tall tower, looking at the world from a great height. He said it to himself again, this time under his breath: *I need a place to put my story.*

CHAPTER 24

You Can't Get
There from Here

Souli had been writing to me for some time already, asking if I would like to work on this book. He asked several times over the years, and several times I said no, until I said yes. And, as if suddenly, I arrived in Palestine-Israel, a place I hadn't visited since I was ten years old. It had felt too complicated to put my body there.

So when I arrived, stepping out of the taxi into the early morning streets of West Jerusalem, arrival was a shock. It put me right to sleep. When I woke up, Souli was at a nearby café, waiting with a friend. He wanted to show me how to get to his apartment in Ramallah—very close, but made far by the circuitous routes the wall and checkpoints demanded.

As we walked through the touristy sections of West Jerusalem, on the way to the bus stop just over the invisible border into East Jerusalem, I looked around. We passed men in black hats, women in wigs and long skirts, teenagers speaking loudly into cellphones. I made an angry sound at the wide streets and fancy shop windows, wondering what was here before the war in 1967, before the war in 1948. But Souli only laughed at me, as he often did when I got too serious.

"Do you feel at home?" he smiled.

"No!" I said, stopping to look at him.

"I need to work on your politics a bit," he said laughing.

"I need to work on yours!"

"Good."

I followed Souli until we reached a dirt parking lot full of buses, not far from the walls of the Old City. We climbed onto one that would take us through Qalandiya checkpoint and into Ramallah. He pointed out the window as we waited for the driver to start the engine. "There used to be a bus here that went to my village," he said. "I would meet my father here after school and walk with him to the barber shop. Hizma is only fifteen minutes away. There's no bus anymore with the wall. You can't get there from here."

We climbed onto the bus when it arrived, offered our coins to the driver, sat by the window. After driving through seemingly endless traffic, the watchtower appeared, along with the open space in the wall that marks the checkpoint. It took, as Souli promised, forever. There were other, less crowded checkpoints, but few that connected Palestinians directly to the most central West Bank roads they needed and were allowed to use. When we finally crossed into Kafr 'Aqab, Souli spoke about how Oslo had turned this area, just before Ramallah, into a no-man's-land, where the PA was not allowed to function, and Israel for some reason did not exert control. He shook his head and pointed at a building with all the windows missing. "I remember," he said, "when it used to be beautiful."

The bus dropped us near the center of Ramallah, crowded with people walking, talking, shopping. Souli spoke about how much privilege there is in Ramallah compared to Area C, and certainly Gaza. I followed him down a main road, then uphill along several smaller streets, until we reached his apartment.

I would repeat this trip many times that year because Souli had encouraged me to live in West Jerusalem, and for the coming months, that's what I would do. I stayed in an apartment on King George Street with other Jewish anti-occupation activists. I lived there for many months, inside an unshakeable unease, crossing into Ramallah several times a week to work with Souli. I would return to Jerusalem to find a large Israeli flag waving outside my bedroom window.

I felt, as I had for some time, that Souli was trying to convince me of something. We'd had the same argument many times before.

He would smile the whole way through: "It's simple. Both our peoples belong here. This is really the truth. With any other *girsa*,[1] with any other theory, I don't see a future at all. I hear both Palestinians and Israelis say it, in different contexts. We love the same water, the same stones. So it doesn't hurt me to say this, to talk about Jewish history here."

I would argue back, "But there are so many Jewish histories you could choose. So many threads in Judaism that claim diaspora as our home, or argue that our connection to this place is not about living here, but something else. Plus, religion, dreams, ancient history . . . it's a tenuous connection, isn't it? What would you do if the Canaanites[2] came back claiming a piece of this land?"

He'd grow tired and wave at me with the back of his hand. "You're missing the point. Let's say it's *khurafiye*, a fairy tale. There are a lot of Palestinian *khurafiye* too. Denying them doesn't help. I've come to see that recognizing Jewish connection doesn't delegitimize our claim, and it's true the other way around. I admit how hard, how complex, how conflicting it is to recognize this. People are worried for losing land, culture, history. But denial of connection is the problem in the first place."

I'd interrupt these conversations to ask when he planned to take me to Hizma, and he'd say, "Soon, soon." He'd stayed away from home for some years, hiding from his family. When he did occasionally visit, he felt a sense of *ghurba*,[3] like a stranger.

The first time he took me to Hizma, he decided that before heading to Sarah's house, we would visit Ta'mira. Since his family land had disappeared into the wall's buffer zone, the Israeli army allowed them one visit a year, during the October olive harvest. Busy with work, Souli never went with them. Years had passed since he'd stood on that little plot of land that lay between al-Quds/Jerusalem and Hizma.

Technically, we weren't allowed to visit. But Souli thought we could manage in a car with Israeli license plates, heading from West Jerusalem through the sprawl of the Pisgat Ze'ev settlement. Souli asked Gadi if he would drive, and Gadi said yes.

In the days before our trip, Souli spoke excitedly about the evidence of Jewish history in the place he was born: "There is an old

graveyard there called 'Qubur Bani Isra'il' in Arabic. Translated literally, 'Graves of the Sons of Israel.' It's from many, many years ago
and it still exists—huge stones, near my village. I don't know the
story exactly. But they say it used to be the Benjamin tribe in my
area. And that's why there is the old Jewish cemetery."

It was not at all clear how and when the gravestones arrived
here, but for Souli, it didn't matter what was precisely true. He was
interested in the echoes the stories left behind. This was his secret
key to everything: narrating the legitimacy of both Palestinian root-
edness and Jewish connection. He confidently emphasized the lat-
ter, because to him—Palestinian connection was obvious, required
little explanation.

But as Gadi drove us into Pisgat Ze'ev, Souli was mostly quiet.
He seemed nervous. "Some of the workers here are probably from
my village," he said, looking out at the houses of the settlement.
"I worked here when it was new." On our left, some slightly gray
(once-white) buildings appeared: the older structures of the Neve
Ya'akov settlement. Souli pointed across a small ravine and up a hill
to some more white and gray houses. "That's Hizma . . . And that's
where we used to play soccer," he said, pointing to a small grove of
dark trees between us and the houses on the hill.

Passing the soccer grove, the small deer standing there with
black eyes under the trees, it took us time to find the right path. It
had been so long since Souli's last visit to Ta'mira. He wasn't sure he
knew the way. And we couldn't take the route he'd used as a child;
wire blocked the path.

When a car wheel caught on a rock and refused to go farther,
Souli said we could continue on foot. Stepping out of the car, he
looked back at us. "My family told me someone has seen settlers
walking around here." Though no one was allowed in the buffer
zone, settlers and Israelis could presumably enter with little fear of
punishment. It wasn't the same for Palestinians.

Souli put on his white trucker hat with the Combatants for Peace
logo: two figures throwing their rifles behind them, with abandon.
As we made our way up and down hills, Souli suddenly seemed to
know where he was going. We kept walking through the sun for
some minutes until he pointed at a shin-high wall of rocks.

"This is my family land, this. The border."

He stepped over the stacked rocks and we followed. It was quiet for a long time except for the sound of wind and dry grass crunching under our feet.

"There used to be a lot of *tin* and *anavim*," he said, using the Arabic word for figs and the Hebrew word for grapes. "But it's dying. The land, nobody can access it."

He began reaching up into the trees, then bringing his hand back down into the broken dry grass covering the ground beneath them. "It used to be clean," he said. "You could sleep here at night."

I kept following him, as though if I walked closely enough, he might start telling stories. But all he said, several times more, was, "It used to be clean."

He found a ripe fig, wiped the dust off. Picked two more, wrapped them together in a T-shirt and placed them in his bag. He bent down, picked up a rock, put it back. This happened several times until he settled on three smooth white stones; he put them away with the figs and sat down under a tree, didn't say anything as he pulled out his flute.

It was made of light wood, slender strips of red and green and white paint on the back. He lifted it up to his lips, let it fall, lifted it up again, played just a few falling phrases.

"I used to be able to play for hours," he said. "I can't now, the smoking."

He didn't smoke any cigarettes on Ta'mira, though in the amount of time that passed, he'd usually have smoked a handful.

"Souli . . . ," I said, and it must have sounded like a question because he shook his head.

"I can't," he said. "You know I like to stay with the positive; I don't want to go with the drama."

Eventually, we left that place of quiet. We got back in the car and Gadi pointed toward the center of Hizma, driving along a rocky path until it became pavement again. Before long, tall gray walls rose beside us and we were very small, driving through the Hizma checkpoint. Though we'd have to reenter Israel through a closely monitored checkpoint, as we headed away from Israel, the soldiers stood looking hot and bored. As we approached one of the village's few entrances for cars, Souli pointed at the houses closest to us. "All of these houses are new," he said. "Some Palestinians come back from America and they build here," he pointed toward the center of the village, which fell under Area B. "Because of the rules of Area C," he explained, "people can't build outside the village. So they build in, closer and closer."

We were quiet again as we drove down the main road of Hizma, stone houses on either side, people walking slowly with vegetables and soda and bread in plastic bags. Souli motioned for Gadi to slow down, pointed him toward a space where he could park the car between Souli's two family houses, facing one another from opposite sides of the street.

It was still quiet except for the small laughter of some children hiding just behind walls, and then the louder voices of the older boys. "My brother's sons," Souli said, as the boys walked up to their uncle with hands outstretched.

When a woman walked out across the rose-and-white checkered floor of the patio, I recognized her from pictures. Souli took his mother's hand, kissed it, and with her fingers still in his, touched his forehead. Sarah removed her hand, pulled at his unruly mess of curls, and scoffed, turning her head away in annoyance.

She started speaking quickly, as if to herself, and we followed her upstairs to sit in the living room where Souli's sister Rashida brought us coffee, smiling.

"What's your mother saying?" I asked Souli. Somehow, he was already on his second cigarette. He laughed and looked away from her as she continued speaking. "She's upset I don't come more. And that I'm not married."

Many cups of coffee later, we headed toward the patio, on our way to Souli's aunt Fatima's house, when his older brother Karim appeared. Or it was more that we'd appeared, and he'd been here the whole time. He stood solidly with his wife in front of their kitchen, a doorway hidden by a sheet. He was a completely different style and shape of man than Souli: tall, broad, solemn-seeming. He didn't smile easily, at least not in front of me. He stood very straight. Souli smiled and fidgeted while he introduced us, and then his nephew Tariq followed us in his bright yellow shirt, jumping in the car for the two-minute drive down the road to Fatima's.

In the car, Souli's fidgeting stilled before he spoke. "For my brother . . . the village is his whole world. For me, it's different. I travel and check things. But for him, he doesn't want to. The land here is holy. It's God."

Before we left that day, Fatima would tell many stories, different decades mixing in the space of a sentence. Souli would hand out the figs and stones from Ta'mira to his brother, to his aunt, to his mother. Sarah would hold them in the palm of her hand like a baby bird.

The silence from Ta'mira stayed with Souli. There were many places in the past that he couldn't or didn't want to touch. Instead of sitting down for interviews, I followed him in his work. When I asked questions, it became clear we wanted to speak of different things. Because he had asked me to help tell his story, I wanted to understand what exactly it was: what had happened in it. But he avoided my questions about 'Ayn Farrah, about torture, about jail. At the beginning, he reduced enormous things to single sentences. It was a natural response to trauma, Souli said; many others who'd been in jail did the same.

"You become a little bit like that," he said one day, "separate from things. Otherwise it destroys you."

It was only through cobbling phrases together, uttered over many hours and days, at disparate times, that the most painful elements of the story revealed themselves. When we visited the Abu Jihad Museum for the Prisoners Movement Affairs in Abu Dis, he walked through the exhibits as if stepping barefoot on hot sand. When I first asked him to take me to 'Ayn Farrah, he took me to a place some distance away. We sat high across the valley, looking down at the monastery built directly, precariously, into the cliff. He was silent for a long time. Then he spoke at length about a plot of grass nearby, where he'd set an accidental fire as a child. He'd been making tea and suddenly the dry field was burning. His mother had reminded him of it often, laughing about how he'd peed on the flames to extinguish them.

He was right that evasion was a natural response to trauma. But there was something else, too. A large part of Souli's work was using his personal story to transform others. As any other storyteller, he'd chosen the parts that served his purpose. He wanted to encourage mutual recognition among the Israelis and Palestinians, for each people (in their many iterations) to understand the past the other narrated. To use that understanding to build a just future. He thought this required not only a recognition of the past, but also some way of surrendering it.

When other Palestinian activists argued that any Palestinian who forgave the Nakba was violating a boundary, betraying the Palestinian people, Souli contested the point, saying, "I don't think that history will bring justice back. We lost a big part of our land; this is a fact. But I don't see justice, I see forgiveness."

He knew that in order to move forward there must be a deep acknowledgment of the Nakba, of all the suffering the Palestinian people experienced and experience because of Israel's creation. He never wanted Palestinians to give up, but there was a way to offer forgiveness and still find just, agreed-upon solutions. Solutions that might make space for both the Law of Return (a current fact that allowed any Jew around the world to become a citizen of Israel) and the right of return for Palestinian refugees (a still-unrealized dream). Souli believed what Edward Said had said, that these two principles would have to be "considered and trimmed together."

With this future in mind, he wanted his people to think differently, to open up a bit. To refuse to live in a "victimhood mindset," which he knew stood in the way of freedom. He'd become very clear on this. Living in trauma and victimhood prevented self-critique; it kept Palestinians from acknowledging the power they had to change elements of their reality.

Kazem, another Palestinian leader in Combatants, spoke about it one day: the very uncomfortable place where Souli stood. We were sitting at Makhrour restaurant near Bayt Jala after a steering committee meeting, under some blue tarps blocking the sun. At a long table, I held a small brown paper cup of coffee as Kazem widened his eyes. He theorized about Souli, how much he had changed. "Sulaiman became Souli, and I miss Sulaiman. I miss Sulaiman the *fellah,*[4] Sulaiman the shepherd. I miss the simple Palestinian guy. Because Souli became the Palestinian Ashkenazi," Kazem laughs. "Sometimes when he's speaking, he says he can't remember a word in Arabic! So he'll say it in English instead." Kazem smiles. "With all of this, Souli is still the simple patriot that we love."

But no one could look away from the change. Other Palestinians were with Souli, Kazem said, when he spoke about jail. But he lost them after that. "It's different with other Palestinians in Combatants," he said. "Think about Jamil." Jamil's family were Nakba refugees. When they fled, his grandfather refused to leave and was killed in the house they left behind. Many years later, Jamil's little brother stepped from the doorway of their home in Dheisheh refugee camp; he began walking down the road toward their uncle's house. There was a curfew then, and when some Israeli soldiers saw Jamil's brother, he began to run. The soldiers fired their guns and Jamil's little brother died right there on the street, not far from the doorway.

"It's different with Jamil," Kazem said again, looking at me, as if to make sure I was listening. "How can he forgive? The suffering is still with him."

Souli felt it. The difference Kazem spoke of made it challenging for Souli to give lectures to groups of Palestinians. In Combatants for Peace, he usually spoke at house meetings of Israelis and internationals. When I asked why, he shrugged.

"Now I don't feel belonging to the Palestinian narrative *alone.* I feel belonging there, and beyond it. So some Palestinians can still relate to me because of a certain stage in my life. But sometimes I feel strange to talk to fellow Palestinians. I have to think before I speak. It's different worlds, cultural dynamics, everything. Sometimes I feel it's really too hard. Sometimes I feel I'm too open, like more than they can accept."

He knew he would never, could never leave his roots, felt sure his impatience came from love and a wish for Palestinian freedom. But it also carried a distance.

"In jail," he said one time, "they used to say, 'The *I* will melt in the *we* . . . '"

He paused.

"You see? I say, 'They used to say.' Before, I was saying 'we.' But now I'm looking from afar.'"

We began to visit Hizma more often, and when Souli's family seemed pleasantly surprised by his presence, we both began asking questions, searching for answers he couldn't remember.

One day he turned to his mother and said, "*Yamma*, I want to ask, because I forgot. Where was I born? Was it here, or the caves nearby, or in Jerusalem?"

"You were born at home."

"With a midwife?"

"Yes, of course . . . I can't believe you don't know where you were born!"

He laughed. "For the book, mother, I was going to tell Penina to write that I was born in a cave. It is stronger for the foreigners to tell them I was born in a cave . . . like Che Guevara . . ."[5]

"So what do you want from me," Sarah said, "to tell them something different?"

"No, mother," Souli said, "tell them the truth . . ."

It was very hard to know how to tell the truth and where to find it. But as Souli's family welcomed him back, he appeared still somehow hesitant, distant. As if—after having changed so much—he was unsure he could stay in this place. But he didn't want to believe it, didn't want to entertain what he'd heard some people say of him, that through his work with Israelis, he'd given up too much, lost something of himself, become less Palestinian.

I watched him try to prove this wrong, to find evidence of his theories here, in this place where he was born. He kept avoiding details of his own lived past. And he often skipped articulating the realities of present occupation in Hizma—perhaps because he knew the signs were all around us and very difficult to miss. Or that I would make sure to find them. Most often, I listened to him speak dreamily of distant history, watched as he searched for traces of ancient Judaism in his village.

He pointed out little huts where some women in Hizma used to light candles to honor dead holy men on Thursdays or Fridays—he wasn't sure which. He wondered whether there was a connection between this ritual and the Jewish practice of Sabbath candle-lighting. He loved these echoes, though this line of thinking seemed dangerous to others. Some felt it mirrored the argument of certain right-wing Israelis who wanted to prove that all Palestinians used to be Jews. An argument sometimes used to justify a "greater Israel," denying Palestinians their right to peoplehood and self-determination. But his friend Jalal took this idea and turned it on its head. Souli had heard him laughing many times, in all seriousness, as he said: "All Palestinians used to be Jews." Though some Palestinians grew angry at this, Jalal meant that Jewish connection to the land legitimized Palestinian ownership, not Ashkenazi Jewish belonging.

Souli took the historical echoes in his own direction.

"Some Israelis could use Jewish history here to say there are no Palestinian places," he said one day. "But what exists is that the whole country used to be Canaan. Every town here is old, except a few. Everything changes, and now if you dig in the ground, you will see the graveyards, you will see these histories, simply. It's a lot of mixing, that's my feeling."

He pointed to the candle-lighting. One might guess that the Palestinian practice came from the Jewish one. But the reverse, as well as any number of explanations, was just as likely. For Souli, the exact origin wasn't important. It was the overlap that mattered: the sense that many Palestinian and Jewish practices were born from the indigenous culture of this place, and then branched out in their various ways.

"For example, some Palestinians will have a pagan Canaanite influence without knowing. Talking about the moon and the sun, counting the stars and singing for harvest. Like the *tatriz* (embroidery) on the *thobe*, the Palestinian traditional dress. I was reading an article that says the *tatriz* has Canaanite symbols," images that come from a time of different gods. "My mom doesn't know this. But some people did research and they know this is connected to that story, like thousands of years."

This was one reason Souli liked to peer underground. The mixing he found there promised to infuriate everyone, to challenge any single notion of ownership, to point toward a more expansive way of understanding our relationship to past, present, and future.

But to say these things aloud was more than difficult—when Palestinians were still living inside a real, present danger. In Hizma, it was all around us. There was the broad, tall wall with the opening that seemed only to emphasize its height and strength. There was the kitchen window, where Said used to peer out at Ta'mira, before the wall took it away.

There were the realities monitored and tracked by the village council. Over time, nearly 20 percent of Hizma's lands had been confiscated to construct nearby settlements, bypass roads, and the wall. In Area C, which made up approximately 90 percent of the village, it was very difficult to get building permits from Israel's Civil Administration. Souli's brother Karim spoke often about how this made it difficult to repair things in the village when they were broken. And soon after I arrived, Karim told Souli that a new bit of wall would go up near the village. Surrounded by settlements, Hizma already felt like an island, like a South African Bantustan in the time of apartheid. The new concrete would only solidify that feeling further.

And then there were danger's everyday signs.

There was Souli's older sister, closing the windows when we heard army tanks in the street, her gesture with its look of routine. There were all the empty tear gas canisters hanging from electrical wires. And there were the words of Souli's nephew Tariq, sprawled on an armchair in his mother's house one day, his hair damp and red with new henna. When his mother told me I should learn Arabic, I smiled and said she was absolutely right.

"Penina," Souli said, "Tariq speaks Hebrew." And then he turned to Tariq and told him to show me.

Tariq looked at me, eyes sparkling and turned up at the edges, as if about to tell a joke. He demonstrated his Hebrew by reciting a phrase he'd clearly heard many times.

"*Aravim klavim.*"

I stared at him. He'd said, "Arabs are dogs."

This sort of sentence, he seemed to be saying, was what Hebrew was for. Tariq laughed at the shock on my face, and the conversation turned quickly to something else.

————•————

Souli seemed to shrug off many of the occupation's signals—maybe because he felt I was overemphasizing or misunderstanding them, or because his distance from home had irrevocably changed his relationship to such signs, as it had many other things.

We were sitting one day at a restaurant in West Jerusalem—up some stairs, blue tiles, outdoor patio—when I shared something that Maya, a close colleague and friend in Combatants, had said. We'd talked about many things. How it felt to be a teenager standing there in the big square the day Rabin was killed. How she'd been afraid to visit the West Bank the first time she went with Combatants for Peace. How in the movement, there was a connection between the work of lifting women's voices and embodying nonviolence.

She'd spoken also about Souli's power to change people, to inspire Jews to come to the West Bank for their first action. He did it, she thought, by telling a story that didn't ask anyone to give anything up. But she wondered if he was the one who lost something in this sort of storytelling.

"It's easy for him not to fight," she'd said, "to be tolerant to all kinds of opinions and to find humanity in the settler. So this is great, amazing. But I think this is difficult for many people to accept. Especially on the Palestinian side. Because you have to have the ability to lose control. And this is very difficult if you're grasping something very, very important, such as a state. Or flag. Or a place to live. Souli represents this ability to be a citizen of the world. But in a way, this contradicts the struggle for independence. I believe people can see this is a contradiction."

Souli listened as I shared what Maya said, nodding with his head down. He paused, then looked up. "I don't want to be open to the Israeli side and the Jewish narrative and closed to my side," he said. "Because the more you understand the Israelis, the more you lose there. The more you show understanding to the other side of the story, the more you might lose something . . ."

"And I did get closer to some Israelis in my mindset along the way. Maybe it had to do with how we were impacted by Israeli culture in jail: newspaper, TV, everything. But I have to say, when you were told all this evil stuff about Israelis and then find it's not like that . . . the circle breaks. This really makes you disappointed. Not just disappointed—this shocks your system. And then it's hard, then you are in trouble in your mind. This is really not easy. So for me, I became kind of skeptical with Arabic and Islamic culture. It became hard for me, honestly."

He spoke slowly, as if frightened to let the words leave his mouth. He kept talking for some time, between cigarettes and long silences, about the worry that his work had opened him too far to *the other side*, had closed him off too thoroughly from the culture and struggle he was born into.

Another day, while sitting by a spring, he told me that Bassem Tamimi had a theory about all this, about where Souli fell on the spectrum of change. We'd decided to visit one of the springs peppering the West Bank's Wadi Qelt valley. 'Ayn Fawwar, like the others, was managed by the Israeli army's Civil Administration. It wasn't far from 'Ayn Farrah, where one hot day in 1986, two young Israeli men had looked at Souli singing and known without a doubt that he was Palestinian. On this day, it was different. Palestinians we passed looked at his long curly hair, his soaking socks and Converse, and kept speaking to him in Hebrew, assuming he was an Israeli. He would answer them in Arabic; their eyes would widen in surprise and they would laugh.

"Why do you think that keeps happening?" I asked him.

"It's because of you," he smiled, pointing at my stereotypically Ashkenazi Jewish face, my whiteness. He paused. "It's also because of this." He pulled at the mess of his curls, pointed at his Converse. "Because I'm a hippy now."

He paused, then launched into Bassem's theory. "You know, Bassem Tamimi told me I have a few personalities. His analysis was like this: 'You don't have all the Arabic vocabulary.' This is really true. I never thought about it before. Bassem said I stored in my head all the words I heard when I was a child, until I was fourteen years old. These are the words of my local accent, culture. This was cut when I went to jail because jail is a different story. There you have people from lots of other places: cities, refugee camps, places with different cultures, different ways.

"Bassem said, 'In jail you collected the language of politics and revolution, of books. Then, after jail, you learned the language of Israelis. So your dictionary,' he told me, 'is not full.' He was laughing when he told me, but it's smart. It's really true."

It was like the time we visited Battir, a West Bank village full of greenery and stone terraces, to drink coffee with Souli's friend. We didn't share a language, so when she began to laugh and laugh, Souli had to explain. "I tried to use a saying, an old saying, about the Prophet. But I didn't say it right." He grinned, and his friend just kept laughing.

We talked about Bassem Tamimi's theory again another day, not long after the trip to the spring, when Souli decided it was time to visit Bassem in Nabi Saleh, a West Bank village north of Ramallah.

Bassem was supposed to be leaving for a US speaking tour with Jewish Voice for Peace, but Souli said he wouldn't be going after all. He'd lost his visa after adding his name to a lawsuit against the far-right billionaire, supporter of Netanyahu and Trump, and funder of Jewish settlements: Sheldon Adelson.[6]

"The others on the lawsuit were Americans," Souli said on the ride over. "No problems with their visas. Bassem shouldn't have done it. His politics are too much. Our politics are opposite."

"Really? Opposite?" I asked.

"Yes, but he loves me from revolutionary times and I love him. Here that matters more. Some people I knew from that time don't speak to me anymore, but not Bassem. He still holds the old principles. But he's not totally stuck there, he's open-minded, relatively. I love Bassem and his wife Nariman—really, they are lovely people, good hearts. I don't agree with everything they do and say, but I like to keep this connection a bit."

When we reached Nabi Saleh, Souli and Bassem smoked on the wide cement porch under the sky. As Nariman sat sorting leaves, interjecting to correct them or make them laugh, they talked about jail. How everyone used to sleep close together on the floor, putting pieces of cardboard between their bodies, hoping to shield themselves from their neighbor's breath. They cinched the bottom of their pants and laughed, remembering the skinny jeans of the first intifada.

When I interviewed Bassem later in a Ramallah café, he told me of everything he'd lost. In Israeli jails, he'd been tortured various times. Once, he'd been beaten into a coma. And when he woke up, he learned that his sister was dead. She'd come to the military court and an Israeli guard, he heard, had pushed her down the stairs. Bassem was released from jail the day of her funeral.

With all of this in the background, with everything, he spoke critically of certain things Souli did: going to peace conferences where Westerners wore suits and explained nonviolence to Palestinians. Using those people's definitions of important words, Bassem said, meant surrendering to their colonial mindset.

When he traveled, he found this mindset everywhere. Once, he was on a US speaking tour with his friend and famous Israeli anti-occupation activist, Miko Peled. After a talk, someone approached Bassem to say, as if giving him a gift, "I respect you because you are friends with Miko Peled."

"I don't need your respect," he said, evenly. "You need me to have an Israeli in my life, to give me credit?" He explained that he gave Miko legitimacy, not the other way around. Miko's father had been a prominent IDF general, and so Bassem said, "This credit is for me, not for Miko. He must thank me, that I accept to have him in my life."

He looked at me. "This is part of your problem. You see Sulaiman, and you chose him, because he has relation with Israelis. I think this is part of the Western mentality that influences and impacts you." Look for it, he said, "and you will find it."

I sat there looking, and finding it. Because while Souli had chosen me for this project, Bassem was also right. I carried all this in me: the complex set of reasons I was interested in Souli's joint work, the notion that I owned and understood all the important words here.

Over the course of this conversation, Bassem made himself clear. Through contact with Westerners who carried this mindset, some Palestinians had allowed themselves to be changed too much.

"Is that what happened to him?" I asked, pointing at Souli sitting beside us, appearing not to listen, looking at his phone.

"A person can change completely. Sulaiman started to, he decided to try, but I think he will not succeed."

Bassem explained that Souli had built two versions of himself, two shapes. There was the fighter who existed before and during jail, and there was the person sitting here, committed to dialogue and working with Israelis. Sometimes it seemed the old Sulaiman was gone, Bassem implied, but it wasn't true. Both shapes were still here. Maybe because both versions of Sulaiman had the same goal: to end the occupation, to win freedom for his people.

Bassem looked over at his friend. "I know the secret Sulaiman. I know the other. I tell him, 'You need our relationship to protect the other Sulaiman.'"

Souli looks up, smiles, and says, "I will delete him soon!"

"But he can't," Bassem said. "I tell him, 'When you call me, you want to search for the other Sulaiman inside you. If you really wanted to change, you wouldn't call.'"

It felt true. Watching Souli drive toward Bassem in Nabi Saleh that day, he'd had the air of a person returning home.

At various times, Souli's friends had tried to find the two Israelis from 'Ayn Farrah—Samuel and Alon. Their efforts had been unsuccessful, so I asked Souli if he'd like to try again as part of the book process. He said yes, though later I wondered if it was the kind of yes you give when you hope a question will simply disappear.

But the question refused to go away, because eventually, Gadi found the two men. Alon worked at a school in Jerusalem. Samuel lived in a settlement not far from 'Ayn Farrah. When I asked Souli what we should do, if someone should reach out, he nodded with a shrug and suggested Gadi give it a try. He didn't want to promise a meeting but was curious to know what the two Israelis might say.

Gadi reached out to Alon and he responded quickly. He seemed interested in meeting about the book, interested in hearing about Souli. Gadi was elated. With the skills Souli had built talking to right-wingers, he thought it could be a good meeting. "It could even," Gadi said, "be a love story."

But the next time Gadi got in touch, Alon had changed his mind and didn't explain why.

Afterward, Souli breathed out a heavy, *o*-shaped breath. He was relieved. He'd been open, curious about the cinematic possibility of it: what if he could recruit Alon to join Combatants for Peace? But when a Jewish friend asked him what he would say, he paused. "Yeah, that's . . . I don't know. I was asked this. But I don't know."

During that conversation, I watched this Jewish friend's anger mount, her deep desire for Souli to apologize for what he'd done. This was maybe one reason Souli felt relief that there'd be no meeting. If he agreed to talk, would they assume he was going to ask for forgiveness? He wasn't sure he wanted to.

That day in 'Ayn Farrah, he'd seen two Israelis wearing the uniforms of soldiers. They were sitting by the spring where his mother had gathered water as a child. On land controlled by Israel that he knew as occupied Palestinian territory. This control was violence, too. It was the context behind Sulaiman's plan to take Samuel and Alon's guns, guns he assumed they had in their big bags. So in that conversation with the Jewish friend who was so eager for his apology, Souli tried to explain.

"Violence has different forms. Maybe in my case it was direct, and you might think, how the fuck did he do this but . . . If you lose your land and you lose your life, your dignity and your everything, you could do any shit. Now I'm calm, I think differently. But as a simple example, when we went to my family land, and they told me there are settlers coming there. Do you know the feeling?"

He spoke about another villager from Hizma who owned a cave near Ta'mira. His cave was now in the "buffer zone." Though he couldn't visit, he could still peer out at it, from a window of his house in Hizma.

"He lives just across. Imagine that he saw them, the settlers, between the mountain and the other mountain. I don't know . . . I expect anything from him, to be honest. He could cry, he could fight, he could give up—everything is expected. And when I see how some soldiers treat people at the checkpoints, I think about this. I remember one soldier, she was treating the people waiting there really shitty, like animals, or worse than animals. And I heard the people talking between each other and yelling. People didn't act physically but I thought, one of them could just lose patience and that's it. It's not easy. I'm not legitimizing violence, but it's really not easy."

But in other conversations, in quieter and more contemplative moments when he didn't feel the need to defend, he seemed more conflicted. Like he was truly considering—motivated by a force from within or without—whether it would be right to say sorry.

We spoke about this once after he heard Peter Yarrow—musician and friend of Combatants for Peace—tell a story. Outside a New York church on Universal Peace Day, Peter had asked the audience to turn west toward Japan. To sing and say in their hearts that what the US had done, using the atom bomb on Hiroshima and Nagasaki, could never happen again. That they would each take upon themselves the inheritance and responsibility of their country's act, until such things disappeared from the world.

When Peter was putting his guitar away, a Japanese man approached him, trembling with the importance of what he wanted to say. He apologized for the crimes Japan had committed against the US during the war, and his words shocked Peter, brought him to tears.

"I saw the impact of this act," Souli said, "of saying sorry. It was very strong. I try to pass this example along, but it's not easy. So, it was really a struggle when we began looking for the two Israelis. And people asked me, 'Okay, what would you say?' I always avoided the answer, because I didn't know. I'm friendly, but to say sorry, I don't know if I would do that. In my heart and conscience, I feel bad for them, of course, for what happened. But in the big picture, it's a different thing. Because while they were victims, I am a victim too."

"I was in jail; I feel I was punished more than I should have been. And when an Israeli does a crime, they don't punish him the same way; I can't disconnect from this. I want to humanize everyone. And I feel there is justification for Palestinian resistance. I don't want to delegitimize my side of the story."

And there was something else. For many Palestinians, he thought, saying sorry would be the breaking point. Any credit he still had among Palestinians would be erased. He wasn't sure he was ready to lose anything else.

"I'm talking to people all the time about the self-critique," he said, "how we need to denounce violence and advocate for nonviolence. This is really my politics, my mind, my heart. But practically, I admit how it's fucking complicated."

CHAPTER 25

The Stone
and the Valley

After a year, I went home to California, and Souli kept visiting Hizma more and more. As he sat on the couch upstairs with Sarah, as he held his little brother Nabil's newest baby, as his sister brought him coffee, he was surprised at the comfort he felt. Certain things that had created tension were now making everyone laugh. For some time, Souli had been concerned that his family didn't like his tendency to bring '*ajanib*, foreign friends, to visit Hizma. But one day, Sarah smiled and told him it had always been this way, since he was little.

Once she said, when he was very young, they'd placed him under a tree during the wheat harvest. She and Fatima were working hard under the sun, and had set him there in the shade, to protect him from the heat. When they looked over at the tree, he was gone.

Everyone dropped their scythes and went searching. An old man found him on the road, getting into the car of some foreigners. He'd gone off walking, and the '*ajanib* had given him chocolate. When Sarah arrived, the man from their village was shouting. "They're going to take him away, make him a soldier to fight against Palestine!" he said. Sarah took little Sulaiman from the car; she headed back to the wheat.

Telling the story, she looked at him knowingly and said, "You see? All your life, you've loved '*ajanib*."

Souli laughed and laughed.

Still, there were difficult moments in his return to Hizma. Sarah talked breathlessly and endlessly about how his hair was too long, how he needed to marry before she left the world. His niece Amira told him, after she saw a film about Combatants for Peace, that it seemed like *tatbi'a* (normalization) to her.

But it was far easier than he expected, especially with his brothers, after all those years they had spent critiquing his work. Now, they said nothing. He knew Sarah blamed them for his absence, so maybe they were staying quiet for her. They saw he could leave and not come back. "Also," he said by phone once, "maybe the years showed them that I'm not fucking selling Palestine. *Shwayya*. It's hard to know."

It was a kind of coming home, and it kept spreading. He found himself more comfortable again talking to rooms of Palestinians in his work with Combatants for Peace; more in place, more grounded.

And as he visited Hizma more often, something kept clarifying. He'd needed to disconnect. But after this long, long time, he was trying to balance a bit, to accept the things he didn't like in the village. Not to fight to change them, like he had before.

"The shift between cultures," he said, "is a bit easier than it used to be. I'm not going to live in the village, but maybe I'm more peaceful with my past now than I was ten years ago."

Sometimes smiling and sometimes not, he would fit all these changes into a phrase. He was on a "spiritual journey," he said. An internal path that ran alongside his more external work. He began studying Nonviolent Communication (NVC), bringing it into Combatants meetings. He sat often in the *sahra*, the *midbar*[1]—trying to learn from its enormous quiet. He took ayahuasca. Over the course of his first ceremony, he remembered things he'd thought totally lost, things he would have liked to forget. He relived the period of torture in jail. He saw his father and grandfather, told them many important things he couldn't recall the next day. On Ta'mira, Said's mother Khadra sat in front of him. Beside him were Samuel, the Israeli he'd stabbed in 'Ayn Farrah, and Yunus, the boy he'd investigated in Hebron. It seemed his grandmother was there to convene some long-awaited meeting, to deliver him a blessing. He woke up feeling clean.

When he sat with Sarah in her backyard and told her about the ayahuasca ceremony, about all the changes that seemed to move through him, about talking to his father and grandfather and grandmother, she was glad. She'd felt that something was blocked, some curse maybe holding him back. She told him something he'd never known: that Ta'mira had come to their family through his grandmother Khadra, the one who'd presided over his vision, facilitated something—though he couldn't quite remember what—between him and Samuel, him and Yunus.

It was a sort of mending, the kind not associated with a wound closing but with something opening up. New memories kept appearing, as when he called, excited one day, after seeing a particular shade of gold. The color brought a word back from some hidden place: *tasat al-rajfa* (bowl of trembling), a small vessel people used when they got worried or afraid from something.

He called Aunt Fatima, as he'd started to do whenever he had a question about how things used to be. She told him they still had it, the *tasat al-rajfa*. When someone became frightened, they put water inside it, took it out when certain stars were in the sky, and left it under their light until the sun came. In the morning, they drank, and the fear went away.

Listening to his aunt, he remembered something. How one time, when he was a boy, a dog had followed him. It was very, very dark. When he got home, he couldn't find his breath. He was so afraid. And his family made this *tasat al-rajfa* for him.

He was looking for more of this, more ways to drink water from a bowl, when his friend Dana came to visit in Ramallah. They sat in the living room and she told him to lie down. She asked him a question. Dana was a Palestinian trauma healer—rooted both in global models and in traditional Palestinian methods of diving into oneself, uncovering truth.

Dana and Souli met through an NVC training, and had recently made a plan. If Souli wasn't going to meet Samuel and Alon, he'd go back to meet the version of himself who was there that day in 'Ayn Farrah. He closed his eyes, the dark his only medicine as Dana guided him, and he spoke in a mixture of languages—mostly Arabic and English. He began as if sitting in the place where, a few years prior, I'd first asked him about 'Ayn Farrah. The cliff where he'd spoken haltingly, struggling to remember and return, answering other questions entirely.

Lying on the floor, with his eyes closed, he spoke. "Me and Penina are sitting at the mountaintop, making tea and mint on the open fire across from a monastery on the opposite mountain."

He spoke of his present self, Souli, and his past self, Sulaiman, as two separate figures. He moved between them, pronouns switching, refusing to be followed.

"Now I'm entering into his heart. Now I'm going to revisit young Sulaiman. I can see him sitting, making tea on the open fire in the front yard of the monastery. I am looking at the sacred stone and the valley. I hear the sound of the waterfall in 'Ayn Farrah. This is our sacred water, the water my mom and aunt used to carry . . . Sulaiman is sitting, ready for the mission. In his shirt he is hiding the knife. He is not violent in his nature, he just wants to protect things. He is entering history because of the water and the sky in 'Ayn Farrah.

"A scene without witness, a swift movement, my blood boiling, I'm inside my heart, he is inside my heart. And here it comes, the split. Here is the original Sulaiman . . . And here is Souli, the Ashkenazi. They are judging each other.

"We, both of us—Souli and Sulaiman—are continuing on this historical path, to correct what went wrong. To save my mother. To save the children of my partners in Combatants for Peace, Avner's children, and Chen's. To allow my sister to live. And for my father in his grave, to give him peace and restfulness.

"There's a wind blowing on me . . .

"Steadfastness, strength, gentleness, childish innocence, purity, morals, embarrassment from doing wrong, love, love, the love, belonging, honesty . . . all the principles that we came from, from my grandfather, my mother, my sister, my brother, from the blood . . .

"Sulaiman is conversing with Souli."

CHAPTER 26

A Small Revolution

After a time, Souli stepped back from the role of Palestinian co-director in Combatants. He kept speaking and fundraising, but needed space to look inward, to find something: some healing, some freedom.

He dove deeper into his NVC training, where he met a woman named Lilach who'd grown up in Kfar Adumim, a Jewish settlement just minutes east of Hizma. As a child, she'd walked like Souli, barefoot through all those springs. She called that valley with its low paths between the cliffs—including 'Ayn Fawwar and 'Ayn Farrah—"my wadi." She lived in Jaffa now, but her family still lived in Kfar Adumim. Souli listened to her explain how that place was—irrevocably, unchangeably—her family's home. He was deeply moved by her connection to the streams and hills he loved so much. They argued about certain things, agreed on others. As their friendship grew, they laughed often, and Souli felt enormous hope in the ways they found to listen to one another.

Still, he could not think of the wadi without seeing his mother as a young girl, singing to herself on the path to 'Ayn Farrah, carrying fresh water home. So many paths were closed to her now. This reality was with him when an American Jewish friend and anti-occupation activist asked a question. She was thinking of making *aliyah*,[1] taking advantage of Israel's Law of Return, which allows all Jews to win citizenship—while Palestinians are not allowed to return home.

"Would you think differently of me if I made *aliyah?*" Souli's friend asked one day.

He paused and said what was hard to say: "Yes."

Souli said they'd always be friends, but yes, he would think differently of her if she took advantage of this system while simultaneously speaking out against it.

He told her he believed deeply in Jewish connection to the land, and he dreamed of a future where Jewish connection could live beside and intertwined with Palestinian connection, a future where there was not a separate law of return for different peoples, where everyone was welcome, where no one exerted control, where he could welcome her to this land without question.

Both pieces of his answer, the recognition of the current unequal reality, the dreaming forward, lived together, and this was a kind of healing.

As he looked for more modes of repair, he traveled to Tamera, a community in Portugal committed to building nonviolent community—designed to transform systems in the world meant to control, extract, and kill. To work on every level at once—personal, communal, global. He listened to people there speak about the healing that could occur by returning home—to the wisdom of trusting elders, to the practices of decision-making and mediation through a council, which were long used to make things right. Thinking about this idea, and its resonance with *sulha*, he met Palestinian women there who kept teaching him things long after he left.

There was Haneen Abualsoud, who'd been born and lived in Gaza until just recently. It seemed her whole life she'd been asking the question: How could she bring peace to her people? In a small space, often without electricity, expecting another war, she felt entirely full of love for life. She sat on the roof with her sisters, looking at the stars. They dreamt about freedom, to decide what they would do and what they would become without a man's permission. To lie on the ground in nature near their house without the promise of more bombs. It was in 2008 that she realized she had to leave her home. That day in the kitchen, the war was all around her. Bombs were falling around her house, very close. She was hiding there under a cabinet, holding her sister's hand, looking into her mother's face, which had turned yellow with fear. Haneen managed to leave years later, and when Souli met her she was writing, working, and dreaming, trying to get her husband and children out of Gaza.

In Tamera, Souli also met Aida Shibli, a Palestinian Bedouin radical feminist, an activist for human rights and ecological justice. She was a citizen of Israel, but had always known she was Palestinian. During the first intifada, at sixteen years old, she was arrested after hanging two Palestinian flags from her balcony. During the second intifada, she worked as a nurse in Hadassah hospital. As bodies came to her, she tried to save them from the violence outside. One of those days, looking at all the people lying on beds, trying so hard to survive, she learned of a new life in her. She was pregnant. As she wrote to Souli one day, "I knew if I would keep this child, I would need to change my life. I would need to change THE life. During the whole pregnancy, life was giving birth to me and to my child at the same time." She held and fought for this love, while also trying to hide her Palestinian-ness in a Jewish neighborhood where to be Palestinian felt dangerous.

Something new was happening in her then. She was trying to reconcile the occupation—all the harm Zionism and capitalism had done to her family's indigenous knowledge—with certain very personal griefs: her relationship with her father, her divorce. She used to blame the occupation for everything, but found she couldn't now. She told Souli, "This took me on a long journey. I am still in it: to find out what are the structures and patterns in me and my society that allow outer enmity to last? What is my contribution to any situation of conflict—personal or collective? How would I act if my heart would be open at all times? What kind of inner change do I need to make, so I can dissolve patterns of war inside me?

"Global war, expressed in local conflicts like the one my people suffer from," she wrote, "is based on the illusion of scarcity, in land, water, love. We are convinced by a system of power that we need to compete in order to survive and thrive. The system wants us to believe that there is an outer enemy that we need to fight against so we can be happy. We buy into it and waste our energy instead of changing the system of power that rules us all. We are all in this journey of healing, healing the collective trauma of separation, ending othering in all its forms, knowing that war outside is based on us believing in war."

Souli was feeling what it felt to hold all this. He was feeling it as he learned to listen to his breath, not just on meditation retreats, but while watching the US move its embassy to Jerusalem: an act that seemed to tell his family that they did not exist, that Palestinians did not exist. He was dreaming of silent marches, and when Netanyahu called louder and louder for annexation, his dreams grew larger still.

As all the frightening news unfolded around him, he stayed mostly light, focused on smaller things. On stories about people changing. About a right-winger who heard Souli speak and wrote afterward to say that he couldn't stop thinking of Hizma.

About a lecture he gave at an NVC conference, to a group of mostly Jewish Israelis. Looking out at the group, searching for a closing sentence, he'd finally said, "In the end, I believe we will all meet each other in Yerushalaim."[2]

When he opened up for questions, a man wearing a *kippa* stood up, crying. "Do you know what Yerushalaim could mean?" he asked, and answered his own question. "*Yeru*," he said, naming sounds that echoed the word *see* in both Hebrew and Arabic.[3]

"And *shalem*—" the tearful man continued, "to see what is *perfect, whole*."

Today, it's still like this with Souli. As more terrible news rolls in, as others focus on what's broken, he keeps finding things that are healed, things that were never damaged in the first place.

I see this again in the middle of a speaking tour. On behalf of Combatants for Peace, Souli has been traveling the US talking about love, about forgiveness, about the movement's direct actions against the occupation. He is still glowing from the work of the Sumud Freedom Camp, an initiative inspired by the Standing Rock protest against the Dakota Access Pipeline in 2016–17. With a coalition of other organizations, Combatants for Peace had successfully reclaimed land. They helped bring Palestinians from the village of Sarura, displaced by an Israeli army firing zone, back to their homes. He is inside this glow when I meet him at an Oakland café, on Ohlone land, a place that doesn't belong to us, that neither of us belongs to.

Right away, he pulls out his phone and begins talking about the olive harvest. His family has just gone to visit Ta'mira, the one day a year the army allows it. Though Souli is in Hizma often these days, he has still not gone with them. He's visited Ta'mira multiple times, but only illegally, with an Israeli who can drive him. He's gone once or twice with a group of trusted Jewish activists to whom he talks about history and land and his grandfather, standing next to the little wall Ayed built.

He only knows the shape of harvest day because his family tells him. Karim says they open a door in the gate and let the family stay just until dark. Sarah says the soldiers have a list of names. They count you on the way in, she tells her son, and they count you on the way out.

Today, Souli's looking at pictures of the olive harvest his nephew Naji posted online. The family has just collected dusty olives clinging to the unhealthy trees of Ta'mira, trees that went untended all year. His family has been counted on the way in, and counted on the way out.

Souli has just skyped with Sarah and, looking at his mother's face, he could tell she was thinking of Said. Of how they used to visit Ta'mira every Saturday, of their careful watering and dusting and cleaning and lunch in the shade. How, sometimes, quiet Said would get bright in the face and maybe even sing.

"The olive harvest is holy," Souli says. "It gives life; it's full of historical meaning to bring the olives back to your house. It brings the family together. Usually this is a happy day, to go to the harvest. But because of the situation, today . . ."

He looks at the pictures of feeble trees on Naji's Facebook page.

"You know, these are trees we ate from back in the days. But not anymore. Because you need to work on the land for things to grow."

He begins reading Naji's post. "It's in Arabic. I'll try to translate: 'Ta'mira is the land of our ancestors. If the olives knew the story of the place and the people that planted them, their oil would become tears.'"

He makes the sound that means he's overcome by something. It's slight, and quickly becomes a joke. "Ohhhhhh shit. Fuck you, Penina," he says, laughing.

He zooms out to a more comfortable distance.

"Today, I am not talking just as Palestinian. I am extending myself more than that. I'm trying to see the picture from outside and both sides. But it's really complicated, *ya 'ni*, because I'm still Palestinian, I still go through checkpoints. So I'm not going to be a Zionist. A lot of shit happened from Herzl till now. And still, we have family land taken. Not in '48, not in '67, but *now*."

He speaks of his cousins in Jordan, still stuck where they were when the 1967 war came, still unable to return home. When Souli visited once, his favorite cousin kept talking about Nibu Mountain. How when he missed Hizma and al-Quds, he would go there, and stand on its peak for a long time.

"My cousin in Jordan, he always tells me, 'We never felt we were Jordanians.' When he goes to Nibu Mountain, he can see Palestine, Canaan, call it what you want. He told me, I go there to breathe from the air of this land. My cousins still feel their soul, their spirit, their heart, their everything, is Palestinian. That's it. They will never be something else.

"We have a saying. Even if they take Palestine from us, it will be in our heart. Nothing will take it away. So they will not demolish the Palestinian people. This is not going to work. Even if you expel all the Palestinians, they will not forget; they will fight forever, seriously.

"But today," he says, "I don't want to be just Palestinian. I'm a bit different in this way. I want to be human, first. I can't disconnect with my roots, but I can extend my belonging, if you want, to include more."

He looks back down at the photos of Ta'mira on his phone. He stares at the oldest stones, the ones his grandfather didn't bring, the ones that were there before. They looked like the much older stones of Qubur Bani Isra'il, like ancient gravestones.

And somehow, without me noticing, he follows those stones and begins talking about Jewish history, how recognizing its presence is part of the solution.

"This is why I personally have a problem with Palestinians who say Jews have to go back to Poland, except the few who were living here before 1948. This is a lot of ignorance. And the other way around, of course. When some Israelis say this is just a Jewish state and Palestinians have to be expelled. *Ya'ni*, this is not going anywhere, this is a heavy, deep problem. This is crazy to think that Palestinians will be drawn to Arab countries or Israelis will go back to Poland. Anyway, they were not all from Poland. And now they are third, fourth generation and all that."

He knew many people understood that everyone on this land was here to stay. But he was looking for something deeper. "People have to come to some middle ground," he continued, "and that's why I don't agree with my friend Samar."

Samar is a '48 refugee from Bayt Nabala, a village now within Israel. Her family has lived in South America, the US, and Ramallah, but is always dreaming of going home. She often challenges Souli for being too close to the Israelis, for giving too much power to their stories.

"I don't demolish her feeling. My family in Jordan feels the same wish to come home. But *ya'ni*, how can I say it, to just carry the same story forever doesn't help anyone, so I don't know . . ." He laughs. "I need a successful story at the end of the day. Which will never be Samar without Chen Alon's daughter Tamar. This doesn't work in my mind."

Tamar is on Souli's mind because she recently refused army service. She did it to protest the occupation, and she went to jail.

When Souli visited Chen during Tamar's jail time, he told people he was going to visit *his brother*. When he arrived, when it was time to sleep, Chen smiled at Souli, joking in their usual way, pointing him toward Tamar's empty room. "You can go sleep there," he laughed. "That's the prisoner's room!"

Now, whenever Souli thinks of Tamar, he thinks of his brother's sons. And when he thinks of his nephews, he thinks of her.

"So for me," he says, downing his third espresso, "I will struggle for Chen's daughter as I'm struggling for my brothers' kids. Really, I don't feel a difference. She deserves life and safety and legitimacy. And the same for Palestinians. How to do this in a one-sided struggle, I don't know. This is why for me, my flag, my principle, is the joint nonviolent struggle to break the cycle. This is my alliance. That's why for me it's important that my family's kids will meet

Chen's kids, create a kind of communication. What bothers my mind is always this question. How can we, in the end, through a journey, a small revolution, mobilize people into joining nonviolent action that *includes* reconciliation and love and dialogue?" I sit looking at him, trying to trace how we arrived here. But this is how it's been in all our conversations, over years. We travel so many places; I can't catch up. Today, we begin in Ta'mira and end somewhere else. But for Souli, it's all the same. Today, everything that happens—whether beautiful or tragic—points him back here, to this shared space.

EPILOGUE

A book is somehow like a relationship, a movement, a small sliver of land. Nothing is stable. And at least on the surface, there is a finite amount of space. I came into this book process obsessed with pointing out where finite space was shared unfairly. Throughout the years of working on these pages, Souli has pushed me to challenge this inclination. To identify places where, if we just think differently, the amount of space widens so drastically that we can't see its edges. But whatever the nature of the space, whether constricted or expansive, it is always shared. Because we are all here. What matters is the shape of that sharing, how we choose to do it. Over many years spent circling in these pages, of which hundreds have been discarded, I have tried to answer this question—both with Souli, and in myself. Over many years, these pages served as one exercise in sharing space. Struggling with whether Israeli stories have, in the end, overtaken Palestinian stories here; with whether my voice has overtaken Souli's. Struggling with what it means for softer language, which may welcome those not already fighting for justice in this land, to overtake stronger language, like *apartheid*. Struggling with both the beauty and heartbreak, with how both Souli and I entered the space of the book in one way, and left it in another.

When I first arrived in al-Quds/Jerusalem and Ramallah, asking endless questions, Souli called me a *choferet* ("digger," in Hebrew) and turned away. He was surprised; when he first asked me to work on the book, he expected I'd follow him around, listen to his lectures, and then a book would be born. He found himself in a different place than the one he had imagined, looking more carefully than he'd planned at all the parts of the story he wanted to ignore. This was one instigator in the process of further transformation he's still traveling through.

I hope the infinite exists here, that all these words point toward it. But I have spent many days with my hands up against the wall of this finite space. If Souli experienced the pain of including things, I dealt with the reality of excluding them. I found myself leaving many things out that were important to me: including a certain feminist reading of his narrative.

I spoke to many women throughout this process, and yet many of them are absent here. It's not something Souli asked for, but it is something that happened. I have wanted to protect the thing most precious to him: the story of his relationship to joint nonviolence. It's a story with many pieces, one that requires many pages. And so in the cutting process, I have left out certain relationships, particularly those he's had with women in activist circles.

I was speaking one day to a woman who knew him well, a close friend who worked with him in movement spaces, when she stopped me. "Don't make him a hero," she said. But it was a hard thing to escape. Many have observed a similar dynamic in Combatants for Peace. Power is distributed unequally—not just between Palestinians and Israelis, but between Mizrahi and Ashkenazi, queer and straight, poor and wealthy, women and men. This power determines which stories get told. Certain stories—often those with a particular relationship to violence—turn people's heads, and they're the ones that are most often lifted up in big moments. They are often stories of men.

These are commonly narratives with a heroic glow about them. I could feel it, talking to other people who love Souli, how they wanted me to leave certain things out in favor of this glow. I understood why. They wanted to protect him and serve his purpose: humanizing all sides, lifting up a joint nonviolent struggle, pointing to a narrative that includes Palestinians and Israelis both. It is nearly irresistible sometimes, the pull of the story people want to hear.

But we're wrong to think that this sort of move is the only way to show protection and care. When Souli's friend warned against making him a hero, she explained how people might not understand what such a refusal means. It means letting a person be real, she said. It means an act of love.

Though I am not sure where all this landed in the text, I know that no matter what I did, my particular reading of Souli's story was always present here. I knew I wanted to make that clear, from the beginning. But it's not obvious how to make a thing clear. In earlier drafts, I inserted the present as non-chronological pauses within the past. I wanted to use these breaths as a space to explore some of the dynamics around gender that did not easily appear in the narrative itself, to also draw out the ways that my politics diverged from his, wanting him to challenge Zionism further, to defend BDS more frequently, to speak about the right of Palestinian refugees to return home. Wanting him to name that while Jewish connection to the land is rooted in real things, it has also been constructed, and we can hold both truths at once. But if there was a sense of justice in these insertions, there was also a potential violation: the insertion of a white Jewish woman's perspective into a Palestinian man's story. In the end, I removed those most explicit interruptions from the text.

There is no map for this, or none that I've found. No flawless set of instructions for how to share space most fairly, in a way that acknowledges all the lines of power running through us, our relationships, our world.

The many hours I spent agonizing over this were rooted in my belief that space—the space of this book, the land where this story takes place, this world we're living in—is finite. Within this framework, principled joint work requires enormous sacrifice. To do it truly, as we ask others to transform, is to look inward—examining which changes we are willing to undergo to win the world we want. We have to realize when we've reproduced certain systems that we set out to transform. We have to claim responsibility, then forgive ourselves and start again.

This is such an important lens. But it's not enough. We need to hold that other reality where Souli lives, one of infinite space. A reality in which, as I've come to understand alongside him, Jewish connection (freed from any practice of domination) can exist alongside Palestinian freedom. In which our stories of liberation are multiple, intertwined, entangled.

Mahmoud Darwish was maybe pointing toward this during an interview with Israeli poet Helit Yeshurun. "It is impossible for me to evade the place that the Israeli has occupied in my identity," Darwish said. "The Israelis changed the Palestinians and vice versa. The Israelis are not the same people that came, and the Palestinians are not the same people that once were. In the one, there is the other. . . . You should know that neither the Israeli of yesterday nor the new Israeli has the power to remove me." Still, he said, "the other is a responsibility and a test. Together we are doing something new in history. . . . Will a third way emerge from these two?"

In Souli's reality, within some third way, we do our very best to keep everything worth keeping. We see the process of mutual transformation as an ever-widening circle, one that creates space for more and more stories to be included, one that invites Palestinians and Israelis—and all people—to create a world where everyone, without exception, feels what it is to be free.

Every day, Souli is speaking his instructions for how to arrive in this place, to find it where it already exists. "Humanization, recognition and acknowledgment," he says, "are deeply important, the keys to our way forward, our way to heal." We must use these tools outside organizational structures, he says, as well as within them. To create coalitions across many lines and "build supportive community spaces together, as part of this new practice, this new reality we are trying, learning to move from fear and competition to trust." His final instruction, always, is hope. "I'm an optimist," he says on our last day of edits, smiling and shrugging, "and we are on a long journey of revolution." Representative John Lewis has just died, and Souli reads me something the American civil rights hero once wrote, and afterward we know there is little else to say: "Do not get lost in a sea of despair. Be hopeful, be optimistic. Our struggle is not the struggle of a day, a week, a month, or a year, it is the struggle of a lifetime. Never, ever be afraid to make some noise and get in good trouble, necessary trouble."

I felt very far from this clarity the day I decided to work on the book. But maybe I was trying to reach it, when I told Souli yes by ripping a piece of paper from my notebook. On it, I copied down a line from Anne Carson's translation of Antigone. Ismene shakes her head (I imagine) at Antigone and says—*you are a person in love with the impossible.* She says this after Antigone describes what she wants, which seems now like a very simple thing: for their brother to receive a respectful burial.

People have called many funny things impossible. Souli talks often about how the night before the Berlin Wall fell, no one was even remotely expecting it.

Right now, as I write, some people feel hopeless about the prospects of justice or peace in the wider world, let alone in the oft-discussed, highly disputed place of Souli's birth. But no place is immune to the currents of change that endlessly, stubbornly, flow through everything. If Souli's right, that one day everything will be okay in his *holy land*, it won't be the first time in the history of the world that a group of people made the impossible possible, simply by believing in it hard enough. For this to make sense, of course, you have to remember that all *true* belief leads to action.

ACKNOWLEDGMENTS

We are grateful for more people than we can name on paper. Thank you:

To all peoples who have taught that land is not a thing to be owned.

To the land itself, which is so much smarter than us.

To our parents—Sarah and Said al-Khatib, Amy Eilberg, and Howard Schwartz.

To Souli's former Peres Center colleagues Tami Chai, Yael Patir, and the incredibly gentle and kind Ron Pundak (may his memory be a blessing).

To Libby and Len Traubman for their deep listening and tireless commitment to peace-building. To Len, specifically, who looked at Souli with his kind eyes and said: *You are holding the vision.* To Len, who changed so many lives before his ended.

To Mindy Mercado, who believed very early on. To Agnes Handal for her written translation and transcription; to Rabbi Amy Eilberg for Hebrew transliteration advice; to Betty Rosen for an enormous amount of Arabic transliteration help in exchange for just a bit of coffee; to Mairav Zonszein for the total trust she inspired as a fact-checker. Any remaining errors are our own.

To Samar Nakleh for her spoken and written translations, hard questions, and companionship on long car rides. To Karen Isaacs and Daniel Roth for modeling the fight for collective liberation.

To Seeds of Peace and the GATHER Fellowship, to Achvat Amim, EcoME, the community of Middle East Dreamers, and the Logan Nonfiction Program at the Carey Institute for Global Good.

To Daniel Moses and Tamar Miller for early support; to Steve Apkon and Marcina Hale for their faith, vision, and guidance. To Huda Abuarquob for her fierce wisdom and mentorship. To Beth Schuman for her tirelessness. To Ashley Bohrer for going with the flow, reading excerpts, and providing deep feedback. To Suja Sawafta, who helped translate an Abu Arab line, advised on Arabic transliteration, and first taught Penina about the sea. To Lily for her lessons on love and home and sleep. To Suja and Lily both, who moved Penina toward action.

To all the members of Combatants for Peace, and everyone who trusted us to include them in this work.

To Gadi Kenny, who shared with Souli many stories of his mother, the woman who taught him about the importance of love and trees and peace. Gadi dedicated so much time and care to supporting Souli and countless other peacemakers, and offered important and oftentimes challenging feedback on this book.

To our agent, Becky Sweren, for understanding this project, making it better, and finding it a home. To Amy Caldwell and the team at Beacon Press for welcoming us in. To Aida Shibli and Sami Awad, whose inspiration becomes a map. To Mubarak Awad and Galia Golan, for the huge honor they gave us in reading these pages.

To Marty Piñol, for literally everything.

SOURCES

While this book is very much a work of memory, we consulted a broad range of documents, and drew on many interviews, to source and corroborate historical information.

Portrayal of historical facts, and numbers of casualties in particular, often vary across different publications. We tried to compare numerous sources and state the truth as best we could. We drew on news outlets such as Al Jazeera, the BBC, *The Guardian*, *Haaretz*, the *Jerusalem Post*, the Jewish Telegraphic Agency, the *New York Times*, the *Times of Israel*, and *+972 Magazine*—trying to hold in mind each source's particular political leaning.

We also relied heavily on information from human rights organizations like the Applied Research Institute—Jerusalem, B'Tselem, Emek Shaveh, Gisha, Human Rights Watch, the United Nations Office for the Coordination of Humanitarian Affairs (OCHA), and the Palestinian Academic Society for the Study of International Affairs (PASSIA). For information on casualties, we also consulted the website of the Israel Ministry of Foreign Affairs.

To avoid unwieldy endnotes, we've compiled a website with primary sources listed by chapter: www.inthisplacebook.com /sources. On that site, we've also indicated which names in the text have been changed.

Below is a small selection of sources, which we've included either because they were used multiple times throughout the text, or because they provided a quotation or an especially important insight.

INTERVIEWS AND PERSONAL COMMUNICATIONS

Penina conducted most of the interviews, sometimes with Sulaiman, in spring 2016—though some were conducted later. Our gratitude goes out to the following people, and all those not listed here, whose stories or expertise found their way into this work: Haneen Abualsoud, Ahmad Aljafari, Chen Alon, Bassam Aramin, Abed Asali, Hillel Cohen, Elik Elhanan, Qaddura Fares, Yehuda HaKohen, Ahmed Helou, Buma Inbar, Maya Katz, Gadi Kenny, Fatima al-Khatib, Sarah al-Khatib, Lilach, Reut Mor, Michal Pomeranz, Itamar Shapira, Yonatan Shapira, Zohar Shapira, Aida Shibli, David (Dudu) Shilo, Bassem Tamimi, Len and Libby Traubman, Waleed Wahdan, Avner Wishnitzer, and Shlomo Zagman.

SELECT DOCUMENTATION

Apkon, Stephen, and Andrew Young dir. *Disturbing the Peace*. Reconsider, 2016.

Cohen, Shaul Ephraim. *The Politics of Planting: Israeli-Palestinian Competition for Control of Land in the Jerusalem Periphery*. Chicago: University of Chicago Press, 1993.

Darwish, Mahmoud. *In the Presence of Absence*. Translated by Sinan Antoon. Brooklyn, NY: Archipelago Books, 2011.

Gibson, Shimon. "The Stone Vessel Industry at Hizma." *Israel Exploration Journal* 33, no. 3/4 (1983): 176–88. www.jstor.org /stable/27925895.

Halperin, Liora. *Babel in Zion: Jews, Nationalism, and Language Diversity in Palestine, 1920–1948*. New Haven, CT: Yale University Press, 2015.

Jabbour, Elias J. *Sulha: Palestinian Traditional Peacemaking Process*. Edited by Thomas C. Cook Jr. Montreat, NC: House of Hope Publications, 1993.

Katz, Sheila H. *Connecting with the Enemy: A Century of Palestinian-Israeli Joint Nonviolence*. Austin: University of Texas Press, 2016.

King, Mary Elizabeth. *A Quiet Revolution: The First Palestinian Intifada and Nonviolent Resistance*. New York: Nation Books, 2007.

Lynd, Staughton, Sam Bahour, and Alice Lynd, eds. *Homeland: Oral Histories of Palestine and Palestinians*. Brooklyn, NY: Olive Branch Press, 1994.

Mandela, Nelson. *Long Walk to Freedom: The Autobiography of Nelson Mandela*. New York: Little, Brown, 1994.

McDonald, David A. *My Voice Is My Weapon: Music, Nationalism, and the Poetics of Palestinian Resistance*. Durham, NC: Duke University Press, 2013.

People's Peace Fund. "June 5, 2007 Peace Events." August 11, 2010. YouTube, https://www.youtube.com/watch?v=1ERak _bPm8c.

Qumsiyeh, Mazin B. *Popular Resistance in Palestine: A History of Hope and Empowerment*. London: Pluto Press, 2011.

Said, Edward. "The One-State Solution." *New York Times,* January 10, 1999. http://www.nytimes.com/1999/01/10/magazine /the-one-state-solution.html.

Shohat, Ella. "The Invention of the Mizrahim." *Journal of Palestine Studies* 29, no. 1 (Autumn 1999): 5–20. https://www.jstor.org /stable/pdf/2676427?seq=1.

Sophokles. *Antigonick*. Translated by Anne Carson. New York: New Directions, 2012.

Team Diary from "Breaking the Ice" Expedition. "Our Peoples Can Live Together in Peace and Friendship." *Guardian*, January 19, 2004. https://www.theguardian.com/environment /2004/jan/19/antarctica.climatechange.

Yeshurun, Helit. "'Exile Is So Strong Within Me, I May Bring It to the Land': A Landmark 1996 Interview with Mahmoud Darwish." *Journal of Palestine Studies* 42, no. 1 (Autumn 2012): 46–70. https://www.jstor.org/stable/10.1525/jps.2012.xlii.1.46.

NOTES

A NOTE FROM PENINA

1. A flexible exclamation in Arabic, often used to express interest, wonder, appreciation.

2. A traditional Palestinian spice typically made of dried thyme, sesame seeds, sumac, and salt.

3. An affectionate term for a loved one, often used widely and casually in Palestinian Arabic. *Habibti* is used for women, *habibi* for men.

PROLOGUE

1. Whether or not you agree with this depends on how you read the text of Jewish history.

CHAPTER 1: TA'MIRA

1. This is a literal translation. But "Abu" can also mean "one who is characterized by."

2. The usual transliteration is Neve Ya'akov. Our transliteration here matches Souli's way of referring to the settlement, giving it a sound of Hebrew and Arabic mixed together.

3. A name for light-haired goats and sheep. The term comes from the name for both Greater Syria and Damascus, al-Sham, and the name for Levantine Arabic, *shami*.

4. In Arabic, *khalas* means "enough," often a word of exasperation.

5. Farmers, people who work the land.

6. A dunam is a unit of measurement left over from the Ottoman Empire. In Palestine, it could signify 900–1,000 square meters.

7. A traditional outdoor stone oven.

8. "The Setback," in Arabic—one Palestinian name for the 1967 war.

9. Local, or indigenous, in Arabic.

10. Thick, strained yogurt.

11. Outdoor bus station.

CHAPTER 2: RA'S AL-TAWIL

1. A village elder and leader.

2. The meal closing Ramadan's daily fast.

CHAPTER 3: A HIDDEN PLACE

1. In Hebrew, Ein Mabo'a.

2. Jews established Neve Ya'akov in the 1920s, buying the land from Palestinian owners, and lived there until they fled the Jordanian army in 1948. The new Neve Ya'akov was established after the 1967 war, close to the original site, but with different boundaries. Israel expropriated land from Hizma and al-Ram for the village's reconstruction, and a new group of settlers arrived. The new Neve Ya'akov was still very much a part of the 1968 "Jerusalem Master Plan"—building Jewish settlements in an eastern ring around the city in order to disrupt continuity between Palestinian neighborhoods and solidify Israeli control of the whole Jerusalem area. See Shaul Ephraim Cohen's book in our sources list.

3. While Sulaiman's family would never sell their land, some Palestinians had. Even when Palestinians did not sell it, land was taken.

4. "The Political Threshing Floor." *Bayadir* is a site used for the threshing of wheat.

5. The title means "The Return"—referring to the Palestinian right of return.

6. Ein Prat, in Hebrew.

7. Arabic word for addressing one's mother directly, in a village dialect.

CHAPTER 4: 'AYN FARRAH

1. A checkered scarf traditionally worn as a headdress in the Middle East. In Palestine, it became a specific symbol of resistance, made internationally famous by Yasser Arafat.

2. An article in the newspaper *Yedioth Ahronoth* (see online sources list at www.inthisplacebook.com/sources) revealed that the two Israeli men were no longer in the army. Given that fact, it seems less likely that they were carrying guns, but it's not certain.

CHAPTER 5: *SHIBL*

1. This was the common torture method of *shabeh*. For more background and testimonies from other Palestinian political prisoners, see the following in our online sources list: Human Rights Watch, *Torture and Ill-Treatment*; and B'Tselem, *Routine Torture*.

2. Congratulations in Arabic.

3. A traditional Palestinian and Levantine dish of rice, lamb, and yogurt.

4. Israeli human rights lawyer Michal Pomeranz wrote that the courts "usually check damage to neighbouring houses, the involvement of the family in the defendant's act, [the] number of minors that will be affected, etc." (Email to Penina, June 2016.)

5. There was more than one visit to Ramallah before sentencing, so we're compressing time here a bit.

CHAPTER 7: *MAYY WA MILH*

1. A Palestinian and Levantine dish of rice, meat, and fried vegetables, served upside down.

2. Souli and Bassam remember a thirteen-day fast. Mary Elizabeth King (see sources list) writes that the strike actually lasted for three weeks, but it's possible she is referring to some of the other participating prisons.

3. "Trouble" is Souli's rendering. The literal Arabic translation is more like *repression.*

CHAPTER 8: *ABNAA' AL-INTIFADA*

1. It was common to refer to prominent members of the PLO leadership by nicknames such as these.

2. The literal meaning in Hebrew is "separation."

3. A van used to transport Palestinian political prisoners between jails.

CHAPTER 10: A NEW WORLD COMING

1. "I became a smoker in a few months," Souli says. "That's shit, right?"

2. Souli's not sure, but this movie may have been *Schindler's List.* If it was, this memory belongs a bit later in the timeline, in 1993 or after.

3. Jews of European ancestry.

CHAPTER 12: LITTLE CHANCE

1. Mizrahi, literally "Easterner," is a term used in Israel to describe Jews from Arab and Muslim geographies, who make up more than half of Israel's Jewish population. Though the category of "Easterner" has roots in the phrase "*Edot HaMizrach*" (the Eastern ethnicities), a concept often paired with European-centric and Orientalist tones of "backwardness," the word *Mizrahi* became a proud self-descriptor for many. Some Mizrahi scholars study the construction of this collective identity, including the way it created one category for a group of Arab Jews from diverse contexts, to describe the ongoing systemic oppression of non-Ashkenazim in Israel and the ways this oppression is tied to the Palestinian-Israeli conflict. See Lavie, Shohat, and Chetrit in our sources list online.

CHAPTER 13: *'AWDA* (RETURN)

1. Palestinian Arabic names for Be'er Sheva and Hebron.

CHAPTER 14: HOLY MOUNTAIN

1. Dessert made with thin strips of pastry, cheese, pistachios, and honey.

CHAPTER 15: HELICOPTERS

1. The literal translation from the Arabic is "Look at me," as when addressing a group. The word has become slang for "show-off"—especially in Hebrew, but also in Palestinian Arabic.

2. According to Souli, the Palestinian narrative claimed the reservists were spies. The Israeli narrative claimed the men had lost their way.

CHAPTER 16: PROPERTIES OF SNOW

1. In Arabic, "Where are you going? To Ramallah!"

CHAPTER 17: SHARED WORDS

1. In solidarity with Palestinian partners, Israelis in the human rights organization Ta'ayush participated (and still participate) in frequent nonviolent direct action against the occupation.

2. When he remembers it now, Souli laughs. "We thought Hillel Cohen was Shabak, for sure!"

3. While Sulaiman and Bassam spoke Hebrew, few of the Israelis spoke Arabic.

4. The foundational Kabbalistic text.

CHAPTER 18: TREES

1. Imran (name changed) actually joined slightly later, in the semi-public meeting that was about to follow.

2. In the account of several sources, two young Palestinian men were involved in the attack (according to pieces by Rami Elhanan and Justin Huggler). Elsewhere (in Nice's review of *The Bombing*), there were three Palestinians involved. See the above-mentioned pieces on our online sources list.

CHAPTER 19: BULLETS & THEATER

1. Years later, Israelis learned that the captured soldiers had been killed.

2. A practice designed by Brazilian theater artist Augusto Boal from the seeds of Paulo Freire's famous text, *Pedagogy of the Oppressed*.

CHAPTER 20: THE YEAR OF LONG DRIVES

1. The first prime minister of Israel.

2. Researching more, we found that the sources paint a complex story. Of course, native Palestinian Jews spoke Arabic, as did many Sephardi Jewish immigrants. Pre-Zionist Ashkenazi Jews also knew some Arabic and incorporated Arabic words into their Yiddish vocabulary. As Zionist Ashkenazi Jews began arriving in the late 1880s, there was certainly a movement to study Arabic and teach it in schools, and it seems that a significant number of Ashkenazi newcomers during this period used some basic spoken Arabic. However, it seems that few learned the language deeply. See Halperin's and Dowty's books in our online sources list for further reading.

3. Many years later, a judge found there had been no stone-throwing at all. She ruled that the police officer who shot the gun had done so in violation of regulations, and she held Israeli border police responsible for Abir's death. She ordered compensation for the Aramin family but did not allow the reopening of the criminal investigation.

CHAPTER 21: IF I FORGET

1. This happened in 2011. It is placed out of order for narrative purposes.

CHAPTER 23: BALLOONS

1. This combines two separate interactions.

2. This may be a combination of memories from several Freedom Marches.

CHAPTER 24: YOU CAN'T GET THERE FROM HERE

1. In Hebrew, "version."

2. According to the Bible, the Canaanites lived on this land before the Israelites arrived.

3. In Arabic, "exile" or "alienation."

4. Farmer, person who works the land.

5. He knew Che Guevara was not born in a cave, but that was beside the point.

6. More recently, Adelson and Netanyahu seemed to have had a falling-out. But Adelson is famous for founding *Israel Hayom*, a free daily newspaper in Israel that many saw as a voice for pro-Netanyahu propaganda.

CHAPTER 25: THE STONE AND THE VALLEY

1. Both words—*sahra* in Arabic and *midbar* in Hebrew—mean "desert."

CHAPTER 26: A SMALL REVOLUTION

1. In Hebrew, "ascent." A word some Jews use to describe moving to Israel from the diaspora.

2. The Hebrew name for Jerusalem.

3. *Yara* is "[he] sees" in Arabic. The letters that begin the word *Yerushalaim* do not map exactly onto the Hebrew word "to see," but they sound related when spoken.